Abu Ghraib

Reflections in the Looking Glass

Michael E. Cannon, Jr.

This book is dedicated to the glory of God with thanksgiving for my many blessings in Christ. It is also given with thanks for my family who has sacrificed for the cause of Liberty understanding their father and husband's service to their country.

It is further committed to preserving the memory of soldiers, our nation's sons and daughters, who have died preserving a liberty that we are only now beginning to appreciate. May God preserve and comfort their families and may their selfless sacrifice inspire another generation to stand in the gap in the ongoing struggle against evil and oppression in our time.

TABLE OF CONTENTS

PART I:

FROM THE LIVING ROOM TO THE WAR ROOM

AN ANATOMY OF A CITIZEN-SOLDIER'S RESPONSE TO WAR

"Courage is being scared to death and
saddling up anyway."

John Wayne

Igitur qui desiderat pacem, praeparet bellum
(If you want peace, prepare for war.)

"In the moral sphere, every act of justice or charity
involves putting ourselves in the other person's
place and thus transcending our own
competitive particularity."

C. S. Lewis, An Experiment in Criticism

"Nothing is easier than self-deceit. For what each
man wishes, that he also believes to be true."

Demonsthenes

There are scant few moments of theater that have
become immortal. Rhett Butler lived in one of those

11

moments from *"Gone With the Wind"* when he said, "Frankly my dear I don't give a damn!" and Jack Nicholson claimed immortality in, *"A Few Good Men"* when he testified from the witness stand that the prosecuting attorney, played by Tom Cruise, couldn't handle the truth. That phrase has wormed its way into the political landscape over and again. A 2004 blog posted by Josh Green creates a fictitious dialog between Cruise's character, Kaffee, and the American Secretary of Defense, Donald Rumsfeld.

> *"Kaffee: Did you order "psyops"?*
> *Rumsfeld: You want answers?*
> *Kaffee: I think I'm entitled.*
> *Rumsfeld: You want answers?*
> *Kaffee: I want the truth!*
> *Rumsfeld: You can't handle the truth! Son, we live in a world that has terrorists. And those terrorists have to be defeated with psyops. Who's gonna do it? You? You, Lt. Weinberg? I have a greater responsibility than you can possibly fathom. You weep for the Abu Ghraib prisoners and you curse psyops. You have that luxury. You have the luxury of not knowing what I know: That the Abu Ghraib psyops, while tragic, probably saved lives. And my existence, while grotesque and incomprehensible to you, saves lives."*[1]

Can Americans handle the truth of Abu Ghraib? Will Americans handle the truth of Abu Ghraib? Should we continue to rant in speculative discussions or dare we open the doors on that prison and look inside? What if we look inside the doors of that terrible prison and see the reflection of our own soul?

Reports have been released from government investigations and the media has hosted numerous expert panels to discuss who should be blamed. There is a significant problem with relying on media and legal experts. We can listen to their views, but we cannot enter into the experience of the people who were at Abu Ghraib through the testimony of experts. Experts faithfully hold the incident under the revealing light of law and justice without prejudice, or insight. It is a practice in observation, verification, and speculation of cause and effect. Motivations often require an explanation found in theology and moral philosophy. Character cannot be explained through the enforcement of legal codes. The character of an individual and the moral fiber of our country is not easily dissected in a five minute segment of news or in a discussion on law. That is why we must perform an autopsy of this crime. We have to examine the entire anatomy in detail or we will lose the opportunity to reconsider the direction of our national ethic.

TELEVISION SOLDIERS

When America goes to war, America's warriors make the journey. Thankfully, not every American man and woman is forced to stare in the face of war. Not every child has to transition from playing war in the backyard with friends to praying God will save them from Hell's playground. Not every husband or wife will have to wonder if they will ever feel the face of their spouse again. Today's war is different from the wars of our past in that it is a managed war. It is a war we hope to keep far from our shores even as it threatens to enter our neighborhoods.

To understand the nature of battlefields far away, we have to learn to empathize with soldiers. We have to see the world as they see it. Their world is not the one we see on our televisions. The smoke that flashes in five second images on our TV evokes memories of putrid stenches in the nostrils of those who breathed it.

Moral philosopher, Adam Smith warned that people without qualifications will imagine they are better suited to tell us about our own lives and even instruct us about our own homes. If we are not careful we are bound to be open to deception and misunderstanding. A deception is most effective when it appears most believable. C.S. Lewis quipped, "The greatest deception is the one that contains the most truth." Another of his sayings from "The Allegory of Love" may bring us closer to the point, "To fight in another man's armor is something more than to be influenced by his style of fighting."

This caution against blind acceptance of another's interpretations of events should cause us to pause and reconsider how we have come to understand Abu Ghraib. Abu Ghraib is more than news. The competence of our leadership and the moral imperative of our mission in Iraq are interpreted in the shadow of Abu Ghraib. It is as if Abu Ghraib was an unredeemable moment of truth. For months after the news of prisoner abuse broke, news anchors led Iraq news and updates with some veiled or incongruent reference to Abu Ghraib. Out of all the tragedy of war, why did Abu Ghraib resonate so pervasively in American Culture? This one event influenced our confidence in the war and America's leaders. More importantly, it degraded our trust and confidence in American soldiers.

As we survey the facts and reflect on the experience, remarkably all we know has come from the information presented to us through our window on the world, the Television. And Television has not served us well.

Trying to understand the abuse in Abu Ghraib prison through the eyes of the press while sitting safely in American living rooms, is analogous to American poet John Godfrey Saxe (1816-1887)poem of the six blind men's encounter with an elephant.

It was six men of Indostan
To learning much inclined,
Who went to see the Elephant
(Though all of them were blind),
That each by observation
Might satisfy his mind
The First approached the Elephant,
And happening to fall
Against his broad and sturdy side,
At once began to bawl:
"God bless me! but the Elephant
Is very like a wall!"
The Second, feeling of the tusk,
Cried, "Ho! what have we here
So very round and smooth and sharp?
To me 'tis mighty clear
This wonder of an Elephant
Is very like a spear!"
The Third approached the animal,
And happening to take
The squirming trunk within his hands,
Thus boldly up and spake:
"I see," quoth he, "the Elephant
Is very like a snake!"
The Fourth reached out an eager hand,
And felt about the knee.
"What most this wondrous beast is like
Is mighty plain," quoth he;
" 'Tis clear enough the Elephant
Is very like a tree!"
The Fifth, who chanced to touch the ear,
Said: "E'en the blindest man
Can tell what this resembles most;
Deny the fact who can
This marvel of an Elephant

Is very like a fan!"
The Sixth no sooner had begun
About the beast to grope,
Than, seizing on the swinging tail
That fell within his scope,
"I see," quoth he, "the Elephant
Is very like a rope!"
And so these men of Indostan
Disputed loud and long,
Each in his own opinion
Exceeding stiff and strong,
Though each was partly in the right,
And all were in the wrong!
Moral:
So oft in theologic wars,
The disputants, I ween,
Rail on in utter ignorance
Of what each other mean,
And prate about an Elephant
Not one of them has seen!

This book will help you transition from blindness to understanding. You will come to understand the 800th Military Police Brigade's odyssey of war. You will experience it through the Brigade Chaplain's journal, observations, and historical records. His personal experiences are representative of an ordinary soldier's stress, fears, traumas, and hopes when leaving their homes and families to serve God and country. No confidential or privileged communication is divulged in these pages yet the author has made every effort to record and interpret their experience.

FORENSIC INVESTIGATIONS

The secret to discovery is in the questions that are asked. Most seem concerned only with the details of the prisoner abuse and then who is to blame. That is the foundation of a legal inquiry but a moral examination must take a different tact. Any real understanding of Abu Ghraib and the impact it should have on America must consider several dimensions of our experience. We saw pictures of naked men stacked in pyramids, heard the commentary from shocked correspondents, and reacted to the political rhetoric of candidates blaming everyone in sight. For Abu Ghraib to be anything more than sensational entertainment and a political device, we must take time to examine each dimension of our collective experience from the early days of the war to the shocking revelation of photos from the Iraqi prison. Examining each of these will resemble an autopsy. An autopsy requires a doctor or forensic investigator to take a body apart or in this case, an incident must be dissected, to gather and examine the pieces in order to understand the whole. The Federal Bureau of Investigations web site claims, "The successful investigation and prosecution of crimes require, in most cases, the collection, preservation, and forensic analysis of evidence. Forensic analysis of evidence is often crucial to determinations of guilt or innocence." This book is a collection of evidence, not only to discover what happened at Abu Ghraib, but what it means.

Often crucial evidence in a court case or answers to infamous mysteries are solved through this process of forensic discovery. People are convicted on evidence obtained from the fingernails of a corpse or from a spot of blood or a hair found on their clothes. Through careful and comprehensive examination of each crucial component, we can develop an informed analysis of the whole. This is not just the story of the 800th MP Brigade. This is an autopsy of the 800th's experience and you are the investigating surgeon. You will examine the collective American experience of Abu Ghraib in the context of Operation Iraqi Freedom.

When the subject of an anatomy is an actual person, the

forensic physician looks for an approximate age, race, sex, unusual or unique marks, features, deformities, or any traumas that could have contributed to the cause of death. An anatomy of the prisoner abuse at Abu Ghraib must follow that pattern of observation.

Your investigation of Abu Ghraib must involve more than a random sampling of reports and pictures. Before the skin of media analysis is cut and the actual facts are laid out for examination, an introduction of the soldiers and experiences that make up the 800th and the meat and marrow of Operation Iraqi Freedom is necessary. We must catalogue the spiritual, moral, and psychological makeup of the soldiers as it existed in the context of war before delving into the more sensational and public aspects of the scandal.

THE INITIAL ARMY INVESTIGATION

The release of General Taguba's scathing report of the 800th Military Police Brigade's responsibilities at Abu Ghraib resulted in a flurry of press coverage and speculation. The report highlighted breakdowns in leadership, logistics, command and control, morality, and morale. The unclassified portions available to the public lack the ability to communicate a perspective only available to those who were there. Now we will take time to consider the people behind the headlines. An officer in the operations section of the 800th wrote a rebuttal to the Taguba Report in an effort to capture some of the unique challenges the 800th faced. That rebuttal adds some perspective but words on paper cannot communicate just how challenging operations are in Iraq to the vast majority of Americans who will never feel the blast of a hot Iraqi breeze on their face.

The Taguba report almost casually mentions the drop in unit morale when they passed the date they anticipated going home. This drop in moral couldn't have come at a more critical juncture in the 800th's mission. Soldiers were making summer plans anticipating going home after the mission to defeat Saddam's army was complete. In fact, the incoming commander, General Janis Karpinski was told that her time in Iraq would be so brief that assuming command of the 800th was impractical. When the change of mission was announced to the Brigade, their heartbreak impacted everything the brigade did afterwards.

Taguba focused on the breakdown in command and control. Many officers retained a healthy and professional relationship with the soldiers. Others were not as comfortable with the challenges of war and they seemed to adopt a strategy of *rank leveling* when they related to the soldiers under their charge. Those familiar with one another from their years of service in the Reserves, relied on one another and the skills they brought to the 800th. Those with civilian experience as prison guards were considered the subject matter experts regardless of their rank just as those with computer programming skills would be relied on to help with automation. Ultimately, this alternate skills assessment would change the way the 800th approached organizational command and control even in the early days of the war. The successful prisoner of war camp near Umm Qsar was organized and run based on individual proficiency rather than Army doctrine. The result was dissention and confusion. Camp Bucca was a successful prison camp due to the innovative efforts of individual soldiers that simply made something from nothing in the Iraqi desert. The organization of the camp became a labyrinth of command and control that defied explanation.

Taguba discussed the sexual perversions at Abu Ghraib but the report cannot capture the hyper-sexuality that was pervasive in every co-ed unit I encountered. The portable urinals had ornate hand drawn murals on the walls depicting every form of sexual fantasy. Rumors were rampant about soldiers trying to slip away to engage in licentious sexual activities. There are many stories of men and women who held to the highest moral standards but at times the conduct of many soldiers reflected a college campus more than a military deployment. Why is there such a moral vacuum? The answer that we discover to this one question may give us the key to understanding Abu Ghraib.

Despite the accurate observations of the Taguba investigation, it remains only a snapshot of life in the war. The report doesn't serve to answer the broader question of "Why?" it only answers "What?"

It is hard to understand the stresses and fears of a citizen soldier unless you have been in a combat environment. Everything changes in that strange and hostile world. The constant stress of hyper-vigilance and alert wears you down physically and mentally. The sense of constant danger from invisible threats takes a toll on your body and emotions. There is never a time or place to retreat and recharge. Without a strong spiritual core, there is nowhere for soldiers to turn for support in the hostile desert of Iraq. If we want to know why Abu Ghraib occurred, we will have to mobilize with the 800th to Kuwait and then on into Iraq. We have to learn to empathize with men and women who received a call to arms. We have to consider their anxiety as they leave their careers and families and fly into the unknown. We must remember the constant news broadcasts predicting high casualties and the certainty of the experts that chemical agents would rain down on soldiers marching to Baghdad. In short, we have to return to the time before hindsight and second guessing, when courage and duty were the only resources to combat fear. Husbands, fathers, mothers, wives, daughters, sons willingly take the yoke of Soldiers, Sailors, Airmen and Marines all with no promise they would ever come home. Only when we take the journey with these men and women will we be able to consider the impact of Abu Ghraib on our nation.

9-11, THE BEGINNING OF A NEW AMERICA

Every American connects with the war in Iraq in a unique way. For some 9-11 awakened a sense of vulnerability, fear, and remorse for those killed. For others, there are more direct associations. The 800th Military Police Brigade is from the New York City area. For almost all of us, September 11, 2001 is personal.

On September 11, 2001, the church I pastored in rural New Jersey passed a prayer request down our telephonic prayer chain for a member that was still missing in the World Trade Center. He worked in one of the Trade Center Plazas and was scheduled to arrive in one of the towers via the subway just as the planes hit. As the afternoon wore on, we received word that he had escaped the burning tower and found refuge in a small café when the towers fell. He choked on the white dust that filled the New York streets as he made his way to a boat leaving Manhattan. He walked into the church later that night as we gathered for prayer. Afterwards, he and his family joined us at my home. We watched the news together. For the first time he saw the towers fall. You could see the reality begin to settle on him just as the white dust had settled on his shoes. None of us realized how symbolic that dust would become. It represented the crushing of the towers and every life that fell with them. Those were our neighbors and relatives. Those were Americans. From October 2001 to December 2002 we counseled together. He worked hard to overcome the trauma, insecurities and fears terrorism had brought into his life. As I left for Iraq, his dusty shoes became an indelible memory that symbolized our purpose. The World Trade Center Towers once stood high over Manhattan as symbols of American financial strength and generations of innovative work. In a matter of minutes they were pulverized into powder. Never again would we passively allow terrorists to surprise us and destroy lives.

AFGHANISTAN IS ONLY THE BEGINNING

In January 2003 I enjoyed the last hours of the day sitting with my family in our den, watching the news and catching up on their lives. As a pastor, my days were filled with event planning and sermon preparations. The nights were spent with church members in our home bible study or at a church board and committee meeting.

The news in early January 2003 was all about Afghanistan and the search for Usama bin Laden. The political situation there was difficult. Afghan clans and tribes were armed and hoped to move into the political vacuum left by the Taliban's overthrow. There wasn't much change from the previous night's news and commentary soon shifted to speculation about Iraq. President Bush had presented a compelling case for Saddam's removal. He highlighted the clear and present danger that Iraq presented to America. I considered Saddam to be similar to a drug supplier. A supplier may never see the children a local dealer destroys with drugs. All a supplier ever sees is the local dealer who comes to be resupplied with his deadly merchandise. But without the supplier, the dealers have no products to sell. Iraq was poised to supply weapons and chemicals to any terrorist wanting to strike America. Iraq's antagonism toward America and frequent missile attacks against our planes made them a logical threat to the US. America was still reeling from the collapse of the World Trade Center towers and the prospect of an anti-American dictator in the Middle East was alarming.

I had 20 years of military service behind me. In that 20 years I had anticipated I might be called up on a number of occasions, but it had never occurred. I can remember where I was standing when Desert Storm began. The Cold War had been won but our modern military machine was yet untested on the modern battlefield. Then, just like now, the pundits all predicted thousands of body bags filled with young Americans. Then, as now, we were sure that chemicals would be used. Then, unlike now, we faced the fourth largest Army in the world that had been hardened by years of conflict with Iran and had been successful in their takeover of Kuwait. As I stood in the church fellowship hall where I was an assistant pastor, someone announced that we had begun bombing Iraqi positions in Kuwait. Everyone in the room was silent as the words began to sink in. The church had sponsored a night of prayer the week before. The entire nation watched as CNN brought us the war live and in living color. But, nothing really prepares you for a call to arms.

In January 2003, the nation was again glued to the television watching war unfold in the Middle East. When the phone rang that night, I answered it and a Sergeant on the line asked me to sit down. Sergeant First Class France had always been great to help me whenever I had a problem. I regret that she was the one tasked to carry this message because whenever you are told to sit down, you always know that bad news is coming. She informed me that I was being mobilized in a few short days with the 800th Military Police. Both the chaplain and chaplain's assistant normally assigned to that brigade were medically disqualified due to long term chronic conditions and they needed a replacement fast.

As I hung the phone back on the wall and walked back into the den where my four children and my wife were sitting, I wondered why the senior chaplain hadn't spoken with me. He would be one in a series of chaplains that either didn't care to speak or simply didn't recognize the need. It seemed to me that if you want to inform a man he is going to war, you shouldn't just delegate the work to someone; you should be compassionate enough to tell him yourself. I actually could have used a chaplain's counsel that night. This scene was repeated in soldier's living rooms all over the United States. No soldier receives the information like another. Some accept the news with disbelief, some consider quitting, but most accept their fate with quiet resolve and a sense of duty.

Because of the hour of the call and the expression on my face, my wife anticipated what I was about to say. I surveyed the room. All I could think about was my family. My four-year-old daughter was playing in the floor with her seven-year-old sister. My thirteen-year-old son was slumped in the chair sitting on the back of his neck playing a video game while my seventeen-year-old daughter sat close by her mother talking about the war. This was a big year for her especially. She had graduated from high school and was planning to begin college in the fall.

My wife sat looking at me waiting for me to speak, her eyes already betrayed the words I had not yet spoken. Finally, I said, "That was the Army, I've been mobilized." All the reports of weapons of mass destruction, the speculation about body bags in the press, faulty NBC (Nuclear Biological and Chemical) suits, and flag-draped caskets flash through your mind. Your thoughts are flooded with a thousand things that need your attention. You feel torn between preparations to leave and reasons to stay home.

FAMILY PREPARATIONS
The next few days were spent making plans for my absence. We reviewed the calendar to see what events were coming up that Bevalie might need help with. I met with a lawyer to give my wife power of attorney in case she had to take any legal actions while I was gone. I verified that my will was accessible and correct. I began to consider the very real possibility of sending my family to stay with my wife's parents for moral, spiritual, and some physical support. I had lost confidence that the church leadership where I was pastor could respond to her in the way she needed and I felt her own family compassion and empathy.

It is odd how far removed most Americans are from the harsh realities of war. The news broadcasts have made life little more than entertainment. The mobilization of thousands of American National Guard and Reserve soldiers seemed like a reality show or soap opera drama to those untouched by the harsh realities of war.

I called my father to tell him that I had been mobilized. His silence spoke louder than words. There are times that a moment cannot find expression in words. He told me that he only wished he could go in my place. He wondered why young men and fathers have to leave children and wives to go and fight wars. He wondered why nations didn't send those who had lived their lives already rather than those with life still largely in front of them. "It doesn't work that way, Dad." I countered. Each generation has a time they are called upon to stand in the gap and fight for the preservation of liberty and defend our nation. Some are called to engage an enemy in the field and others are not. This was simply my time and we couldn't question why.

The days flew by and as we waited for our last day at home together, Bevalie asked to take a family picture. We set the camera on a tripod and posed the family in front of our fireplace. We took several shots and in each of them misery is written on our faces. We never said it out loud but both of us wondered if that would be the last picture our family would ever have together.

I emailed a message to the elders on the church board and asked them to meet with me before church on Sunday. I emphasized that this was an important meeting. I was the second pastor in the history of the church to leave for war. The first was hanged in the Revolutionary war. I hoped that I would beat that trend in my own wartime experience.

Three out of four elders on the church board came to the meeting. One elder was contentious about everything in the church. There seemed to be no action that I could take or decision I could make without his challenge. Churches, board rooms, Army staff meetings, and even the family dinner table all have power struggles. It is a part of our human nature to struggle with whoever has authority over us. This particular man fought me at every turn and even at this point, he couldn't respond and support me.

This was my first real encounter with "Narcissism". I didn't really understand it at the time but throughout the deployment, I would see manifestations of it and come to recognize it for the destructive force that it is. I mention it here to illustrate that the 800th MP Brigade is not unlike any other group of people in this respect. Members of my own church board treated me in ways that the Army would never allow. I realized that my wife would not be able to remain in the church. For her to remain in New Jersey, I would need to count on the elders to care for my family while I was gone. I suspected I could not count on them. I spoke to a realtor about possibly putting my home on the market. Two events convinced us to sell our home. The first was my resignation as the pastor of the church. The decision to resign was one of the most difficult decisions of my life. Beyond the employment, I felt a sense of purpose and personal investment in the church. The other factor was the possibility that I might not come home from the war. I didn't want to be fatalistic but I have seen and helped too many people as they had to make decisions in a time of grief. I did not want my wife to be burdened with making decisions about the house if that time ever came.

While the leadership of the church was a disappointment, most of the membership was sympathetic and supportive. One woman stitched together a flag using desert camouflage material and sewed a cross on each side. She came over to our home and presented her prize to me. I was genuinely grateful and used the flag many times during the deployment. Some called and offered prayer support while others offered tools for ministry and religious literature for soldiers. Later that evening the church held a prayer service and asked God to bless me and keep me safe.

I suspected that would be my last night as the pastor of the little country church we had come to care for so much. We had been called there when the church was in a hard nosedive. Attendance was down. It was as if someone had sucked all the air out of the room. I left active duty to take the call and we had worked hard to turn the church around and make it viable again. We were both excited about the progress the church had made in the two years of ministry we enjoyed there. Our children had made friends there and we had come to feel a great attachment to the members that had become our friends. One man who recently joined the church donated a lap top computer for me to take along for my work. That proved to be a valuable asset as I needed it to complete a number of projects for the brigade. A friend that had always supported our vision there promised to check in on Bevalie and the kids often. Not only did he keep his promise to do that, but he was faithful to email me with the news while I was deployed as well. Their family prayed for and demonstrated their love for my family while I was gone and that meant the world to me. An elder in the church donated a box of literature for me to pass out. So with these tokens of love and support, we packed my bags and waited for the evening to come.

After the short prayer service and after everyone finished saying good-bye we went home and I tucked the children in bed. Sometime in the middle of the night I got up to check on the youngest two girls. Their room was a light bubblegum pink color and they slept in matching princess beds beside one another. Never have I seen anything as beautiful as those girls asleep in their beds that night. I stood at the end of one bed and took in each moment as if it were my last to ever see them. My mind didn't have a thought. My eyes couldn't take enough in. I couldn't contemplate the possibility of never seeing them again and so I just stood there, looking, weeping, and wondering. That picture is forever burned into my mind.

INTRODUCTIONS

The next morning we loaded my bags and left for Uniondale, New York and my introduction to the 800th MP Brigade. From Arkansas to New York, men and women were making their way in to the 800th Headquarters. I met the staff and began to take inventory of their dispositions. The JAG was warm and approachable, the chemical officer seemed to be nervous and to lack confidence but he was knowledgeable about chemicals on the battlefield. The assistant intelligence officer was helpful and the Brigade Operations officer, Major Anthony Cavallaro was competent and self assured. The personnel officer, MAJ David Hinzman was also competent and approachable. They all seemed genuine and receptive to their new chaplain as I began the process of collecting data about the soldiers, their mission, their expectations of the chaplain, and an inventory of equipment.

I was facing an assignment unlike any I had experienced before. I had served as a battalion chaplain with the 101st Airborne and as a community chaplain in Germany, but never had I served as a brigade chaplain in a time of war, especially in a brigade that would be the largest in the theater once all the battalions arrived. The chaplain who had served in the position was a colonel. I was a Captain and I had not even been to the Army's Chaplains Advanced Course. That is a where you are taught how to be a brigade chaplain. Yet, I was going to war with a unit I didn't know and in a position I was under qualified for. That is what most Americans call opportunity! I call it intimidating.

I searched for the Brigade commander, Brigadier General

Hill. I had spoken to him on the phone before I arrived in Uniondale, NY, and I was impressed with his determination to take a chaplain with the 800th to Kuwait. A somewhat soft-spoken man, he was a devout Roman Catholic, and he understood the spiritual nature of life, and the needs of soldiers to have a chaplain in a crisis. Brigadier General Paul H. Hill was commissioned a second lieutenant in the Infantry Branch through the Reserve Officer Training Program [ROTC] program at Duquesne University, Pittsburgh, PA. He served as a platoon leader with the 82nd Airborne Division at Fort Bragg, NC. Following his assignment to the 82nd Airborne Division he served with Army Special Forces in various positions at Fort Bragg, Thailand and with a mobile training team in Vietnam. His final assignment with Special Forces was as the commander of Special Forces Team 41, Lopburi, Thailand. After he transitioned from active duty to the reserves, General Hill served in various units and in several different leadership and command positions. In May of 1999, then, Colonel Hill, was to command the 800th Military Police Brigade (EPW). He commanded the Brigade from 1999 to 2003. He had the requisite experience and institutional knowledge to command the Brigade well and his command influence was manifest everywhere. All that I spoke to held him in high regard. The only significant complaint against him was his toleration of soldier's misbehavior. He seemed willing to overlook unprofessional behavior. I attributed that to the nature of the reserves. Part-time soldiers are hard to recruit and even harder to keep. Because commanders are required to retain enough manpower to accomplish the mission, they sometimes feel compelled to tolerate a lower standard of conduct. The limited exposure commanders have on two-day drill weekends doesn't allow enough time for them to see all the soldiers in every context. Most of the soldiers are on their best behavior on drill weekends and their shortcomings remain undetected until they transition to full time service. When the National Guard or Reserves deploy, commanders are not able to replace personnel. They are forced to deal with bad conduct in creative ways just to retain enough soldiers to accomplish the mission. When the 800th was extended after the end of hostilities, the attrition of personnel had already taken a toll and their indulgence of immoral conduct manifested in ways the commander and the nation would come to regret. On balance, a minority of soldiers struggle with their conduct. The vast majority of National Guard and Reserve soldiers are honorable men and women. They are Americans answering a call to duty in service to their nation. They sacrifice their time, talents, vocational advancement, and too often their lives for little extrinsic reward. Their heroism and selfless service shouldn't be overshadowed by the few that taint the service of the Guard and Reserves by their lack of discipline and moral foundations.

After my introductions to the staff, I began the process of collecting my equipment and supplies for the journey ahead. Conspicuous by his absence was the brigade chaplain assigned to the 800th prior to my transfer. I expected him to be there to hand off his brigade and show me the supplies that were available. I soon discovered that there were no supplies, there was no deployment plan, there was no continuity folder, and there was no record of the brigade's religious preferences. In fact there was nothing to indicate a chaplain had ever been there except a few brief entries in the brigade's tactical standard operating procedures [TACSOP] manual. Even that was oriented almost entirely toward Roman Catholic issues and the proper burial of Muslims. Rather than a curse, this was a blessing. I have my own style of ministry and I now felt at liberty to develop my ministry to the 800th. The outgoing chaplain did come to deliver the prayer at the official ceremony where city dignitaries and New York Senator Schumer spoke.

The next few days were spent packing and preparing for our movement to Fort Dix. I began to get better acquainted with the brigade staff, particularly with the Judge Advocate, the personnel officer, the headquarters commander, the doctor, the chemical officer, and the headquarters first sergeant. I also met the Command Sergeant Major soon after arriving but knew instinctively that I needed to be guarded and careful how I handled my relationship with him.

I was very impressed with several of the enlisted men and women who worked with great enthusiasm and thoroughness. They were personally invested in the mission. Almost all of the members of the 800th had been affected in one way or another by the events of September 11, 2001. Living in and around the Metro New York area, many of them knew victims of the terrorist attack on the trade towers and several were policemen with the New York City Police Department. For them, this deployment was personal. This can not be overemphasized. The men and women of the 800th MP Brigade felt they had a personal investment in Operation Enduring Freedom. Their homes had been affected by terrorism. Their friends had been a part of the carnage or the rescue and clean up of the World Trade Center towers. They talked about how the towers had bled the blood of their friends and family that day. There are images in their minds that will never go away.

The Brigade Operations officer, Major Cavallaro, had worked on the 30th floor of Two World Trade Center when One Trade Center was struck by the first airplane. He checked the offices and evacuated when the second plane hit Two World Trade Center. Everyone stopped moving as the towers swayed. They could see people standing at the windows of the first tower looking for escape. Once out of the building, he and many others watched as their world crumbled with the trade towers collapse. Terrorists brought violence to an unsuspecting, free, and industrious people.

Now they were going to the terrorist's hometown. They were to be part of a pre-emptive strike against a supplier of materials and provider of a safe haven for terrorists. The departmental seals for the police and fire departments of New York City went with the unit every where they went and they were hung on the walls wherever the 800th set up shop. The internment camps were named after fallen fire-fighters; Camp Bucca was the first.

LAUNCHPAD

Fort Dix was a dismal place to stay before our deployment to the war. The conditions in the barracks were terrible. I have never been sick in all my adult life like I was there. Just breathing the air full of mold and spores was enough to warrant a purple heart! It was through that sickness that I came to know the brigade's medical team. 1Lt Ken Rameriz, the Brigade's Physician Assistant (PA) became a good friend. He and I stayed close together throughout our stay in Kuwait. I also developed solid friendships with Lieutenant Colonel Roy Shere, the Public Affairs Officer (PAO) and Lieutenant Colonel James O'Hare, the Staff Judge Advocate (JAG) throughout and after the deployment. These are God-fearing men, one from Little Rock, Arkansas and the others from Staten Island. O'Hare married his wife Renee in April 1987. They have three children together and like all the other parents called to the war, leaving them was the hardest part of serving. His son's Cub Scout Pack held up his crossover into Boy Scouts a few weeks until O'Hare returned. Just missing out on routine events like ball games and school activities hurt, as did not being able to just hug your wife. We all came from different parts of the country and experienced life from different perspectives; yet we all three found common ground in our desire to have close companionship that was trustworthy, encouraging, and faithful. Ken was a particularly sensitive man. Each night when the lights were cut out Ken would set his personal laptop computer on a stack of footlockers and watch the same slide show over and over. His wife Mary and his children were featured in digital pictures that played every night until he fell asleep while staring at them. The separation was hard for all of us but my heart really went out to Ken.

In addition to the "luxurious" accommodations, the chow hall was over-filled. The lines were long and the tables were difficult to find in the mass of people waiting to sit down. Often we would stand in the rain or snow outside while waiting in line. There was no television in the barracks that would receive anything but static. Cell phones had no reception except on the second floor standing by the urinals in the men's bathroom, and there were no pay phones in the barracks until a week before we left. I wondered if someone forgot to tell Fort Dix they were having guests!

Our mission at Fort Dix was to attend the training that the Army required for certification. When National Guard and Reserve Units are mobilized, the Army wisely requires them to attend various classes on chemical warfare, first aid, and other classes to reinforce common soldier skills that may have been lost to citizen soldiers. In addition to the training, active duty allows these part-time soldiers to come together as a team.

One of the critical tasks soldiers must accomplish for certification is weapons qualifications. Days on the firing ranges can be long as soldiers become reacquainted with weapons they rarely have an opportunity to fire when drilling on the weekends in Uniondale. Weapons control was particularly tight while we were processing through Fort Dix. On one occasion, it was rumored that a Lieutenant Colonel discharged a round when he carried his weapon to the clearing barrel. The clearing barrel is set up to test your weapon after you have cleared it. He had inadvertently left a round in the weapon and it fired into the barrel just as it was supposed to. There wasn't an injury but the Lieutenant Colonel allegedly received disciplinary action for the incident. That sort of peacetime safety and caution would not traverse the ocean to the desert of Iraq.

On January 27th, I met Chaplain (Lieutenant Colonel) Ellis. Chaplain Ellis is a National Guard chaplain that initially appeared to be a little backward. While he admitted his lack of experience, fear and apprehension about being on active duty, I would learn to respect him for his honesty, sincerity, and his willingness to do what is right regardless of conventional wisdom. On the same day, I received a call from the Forces Command (FORSCOM) chaplain's office. They were adamant that I should have a chaplain's assistant. I listened carefully and promised to bring the issue up with the Brigade. Since the Brigade commander was already in Kuwait, I struggled to get the issue before anyone that felt responsible to bring in a new assistant. The 800th had a chaplain's assistant assigned, but like the chaplain that was assigned, she also was medically unqualified to deploy.

When I called home that night, my wife gave me disturbing news from the home front. The water pipes had burst in the garage and the flow of water from them had created an enormous sheet of ice down from the garage to the bottom of our sloping driveway. She had taken the kids to church but she returned home to try and shut the water off which was coming out in gallons per minute. I asked if anyone had come to help her from the church. The answer was a disappointing, "no." She also informed me that one of the elders at the church was beginning to make changes to the worship service program. These bits of information seemed to affirm my intuition that I wouldn't be able to return to the little New Jersey church that had been our home for two years. I wondered what God had planned for us on the other side of Operation Iraqi Freedom.

Just after we were issued our DCUs (Desert Camouflage Uniforms) the snow began to fall. Snow drifts pilled up against cars and driving was impossible. Only in the Army can you wear desert uniforms in snow that reaches your waist.

The preparations for deployment continued and most of us were anxious to leave. One of my roommates had been to Camp Doha, Kuwait, before and promised us that no manner of misery was worse than standing in the desert with 115 degree temperatures all day long. Still, Fort Dix didn't do anything that made you want to stay any longer than necessary.

The closer we got to deployment, the more the soldiers wanted to visit with their families. The post commander, Colonel Lowery, had issued a decree that forbid soldiers to leave the post and their families were discouraged from coming on-post to visit as well. This decision had a horrible affect on the unit's morale and flew in the face of American tradition that demonstrated a respect for families and the soldier's sacrifice in a time of war. Since both the commander and the deputy commander were already in Kuwait, the Headquarters commander for the 800th and the 220th MP Brigades went to speak to the installation commander about the policy. They invited me to come along as well. When we entered the commander's office, we were invited to sit down and we noticed right away that the commander was not alone. There was a considerable-sized group gathered in the office. All but his Sergeant Major outranked us. The three of us sat lined up side by side on the couch like school children visiting the principle's office. The Colonel walked across the room to join us. After brief introductions he tossed a pile of papers on the table in front of us.

He pointed to a bar graph on the top and asked, "Do you know what that is?" Of course we had no idea. "That is the soldiers I am responsible for on this post! I have to see that each one of them becomes proficient enough to send to war. More and more soldiers are arriving here and I have as many troops here under my command as any other major installation. If I do not do my job, soldiers are going to get killed. I know you three think you are watching out for the soldiers but you need to learn this lesson, you are not helping them at all. In fact, you're going to get them killed! When soldiers come to Fort Dix, they have already said their good-byes and there shouldn't be any unfinished family business."

A major joined in to explain that we had no idea just how bad this war was going to be and the soldiers had to be prepared for it. Seeing their families before they leave was not part of the preparations for war. The discussion continued on for several minutes. I tried to point out that the bars on his graph were not soldiers but there were in fact real flesh and blood soldiers that were afraid for themselves and for their families. There were mothers that wanted to see their children perhaps for the last time and husbands that wanted to see their wives. There were mothers and fathers wanting to send their sons and daughters off with one last embrace. The deployments had been so quick and with such short notice that the reality of it was just now sinking in and the soldiers were brooding about being locked down on post.

The commander was unmoved and uninspired to allow soldiers time to visit with their families. I remembered reading someplace that many leaders are good at graphs and drawing arrows on maps but precious few know anything about the soldiers at the tip of the arrow. Our First Sergeant did what First Sergeants are supposed to do, he took care of his soldier's emotional needs in order to keep them emotionally fit to fight. They visited with their families even if it was without the commanders blessings.

While we were at Fort Dix, we went through several key events that helped us bond together. My first official service to the Brigade was the observation of the Martin Luther King Jr. day. I remember that I spent a great deal of time pondering just what he stood for and after I finished, a number of the soldiers affirmed that I had hit the mark. I read Galatians 5:1, 13-15.

"For freedom Christ has set us free; stand firm therefore, and do not submit again to a yoke of slavery. For you were called to freedom, brothers. Only do not use your freedom as an opportunity for the flesh, but through love serve one another. For the whole law is fulfilled in one word: 'You shall love your neighbor as yourself.' But if you bite and devour one another, watch out that you are not consumed by one another."(ESV)

I focused on our need to depend on one another and fulfill the prophetic dream that MLK shared in the infamous "I Have a Dream" speech. The conduct of radical Muslims since the liberation of Iraq has affirmed that there is no place in America for petty racist issues. Those that hate America do not care if we are black, white, or any combination of the two. They will decapitate anyone who opposes their oppressive cult of death and hate.

After we observed MLK day, we also mourned the space shuttle Columbia's tragic crash. From September 11th to the shuttle crash, we began to feel that things might not always go perfect even in the most well organized operations. No one mentioned it directly but the Columbia tragedy had an impact on our confidence especially with the assurances we were getting about Saddam's use of weapons of mass destruction.

As the time to fly to Kuwait drew closer, I again became concerned about an officer in the Headquarters Company and the Brigade Sergeant Major. My journal entry from January 29th reads, *"I'm not sure the officer is adjusting well. She is capable I believe, but her insecurity causes her to be withdrawn and reserved.*" She left most evenings to spend social time with another officer in a subordinate battalion. That relationship would eventually earn her disciplinary action in Iraq. At Fort Dix, she came in late most evenings, and after arriving back late, she had little time to interact with the soldiers. This was a crucial time for the unit to come together as we were transitioning from part-time soldiers to the active Army. I wondered how her consistent absence would affect the confidence of the soldiers in her command. Eventually, she did seem to build some strong relationships with some of the females in the Headquarters Company but they became more like friendships between peers than soldiers working with their commander.

The Headquarters First Sergeant consistently stepped in and filled the role she left vacant. He also stepped into the role the Brigade Sergeant Major left open by his absence from unit formations and training. The Sergeant Major was usually absent from the unit and he was always flirtatious with females. He played some sort of cell phone message game with one of the young soldiers. I wondered if they took offense to his forwardness, putting his arm around them and making jokes that were always borderline. His behavior seemed more akin to a high school jock that played fast and loose with the cheerleaders than a Command Sergeant Major in a high profile unit preparing to deploy to war. I approached the JAG about the issue and learned that he was aware of it and that he was as concerned as I. He verbally counseled the Sergeant Major who never admitted to wrongdoing. He was told that his actions constituted sexual harassment and that it would not be tolerated.

The Sergeant Major was ultimately removed from his position in Iraq and sent home because of his fraternization with other soldiers. Sexual preoccupations emerged as a dominate theme in Kuwait. The urinals became canvas for many young artist who had become adept at drawing the female anatomy. Pornography is not allowed in Islamic countries and magazines weren't available in the bookstores. The sad testimony from the murals on the walls bears witness to the depraved thoughts and hyper sexuality of the young people in America. This sex saturated culture was evidenced in the pictures that eventually came out of Abu Ghraib as well.

One of the most disturbing incidents I recall took place on January 29th. I was working the processing table for the installation chaplain, giving religious support and counsel to soldiers processing for deployment when a young female asked if she could speak with me in private. She was about 26 years old and had been married four years. We began to talk and she mentioned her three-year-old child. Tears poured from her eyes each time she mentioned him. She missed him and wanted to hold him. Her maternal instincts pressed her to return home and her fears of never seeing him again weighed heavy on her mind. The part-time money from drills and the college grants the military promised seemed unimportant to her now that she faced deployment to hostile territories and an uncertain future.

Everything in me affirms her desire to return home. I wondered about the sanity of a nation that sends its young mothers to war leaving the children with capable and able bodied men. I only wished that the situation had been forced upon us but we have to realize that as a free people, we have created this madness ourselves. I counseled her using the five steps of grieving that a person transitions through after the death of a loved one. We talked about her adjustment time and our mutual hope for a short conflict and quick flight home. She calmed down and left encouraged. For every bit of encouragement she felt when she left, I was a little worse off.

PUTTING ON A WAR FACE

I became concerned with what I began to call, the "Drill Mentality". All day and all night, I heard planes taking off from the nearby airfield. It seemed as if they were always taking off and never landing. The truth of what lay before us was just out of reach for most of the soldiers in the brigade. They laughed and joked without any reference to the upcoming conflict. It is natural to avoid thinking about something unpleasant or dreaded but these men and women needed to think about it for the sake of their families.

Soldiers have a dual responsibility to prepare themselves as well as their families. I asked some of them what they thought about going to war and the blank expression on their face explained it all. I asked for a training time to work on this issue with the soldiers of the 800th. I was granted a full day to present several briefings to them.

After some fairly generic classes on Accommodating Religious Practices and Suicide Awareness, I began to search for a means to help them transition to the realities of war. I conducted two classes I called, *"The Emotional Process of Deployment"* and *"Family Separation and the Fear of Death"*. I decided to use the movie, "We Were Soldiers".

The first half of the movie is about the unit's preparation for war and the process of family separation prior to their deployment to Vietnam. I required all of the soldiers to sit through the first half of the movie and then we discussed it afterwards.

After a short break, I presented the second half to those who chose to stay and watch. The second half shows the tragedy of war and the face of death. This was a reality check for most of the soldiers. After the movie a number of the soldiers were moved and a somber atmosphere remained for sometime. I noticed a different mindset after that. Soldiers began to take this war more seriously and most important for this phase of our deployment, they began to talk to their families with a more realistic and serious tone.

As I worked towards putting together an accurate picture of the Brigade and the Battalions that would soon join us on active duty to serve under the Brigade, I became aware that the battalions we would work with were not the same battalions that the brigade worked with in peacetime. A bizarre structure in the Reserves has the 800th commanding different battalions in peacetime than she would during the war. This meant that the operational procedures and the ability to anticipate a unit's real capabilities were not able to be known until after we deployed into the theater of operations. The brigade commander would be introduced to the battalion commanders during the conflict. This situation handicapped the brigade since the usual relationship that developed between units couldn't exist until after the deployment to Kuwait.

Even then, the separate battalions trickled in at such a slow rate that proper attention couldn't be given to integrating them into the brigade as it should have been. Each battalion would be given a mission to accomplish and would be expected to brief the brigade commander on their progress. This unfamiliarity would be detrimental to the predictability of the 800th MP Brigade after it was finally constituted in Kuwait. Later, the situation was exacerbated when the brigade was reconstituted for the second mission to supervise the civilian prisons like the one at Abu Ghraib while they planned for a change of command. There simply was not enough Brigade staff to supervise all the separate battalions and there was no institutional knowledge of where problems might occur.

WHEELS UP

Getting to the battlefield is much more complicated than I used to think. We were scheduled to fly and packed to leave. Hours before we loaded up in the buses that carried us to the airfield, the giant C-5 transport planes were grounded for maintenance. We went back to the barracks rooms to unpack the necessary items and stay another day. This cycle of loading on the bus and returning to the barracks continued for several days and then finally, our first group was airborne in the C-5. The rest of us waited for our flight time and the word came that our C-5 was down for maintenance again. We eventually made it as far as the air terminal and I led the group in prayer to ask God to watch over us as we traveled.

As we moved into position to load, we were told the plane was down for maintenance. Over the next several days we would go to the terminal, I would lead the group in prayer, we would stand in line to load, and then go back to the barracks because the planes were down for maintenance. Once when we were onboard and belted up, word came that the plane was grounded and we had to get off again.

The Command Sergeant Major stood at the front of the plane and let loose a string of obscenities that would make a sailor blush. The Headquarters First Sergeant chided him publicly. The Sergeant Major retorted that he had enough stripes to say whatever he wanted in public. I had never heard rank used as an excuse for childish emotionalism before. His answer confirmed his lack of character and his self-serving and myopic view of life. The stripes he wore belonged to the Army and should represent maturity, selfless service, and experienced leadership rather than being permission for grandstanding and public exhibitions. The Headquarters First Sergeant grew more frustrated over the Headquarters Commander's dependence on him like a father and the Sergeant Major's lack of contribution to the unit. He continued to fill in the void left by them both but even he would eventually wear down before we arrived in Kuwait.

We waited while the first group landed at Dover Air Force Base and was grounded there for maintenance. After several days, we boarded a C-5 for the last time. I stood to give a prayer and MAJ. Cavalero joked that I should wait until we were airborne because my prayers for safety seemed to result in more airplane maintenance. I waited until the plane took off and the second group was on its way before I stood and prayed with the group. Ironically, when we stopped to refuel, we were once again grounded for airplane maintenance.

We spent several days at an Air Force Base waiting to fly again. In the meantime, the first group had made it to Kuwait. On February 23rd, we finally were on our way to Moron Air Force Base, Spain.

When we arrived at Moran, AFB the Air Force seemed more interested in quarantining us in a warehouse than hosting us as guests on our way to Kuwait. Other than the austere warehouse accommodations and the nasty bathrooms we had to use however, Moron was a great place to get stuck. We were able to catch up on our email at the library and use the gym. The scenery looked tropical. It was a great place to transition from home where the snow was waist deep to the battlefield where the sand never melts.

Moron AFB turned out to be some of the best time I had to spend time with the brigade personnel officer (S1). Major Dave Hinzman was another of those men with great character who has a way of growing on you. One particular afternoon as we ate lunch with a small group of other men we began to discuss religion. He felt that whatever church you wanted to go to was fine and in fact, all that you need to do is believe and going to church is an optional activity. He expressed his disappointment in the human failings of the church.

I emphasized that a personal relationship with God is indeed possible by faith alone but that the relationship required obedience to be authentic and God has commanded that Christians gather for worship regardless of our disappointments in other people. We engaged in a lengthy debate that culminated in his reading Lee Stroble's, "The Case for

Christ." He was a changed man after that and saw the need to have his family in a church where they would be able to grow in their faith together as a family.

As we continued to enjoy meals and walks together, I forged deeper friendships with several of the soldiers, Master Sergeant Wilson Beamer, Major Stephan Petranker (a practicing Jew), Lt. Ramirez, Lieutenant Colonel, O'Hare, and Lieutenant Colonel Shere, and Maj. Hartman. My prayers at meals expanded to include our families, fears, health, and the mission. Prayers are intangible factors that are often forgotten but they are powerful means to draw a unit together. Through the merging of our lives and views, a new creation was sculpted from the old. Despite the shortcomings of a select few, the 800th MP Brigade was beginning to mature and come into her own.

After a week or so, our stay in Spain was over. Each of us wanted to have our picture made standing by the "Moron Operations Center" sign. At last we boarded the C-5 and continued on our journey to join our comrades in Kuwait. A couple of weeks had passed since we had seen them last and they had already settled into the warehouse accommodations at Camp Arifjan, Kuwait. We arrived, set up our cots and began to look around our new home. There wasn't much to examine. A line of warehouses was home to thousands of military members. The bathrooms and the showers were in portable trailers. Tents were set up around the perimeter of our area that had air conditioner units attached. We began to wonder how we might be able to rate one of those tents in the future. Flags for the state National Guard units were flying outside many of the tents. Tents, warehouses and sand pretty much describes Camp Arifjan.

It didn't take long to realize that sleeping on a cot for a long period of time was going to be difficult. Lieutenant Colonel Shere, the Public Affairs Officer who had become my close friend at Fort Dix, flew out with the first group and arrived in Kuwait more than a week before the second group did. He had bought a foam mattress to lay on his cot and a bright red fuzzy blanket. In the couple of weeks he had been at Camp Arifjan, he had learned to make himself comfortable. I scoffed a little at his cosmopolitan look in a combat environment. But, under his careful direction and tutelage, it wasn't long until I had invested in a mattress and blanket as well.

TOO CLOSE FOR COMFORT

Without private rooms, changing clothes was a chore. Either you had to forget about modesty or walk one hundred feet or so to the bathrooms every time you needed to change your clothes. I decided to use my rain poncho as a private dressing room. With the close co-ed quarters, this innovation worked pretty well. I waited until dark and then slipped my poncho on and changed clothes underneath. Co-ed living situations have always been a challenge for me in the military. I have struggled to maintain a proper respect for myself and the women in my unit while at the same time being efficient in my use of space and time. Hygiene is often neglected by some soldiers in these sorts of environments because of the lack of any privacy. I have showered in gyms with guys since high school and that never bothered me, but even in a set of Army BDUs, a woman is still a woman.

Others also were aware that there were two sexes in the warehouse. It wasn't long before I first noticed the odd relationship between a female major and a senior NCO. When I asked why they left the warehouse together late in the night and why he provided her with personal service like hot coffee in the morning I was told that they had served together in another unit and that their relationship was close but professional. I decided to take that at face value since the senior NCO had earned my respect by his professionalism in every other area that I had worked with him. Both of these soldiers are mentioned in the Taguba report for inappropriate behavior and for drinking alcohol together. The interpersonal relationships in the brigade were beginning to look like an episode of *Friends* or *Sex in the City*. Rather than fiction being taken from reality, reality was taking its cues from fiction. Already the Sergeant Major and now a field grade officer and senior NCO was suspect for inappropriate relationships.

Soon after these observations, an officer in the leadership of the headquarters company became entangled in a fraternization drama with a junior NCO. The officer tried too push the soldier away but his emotional attachment was to strong. I soon found myself sitting with the officer and First Sergeant along with General Hill to discuss the issue. It seems that the soldier had fallen in love and would not forgo the relationship to maintain a career in the military.

General Hill did not want to deal with this issue. He evaded the allegations of sexual misconduct and fraternization and instead discussed the soldier's potential need for psychological counsel. Several officers decided that the commander's conduct was unacceptable and they were not willing to cooperate with the company commander at all. She began to see her position and responsibilities erode to simply manning a mail room and other house cleaning duties. This was my first real disappointment with the 800th. I had assumed that a general officer would not tolerate this sort of behavior from junior officers and yet, we left the office never dealing with the real issue in order to preserve the career of this young captain.

Where do you turn from a discussion with a General? While the Army answer is to carry a problem up the chain of command, you don't want to embarrass your commander if there is no concrete proof of misconduct. You begin to question whether this is serious enough to take higher or if you will look like someone who is a malcontent and a trouble maker. If I decided to push this issue now, I would be ostracized from a large portion of the group, I wouldn't be trusted (ironically for doing the right thing), and my ministry to the group at large would begin to evaporate before my eyes. Was this a big enough problem to raise the issue higher when there was no evidence to back up allegations?

In addition to those considerations, the larger issue was our role in the war with Iraq. Did I want two key players removed from staff just before we went to war? This would mean the unit would be less capable to accomplish the mission and other soldiers would suffer as a result of the lost leadership. Reserve Component units do not have an individual replacement system to mitigate medical or other losses. Over time, the 800th MP Brigade already suffered from critical personnel shortages due to medical releases and individual demobilizations. It was at this point that I began to consult with the JAG, Lieutenant Colonel James O'Hare regularly for advice. I learned to trust his advice about when to push and when to back off. We ordinarily agreed when there was a cause to be championed. He proved to be knowledgeable, trustworthy, and compassionate. I was just beginning to learn what life was like as a brigade chaplain.

This was not the end of the soap opera like dramas in the 800th. Later in the deployment an allegation of a same sex relationship between an officer at Camp Bucca and an officer in the Brigade Operations section presented yet another sexually oriented distraction for the brigade. This particular allegation was neither proved nor disproved. The officers were separated to avoid any future speculation. This series of revelations caused me to doubt my own ability to make accurate observations of human behavior. I wanted to believe that each allegation of sexual deviance was an unsubstantiated rumor but much to my chagrin, each one of the accusations began to materialize as true. Most avoided any significant legal actions until the deployment neared completion.

Pushing problems to the side by separating troublesome soldiers seemed to be the strategy of choice for the Brigade Commander. One after another, soldiers were separated geographically by assigning one to work at Camp Bucca while the other remained in Kuwait. Had the Brigade redeployed in the summer of 2004 as they anticipated, this would probably have worked but instead, soldiers were reunited as the mission changed from EPW operations to the rebuilding of the entire penitentiary system in Iraq.

The brigade established a Tactical Operations Center (TOC) in one of the better equipped warehouses on Camp Arifjan. I was able to get a lap top computer and I began to work on my systems to track and manage the chaplains of subordinate battalions. We all paid close attention to the news and imagined that every sunrise might begin the push to Baghdad. There was only one battalion in Kuwait, the 724th MP Battalion from Florida. The battalion chaplain had previously served in the Marines and seemed to be a godly man. From the beginning however, he was in conflict with his commander and executive officer. I had been urged by a training officer at Fort Dix to have him removed from his position as Battalion Chaplain. While I had some concerns, I felt that was an extraordinary request to make since the unit was soon to leave for Kuwait. Neither the chaplain nor the executive officer seemed to be inclined to reconcile their differences and I worked to serve as an intermediary and peacemaker between them. In time, they found a way to work peaceably together but the efficacy of the chaplain's ministry suffered terribly in the first half of the deployment.

The 724th was the battalion that would begin building Camp Bucca, the Enemy Prisoner of War Camp (EPW) in Iraq. One battalion wouldn't be enough to man the camp however. We would need at least three battalions in country and there weren't any that had flights planned in the next few days. We waited for word that help was on the way but each night at the staff briefing, the news was the same. No battalions had left the states for Kuwait. The personnel we had was all that was available. Part of my mission involved staff relations. Not only would I need to strive to keep an open relationship with members of the staff but I would need to keep their relationships with one another in good repair as well.

One of the most difficult situations I faced in my position as brigade chaplain was just how many waves to make and how hard I should push for conformity to Army standards. The textbook always demands conformity with zero tolerance for non-conformists but what do you do when the irregular behavior is so widespread that enforcement would affect the unit's ability to accomplish the mission in a time of war? I desperately wanted to be the one bringing it to the commander and for him to take aggressive action against it. Unfortunately, the commander was already in Kuwait when I struggled with the 724th chaplain at Fort Dix and once we arrived at Camp Arifjan, everyone was heavily engaged in the mission. We needed more people not less! I tried to establish relationships with those needing behavioral adjustments but soon found that they felt untouchable given the brigades tactical situation. Since they imagined they were too vital to be relieved, their self-restraint eroded further. I decided to invest my energy where I was able to accomplish positive results, and I began to steer away from those who were flagrantly violating Army policies and regulations. I used the email system to publish a "Thought of the Day" with the hope that the posts on everyone's computer screens might begin to have some positive affect on the consciences of the offenders. This is a chaplain's version of covert warfare. I posted the slides in both English and Spanish but without the commander's passion for integrity in the unit, I wasn't able to influence them.

As time passed, our apprehension and tension rose. Issues surrounding the misconduct or incompetence of a couple of the Brigades soldiers had evaporated. Larger issues were now coming into focus. Every night the briefings informed us of the positions the Iraqi battalions occupied and their preparedness for battle. We kept up with Chemical Ali's position because we expected him to release the chemicals employed against the coalition. Our own mission remained on hold. The Kuwaitis refused to allow us to build an EPW camp in Kuwait and the Saudis likewise refused. The Brigades Deputy Commander was adamant about commanding a mission to build camps in the north but that would depend on the responsiveness of Turkey. Turkey was in the coalition one day and then out the next. Without their participation, we couldn't build a camp before the actual conflict began. That meant that at least one camp or up to three camps would have to be built inside Iraq after the war began. The logistics of having prisoners without a finished EPW camp were complicated. All we could do until we went into Iraq was coordinate and plan.

I continued to get a feel for the command, staff, and soldiers of the 800th MP Brigade. There was a tension between many of the female officers on the staff. Rarely did it manifest itself in the open but nothing seemed to flow as smoothly as it should. Tasks and information were not being shared between them. One occasion in particular involved housing for the soldiers. The advance party had voluntarily withdrawn the brigade from the housing list and instead volunteered us to remain in the warehouse. Most units remained in the warehouses for only a short time and then either moved forward to preposition themselves for movement into Iraq or they would move into tents around the perimeter of the post which were air-conditioned.

One of the first nights we were there, a dust storm came

through the camp. The dust in Kuwait is not like the sand on American beaches. It's more like finely-ground dust. When the wind picks it up in the air it turns the sky orange and obstructs much of the sunlight. At night you can't see to travel and you can hardly breath at all, even with some sort of filter over you mouth. The dust storm that hit that night filled the warehouse with a cloud of dust even with the doors closed. We all slept with something over our face to try and breathe and we were covered with dust. The next day everyone coughed and hacked trying to clear it out of our throats. My glasses were destroyed by the sandblasting they took and whatever clean clothes I had were layered with the dust too.

The company commander began to work the issue of improving our housing situation when she arrived but found herself obstructed by other officers already involved and unwilling to surrender the role of arbitrating the housing situation. The job clearly belonged to the headquarters commander but the staff was determined to block her efforts to work on the housing issue. This was just one more distraction that involved the Headquarters Commander. Her First Sergeant would seek refuge in the EPW camp and live there just to get away from her and the issues she was involved in. She was not an unpleasant person to be around, but she was terribly insecure and her inappropriate relationships with soldiers of all ranks made everyone apprehensive around her. When I accompanied her to talk with the brigade commander about the housing issue, he was irritated at first by what he considered to be whining. Certainly he had more important things to do than referee internal strife over petty issues and he was concerned that soldiers were complaining about their spartan living conditions when the infantry was living in fox holes. It seemed to him that the staff ought to be able to negotiate this without having a general officer get involved and he was correct.

The issue was not discontent over spartan conditions but instead, command and control was being confused. The company commander should have had the housing mission but she was not allowed to carry out that mission by other officers in the brigade. This incident demonstrated to me the headquarters commanders need for a paternalistic figure to turn to and the internal distrust and lack of communication skills by several members of the brigade. Her insecurities were also evident in her repeated complaints about a small picture the PAO had displayed in his personal area of himself on the beach with a couple of girls in swimsuits. She did eventually succeed in moving us from the warehouse to air conditioned tents. While they weren't perfect, they were an improvement over the dust and noisy conditions of the warehouses.

These issues spilled over into other areas as well. As the northern option for EPW camps began to evaporate, the deputy commander positioned himself to be the commander of Camp Bucca, even though there was a brigade detachment commanded by a Lieutenant Colonel that should come in to take over the coordination with the brigade staff. Instead, a full colonel serving as the deputy brigade commander took charge and kept charge over the camp operations. In fairness, the brigade commander endorsed the plan and demonstrated full confidence in his deputy. General Hill felt that his deputy commander was a subject matter expert on EPW camp construction and administration. The unfamiliarity of the battalion commanders and the lack of an historical working relationship with the brigade could have fostered an atmosphere of concern for the competence of inexperienced battalion commanders to accomplish the mission effectively. There was only one shot at success and the margin for mistakes was thin and costly.

While the deputy's pursuit of absolute control at Camp Bucca was the clearest case of solipsism (or narcissism) I saw, it was not the only one. In several units in the active and reserve forces, egos in need of public praise and reward are driven to make decisions that may bring personal fame or glory to themselves. Often these decisions disrupt the normal operations of a unit and cause others to have to compensate for the narcissistic motivations of a few of the leaders. It would be unfair not to also note that there are many leaders that are just the opposite. They do not desire the attention and recognition for their work that some seem to need. They are driven by other forces such as a vision for a strong America, a desire to reach their personal potential, or maybe just an awareness that the quicker we get it done the quicker we all go home. Whatever it is, be it for God and country or something else, many leaders performed self-lessly for the good of the Army and in service to the country. *"For we are taking pains to do what is right, not only in the eyes of the Lord but also in the eyes of men."* 2 Corinthians 8:21 (ESV)

Despite some serious dysfunctions among several of the brigade staff, construction plans for Camp Bucca continued to develop. The progress was due to the compartmentalization of the tasks. The brigade was not working well as a unit but the individuals accomplished the necessary tasks even when it meant working around individuals that should be cooperating. Compartmentalization allowed each individual to do his or her job in isolation from others. Their portion of the plan was handed on to the next planning cell almost like a production line. Supply kept up with their issues, the legal team focused on their issues, and so it went with each of the brigade sections. This was a short-term solution. The soldiers that were focused on their tasks were working double time to make up for the soldiers that were biding their time.

I talked with the unit JAG daily at this point and was fascinated with his work and the Geneva Convention. He would have the most interesting role as he interacted with the prisoners. He worked to find a way to transition the prisoners from British to US control. The British don't allow the transfer of prisoners to nations that promote capital punishment. Because the US allows for capital punishment, the Brits weren't sure they could legally hand their prisoners over to the US. As Lieutenant Colonel O'Hare continued to work this issue, his team of lawyers began to come together and focus on their task.

As a brigade, we were all dependant upon them for sifting out the non-combatants from the real EPWs. Many civilians were scooped up on the battlefield. The Iraqis tended to wander around all over the desert and whenever the massive American columns of tanks and vehicles rode by, it invariable drew a crowd of curious Iraqis. Additionally, in the days leading up to the conflict, leaders of the Baath party burst into many Iraqi homes and demanded that the males of any reasonable age report for military duty. If they resisted they were killed. Those pressed into service surrendered quickly to the Coalition forces and just wanted to go back home to tend to their sheep and families. The team of American and British lawyers conducted Article 5 tribunals to try and discern who really fell into that category and who was just trying to escape.

The Arabic culture allows for a great deal of latitude in communication that westerners cannot appreciate. In fact, our term for it is "stretching the truth". In contrast, western communication is highly technical and detailed. Court cases are often won or lost on the smallest detail. Western lawyers are trained to strain at gnats and require solid alibis.

The Arabs that appeared before the Article 5 tribunals couldn't grasp the importance of detail and truthfulness in their explanations. They were asked for proof of their identity, their vocation and record of military service, and they were asked to explain how they came to be captured by the coalition. The tales that were told ranged from boring to mythical. In every case that I saw, the American and British legal teams displayed remarkable patience and tenacity as they kept their focus and searched for the truth. Since many of the non-combatants wanted to stay in the camp, they often wove a story to make them suspect but not guilty. Their story-telling is an art. Camp Bucca provided the first and best medical care many of them had ever had. The food they were served may have been the best they had eaten in their entire lives. Westerners can't begin to understand just how low the quality of life had been for most Iraqis not privileged to live in Baghdad.

As I began to construct my own contribution to the Brigade effort, I became concerned about the soldier's reactions to incidents in the Interment Facilities. Should an Iraqi prisoner attack a soldier or if a mortar round exploded in the compound, I wondered how the soldiers, many of them only 19 or 20 years old, would continue. I approached General Hill and asked his permission to establish a procedure for helping soldiers with post-traumatic stress. I wanted to initiate a plan for critical incident debriefings. I explained to him that it is not natural for people to see a human, much less their friends die. It's not natural for young people to shoot and kill another person, even if they are threatened. Just a couple of months before, many of these reservists had been roaming through college cafeterias looking for friends to sit and discuss their classes with. They enjoyed late night TV and microwave popcorn. Now they were standing guard over Enemy Prisoners of War in Iraq. The prisoners would shout and plead with the guards in a language the guards couldn't comprehend. They stood for hours in the harsh Iraqi heat and remained alert to any threat or escape attempt. They needed help overcoming the impact and shock of war if they were to be expected to continue to function in a predictable way. He agreed that I should be the one to respond and he also agreed to encourage the battalion commanders to give me both space and time to help the soldiers return to normal and ease the tension that could make them a psychological casualty.

Unfortunately, when a prisoner was shot in self defense at close range I could not implement my plan. The pace of the conflict, the shortages in manpower, and the priorities of reporting and moving on precluded my having any effective post-traumatic ministry. Arranging transportation for a chaplain to perform counseling didn't rate as high on the priority list as other convoy missions waiting for security details. I simply couldn't arrange for a secure convoy to get me there in time to be affective. The Battalion Chaplain provided individual counseling but soldiers always answer that they are fine, it is just their job, and it's no big deal. The accumulation of incidents takes a toll that is so gradual, however, that commanders struggle to understand why the morale and discipline of their unit is degrading.

TO ANY SOLDIER

The emotional lifeline for soldiers has historically been letters from home. There have been stories written and songs sung about letters written in the peaceful surroundings of home where there is love and familiarity. Sending those letters to foreign lands where there is hostility and mystery has eased the loneliness and fear of soldiers in every era. Letters from home poured into Kuwait and with them all sorts of delectable treats. Peanuts, candy, and even vacuum sealed cookies. Most of the letters, particularly the Easter cards, were positive and uplifting. General Hill handed me a stack of letters he received from a school in Pennsylvania. He asked me to handle them and distribute them to soldiers that did not receive mail from home. I took the letters back to the warehouse and opened one. What I read disturbed me so much that I decided that I would only give the letters out after I read them. One after another I opened the letters and in almost every case they read the same. Students wrote in the letters that they supported the soldiers and they went on to describe their admiration for their courage and bravery. Then the letters became depressing. The high school students wrote that they didn't support the war nor the President of the United States. One student wrote,

> *"Dear Soldier:*
>
> *Hello my name is Doug. I am 1.7 decades old. I live in a small town in western Pennsylvania called Coraopolis. A possible war makes me feel angry. I don't think we should go to war period. My concern about possible action is that we should not take any actions. I think the US will go to war because they would not send a lot of soldiers over there in the first place. I do not support George Bush's actions because I think he is trying to finish what his father started.*
>
> *Thank you very much for fighting for me, the US and everyone else. Good luck to you and all of the soldiers. Don't be discouraged in any way because everyone is supporting you. If you would like to write back, refer to the address above the date."*

In addition to the schizophrenic style and the unintentionally inflammatory tone of the letters, the consistency of phrases the students used betrayed the philosophies they were exposed to from the media and their teachers. That philosophy is largely anti-authoritarian and anti-nationalistic.

HUMANISTIC THEISM

There is an emerging cultural shift that I have dubbed, humanistic theism. Simply put, humanistic theists are those who believe in God but don't know much about him or don't actively trust that he has some control over the world and events are humanistic. Their view of success is a united world free of ethical and cultural bias orbiting around absolute human freedom. They believe (despite all of history that demonstrates the opposite) that mankind is selfless and will do what is best for the common good when the restrictions of bias are removed. Therefore, while most of us grew up believing that strength comes through unity of vision and purpose, non-sensical phrases such as "strength through diversity" emerged to encourage parting ways and tipping the American melting pot over to dump the contents out. This is the humanistic philosophy being taught to young Americans. While it is not atheistic, it certainly is not genuine theism and shares little with America's Christian heritage.

As my wife was finishing her Master degree in elementary education, a professor insisted that the class understand the importance of placing a picture of someone in every ethnic group on the wall. He suggested that this would be a symbol of unity in the classroom. Unity through diversity became the slogan. My wife suggested to him that the American flag would suffice as a single symbol of national unity testifying that we are all American no matter what our historical or ethnic backgrounds. She was sternly rebuked and told that the American Flag was a symbol of oppression and everything that is wrong with America rather than a symbol to be cherished and held up. In her startling expose of the Government school system, *Cloning of the American Mind*, B. K. Eakman describes the intentional Balkanization of America. She calls it deculturization[2] which she describes as the loss of a national consciousness. *"The goal is to unravel, rather than to weave together bodies of knowledge, thereby contributing to further ethnic isolation and destabilization of Western values."* Eakman describes some of the linkage between the National Education Association in America and the United Nations. The NEA provided a grant for the production of a *"series of nine volumes aimed at kindergarten and elementary school teachers titled Toward World Understanding. The series was quite specific: the teacher was to begin by eliminating any and all words, phrases, descriptions, pictures, classroom material or teaching methods of a sort causing his pupils to feel or express a particular love for, or loyalty to, the United States."*[3] The root of all this seems to be the Utopian dream of a world government. Besides the obvious dangers to our national political identity, our moral conscience is also a stumbling block since a common morality is necessary to enjoy a world governmental agency. There are two Americas today. One is traditionally theistic, trusting that God has guided the cosmos since time began and that man has an obligation to obey Him. The second is humanistic. This humanism may indeed believe in God, but they believe the future is theirs to sculpt according to their own vision without deference to God's will. In fact, notions of religion and faith only seem to complicate their quest for man-centered government and sovereignty.

Since family and religious institutions are the source of faith and moral teaching, the educational establishment has become unfriendly towards them. Education has become the domain of professionally educated teachers who care for our children from sun up to sun down and the exaggeration of the separation of church and state has made it difficult for students to even pray in the schools much less practice an active religious faith. Peer groups and socialization have been billed as more important to proper psychological development than family relationships and religious instruction. Eakman concludes that those pressing for global education see the *"family, nationalism, and conscience as the chief culprits leading to international hostilities and eventually, to war."* They are *"psychological pestilences that lead to authoritarian governments and international conflict.*"[4] That is why students and others feel they can support the soldiers while simultaneously disapproving of the government and the soldier's actions.

The impact of this senseless rhetoric on soldiers when they hear it is disastrous. The whole idea that you can support a soldier and not support his mission or commander implies that he is a victim. It tells the soldier that if he should die, Americans will be sorry but that it was for nothing and the American people were not committed to his cause. I took the time to answer each and every one of the letters personally and encouraged each student to reconsider the purpose of this war. Some of the students wrote back and seemed to understand. Others wrote back and I could tell that they really didn't even know why we were there to start with. I struggled for the rest of the deployment with the lack of vision our students receive in their schools.

WEAPONS OF MASS INSTRUCTION

One of the more interesting dramas that unfolded concerned the Bible. Not just any Bible but Bibles written in Arabic. After I received word that I was being mobilized to work with an EPW Brigade, I e-mailed a friend and advisor, Chaplain (Colonel) Dave Peterson, and asked him for advice. Chaplain Peterson had served under General H. Norman Schwarzkopf in Operation Desert Storm as the Forces Command (FORSCOM) chaplain. He was the senior chaplain in Kuwait during the war. He warned me that one of his biggest challenges was to provide religious literature and scriptures to the prisoners. He found it fairly easy to get Qur'ans to them but most contemporary thinking in the west categorizes all Arabs as Muslims. Most westerners don't realize that Iraq has a significant Christian population. Terik Aziz was a Christian serving under Saddam Hussein. The Geneva Convention requires that all prisoners, regardless of their religious convictions, be allowed to worship as their faith requires. That means a tent has to be reserved for both Muslims and Christians in the EPW camp. It also means that scriptures have to be provided for both Muslims and Christians as well. Chaplain Peterson discovered that there was little motivation or energy to provide Christian scriptures to EPWs. Political sensitivities seemed to require that Christianity keep a wide berth from Muslim lands.

Chaplain Peterson suggested that I begin to move on this issue right away and make sure that the commander understood the requirements of the Geneva Convention. I received permission from the commander to supply the Bibles to Christians and if the resources were available, he would also allow for the separate tents. Now that I had permission, I still lacked funding. I had requested three boxes of religious supplies while we were at Fort Dix and they never arrived. I had little confidence that the supply system could deliver such a unique item before this war was over and the next one had begun. I contacted several civilian agencies but they couldn't provide me with the necessary Bibles. A friend from my New Jersey church came to the rescue. He researched a company that would sell the Bibles and he funded them from his own resources as well. Ironically the Bibles came from a publisher in Kuwait.

After I arrived in at Camp Arifjan, I spoke to the senior chaplain about the Bibles and immediately, red flags went up. He suggested that I needed to quarantine the Bibles until I received permission to distribute them from the Chief of Chaplains. I argued that I valued the opinion of the chief's office but that he couldn't override the Geneva Convention and I couldn't lawfully withhold the Bibles from the EPWs. It took almost a month for the chaplain community to settle down about the Arabic Bibles. In the end, the EPW situation at Camp Bucca moved so quickly and the prisoners were sent home so fast, that I was never able to determine who should receive them.

This event brought one other dynamic of my experience to light. There wasn't a chaplain in either of the two higher commands over me. The 377th Theater Support Groups chaplain didn't arrive until the war was over. When I began to look for input to the religious support section of the Brigade Operations Order, I discovered that I was on my own. By the end of the war, I was bitter because I was placed in such an unique assignment with a wartime mission without the benefit of someone to consult with except my own friends. In the highly transitory Army of today, it is not unusual to have limited resources and almost no institutional history to guide you as you strive to achieve the objectives placed before you. The Army has struggled for years to retain the brightest and the best officers in leadership but the officer corps continues to hemorrhage from the active duty ranks.

IN THE BEGINNING

Eventually, the 724th MP Battalion deployed to Camp Coyote, a staging area close to the Iraqi border. Life at Camp Coyote was more of a challenge than life at Camp Arifjan, yet they managed to create many of the luxuries of a home. Luxuries like toilet seats and a wooden wall to give you some privacy when you needed to answer nature's call. This was no insignificant issue. Before the deployment ended, hygiene and sanitation became a critical issue. Inadequate facilities resulted in most contracting what became known as the *Camp Bucca Grunge*. Females cut the liter sized water bottles in half and used them as bedpans. This resulted in some injuries and cuts to the more sensitive areas of the female anatomy. The men were provided long pipes several yards from the tent that petruded from mounds of sand. They filled to the brim in short order and a visit to the pipes at night could result in wet boots from the overflow.

Males began to move away from the tents for privacy,

but in the dangerous environment of Iraq, wandering away from camp for a little privacy could result in abduction or injury. There was not a case of abduction or injury resulting from going to the bathroom that I was ever aware of but nevertheless, this became a source of tension and stress as the weeks and months passed. Every category of life was a challenge. From relationships to urination, nothing was easy or automatic.

One week before hostilities began, the 320th MP Battalion arrived at Camp Arifjan. There wasn't a mission for them when they arrived. That was a good thing since their equipment was nowhere to be found. Units deploying from the states loaded their equipment up on ships that took as many as 4 weeks to arrive in theater. My HUMVEE was commandeered for the use of the 320th as they began to settle into their own warehouse. Chaplain (First Lieutenant) Ann Tang arrived with the 320th MP Battalion. She was a new chaplain, fresh from the chaplain's basic course. She voiced her concern that she had never been assigned to a unit before nor had she been on active duty. Despite her lack of experience, her compassion for soldiers was evidenced by her hard work and her availability. She strove to provide comfort to the soldiers in the remote and foreign world we all found ourselves in. Ann was small in stature, not even 5'7" in height and less than 120 pounds with all her gear on, but she had a big heart. Unfortunately, Ann didn't adjust well to the harsh desert environment. She always seemed to be hot and tired. After a couple of weeks, she was hospitalized for cellulitus.

While she was in the hospital I was invited to visit the 320th MP Battalion and lead them in prayer. I read a few comments from the US Constitution regarding every person's God given inalienable rights and then a couple of verses from scripture. About 150 soldiers were present in the 320th formation. When I announced that we were going to pray, a soldier from another unit interrupted and asked if his soldiers could join us. They were without their own chaplain and were about to begin traveling north to Iraq. I asked the 320th Sergeant Major if he would mind. He invited the other soldiers over and another 150 soldiers joined the formation. This was just one example of how soldiers desire to invoke the blessings of God when they are going into harms way.

The hospitalization gave Ann time to become acclimatized and when she recovered from cellulitis, she adjusted much faster to Kuwait.

The 320th received national attention after they were assigned to Abu Ghraib. They had lost their sense of unity and command structure when soldiers were assigned jobs in small groups. The chaplain serves the commander as the moral barometer for the unit and when events begin to accelerate too quickly the chaplain sounds an alarm for the commander. Without this prophetic warning from a chaplain, events can begin to cascade on the command group and spiral out of control. It is the chaplain that must recognize the dangers that emerge in the attitudes and behaviors of the unit. The fears and isolation of war creates an emotionally fluid environment that must be monitored continuously. The chaplain has to maintain a personal sense of civility and continue to distinguish between right and wrong in the midst of war in order to keep the light of sanity lit in an otherwise insane environment. When soldiers feel threatened or neglected, moral relativism finds fertile ground to develop.

I feel that Chaplain Tang was handicapped only by her lack of active Army experience and her access to the soldiers at Abu Ghraib. She was actively engaged with her soldiers in Bible studies and counseling but she would not have been able to recognize the irregularities in their professional behavior since she has not seen soldiers when they are acting normally in a wartime environment. Her gentle disposition was an asset when she counseled but became a handicap when she needed to aggressively maintain contact with soldiers in far-flung places. Without a chaplain to sound the alarm, the lack of command and control the situation presented, and the reconstitution and restructuring of the command when the prison mission was assigned, there were no moral safeguards built in to warn the command about changes in soldiers attitudes and behaviors at Abu Ghraib. Too much was assumed and morality was left to the immature and inexperienced solders.

INTERPRETING A NEW REALITY

The human mind is a remarkable device. It is always sifting through new data and assimilating information. As we grow older, we construct paradigms that help us assimilate information much quicker as we compare new information to existing knowledge. Each new situation we engage presents different information. If for reason of insecurity or inflexibility, we cannot change our paradigms, we will erroneously interpret new situations and develop wrong responses. War presents the human mind with a reality different from anything ever experienced before. The desert sand, scorpions that find refuge in your boots, the constant threat from hostile people and the sense of fear and isolation cannot be understood from a distance.

As hostilities appeared immanent, several of us on the Brigade staff assigned to the professional branches of the Army, the Judge Advocate, the Chaplain, the Doctors, and the Public Affairs Office began to meet for lunch in the chow hall to make sense of ourselves and the war. It became a time to relax, discuss the operations, and offer suggestions on what we should do. Other officers joined our discussion like Major Tony Hartman, the brigade's communications officer (S-6). Tony worked as a bailiff for the New York State Courts. While he was deployed with the 800th he missed a promotion opportunity and a promotion exam. In fact, this was his second trip to Kuwait. He had served at Camp Doha a year before. The deployment tempo of 2002 and 2003 placed a big strain on his and all of the soldier's family relationships. His 16-year-old daughter had a difficult time with her dad's deployment to Iraq. Many children struggle with nightmares after they watch the news and imagine their parents in battle. Computer games and movies have created an image of war and battle in children's minds that leave them with horrible images of their parent's experience.

Tony was in charge of radios and computers. Radios and computers become a sort of status symbol in the military. *Important* people are issued a computer and a radio so of course, everyone wants one. Whoever is left out is clearly not a key player. Tony's job was to try and satisfy all the egos by supplying the necessary automation they required. While I never received a radio, he did manage to get me a laptop computer so my own ego was assuaged.

This was also the time for speculation on the date the war would commence. Lieutenant Colonel O'Hare suggested that we should watch the food served in the mess hall. We already watched the food since it was prepared by Arabic men from nations other than Kuwait. We all imagined the best place to attack the coalition was the American Chow Hall. In fact, word came to us that an Egyptian man had driven his car into a line of American soldiers waiting for the chow hall to open. *"On the night before the war begins"*, O'Hare said, *"they will serve really good chow like crab or lobster."* There must have been a number of false calls because they served both crab and lobster several times. While the quality was less than most would accept from an American seafood restaurant, we were embarrassed to call home and try to explain that we had lobster while we were at war.

A couple of nights before the first American combat units crossed the border into Iraq, I approached General Hill about my role after the conflict started. Since the mission of the 800th MP Brigade would not begin until a couple of days into the conflict, I suggested that he release me to ride on the Mass Casualty Helicopters that were staging from Camp Arifjan. I spoke with the hospital chaplain earlier and he had no plans to ride on the helicopters. My experience as an aviation battalion chaplain and my time riding on Mass Casualty Helicopters as part of training exercises had prepared me for this ministry. After some discussion, General Hill agreed to allow me to go. I began to try coordinating the mission through Chaplain (Colonel) Doug Carver, the V Corps chaplain. After several attempts to reach him, I realized that I would not be able to contact him and I decided to abort the idea and focus on the spiritual and psychological adjustment of the 800th MP Brigade staff as the war began.

IT ALL BEGINS SOMEWHERE

We had been through countless drills anticipating a scud attack. A loud horn sounded and we rushed to put on our chemical protective gear (NBC suits). The horn blasted three times and a voice announced, "*Exercise, exercise, exercise.*" Later, the all clear sounded and we packed our gear back up again until the next drill.

On March 19th, just after hostilities began, we gathered as usual for lunch and despite our concerns about the foreign nationals who prepared and served the food, we enjoyed it. Then we heard the horn blast followed by the familiar voice, "*Lightening, lightening, lightening*" This was the first time I had felt threatened. "*Lightening*" was the word reserved for an actual missile attack.

There are moments in life that make you aware of your own mortality and vulnerability but there is no way to accurately describe it. It reminds of the biblical book of Revelation. The English language is inadequate to convey the reality of the moment. You feel helpless, rushed, and exposed. You are in a controlled panic as you grab for your protective gear. You feel like your movements are in slow motion. You wonder if the patriot missiles will succeed in taking out the scuds. You wonder if you will ever know the answer.

We all grabbed our gear to put it on. I looked over to Roy Shere, the PAO. Roy always offered an encouraging word. He had a big-brother personality that is better suited to operate a gas grill than a gas mask. He stood there with his mask on but without the protective overgarment. I asked him why he wasn't putting it on. "*I left it in the tent*" was his reply. I stopped putting my own overgarment on and looked at it. It couldn't have been but a few seconds but it seemed like an eternity. I thought about my own family, my children, the risks of chemical attack, and my present obligations.

I looked at Roy. He stood nearly a half foot shorter than me but height is no indication of the worth of a man. He had been drafted into the 800th just as I had. He was self-employed with daughters in college. He responded to his nations call to arms with short notice like so many of us. When you leave your family so suddenly it makes you feel like you never really said good-bye. He and I had shared family photos and talked about getting together after the war was over. I offered him my suit. Without hesitation he declined and didn't really seem concerned. I felt guilty that I was relieved he had declined the protective suit. We all moved to the wall as we were instructed and sat to wait until we were either hit with the scud or the alert was over. After about 20 minutes the crisis passed because the scud had been intercepted by a patriot missile.

We remained in the chemical suits from Thursday to Sunday. I even preached in it during chapel services on Sunday morning. The message that day was on loving our enemies. The command of Christ is that we are to love our enemies and pray for their salvation. It is easy to forfeit your own humanity and learn to hate those who persecute you and desire your destruction. Christianity has always created an ethical paradox. When a Christian is attacked, they are commanded to turn the other cheek. When their enemies rage against them they are required to love them and pray for them. When a persecutor desires to take their physical belongings away, they have to give them up without reservation.

Why are Christians required to rise to an ethical standard that seems irrational to the common man? A Christian has a unique perspective on life because he has placed his hope in the life that follows death. A Christian understands that the judgment of man is nothing compared to the judgment of God. Our appraisal of another human being is inconsequential compared to the eternal judgment of God against those who persecute his people. There have been many wonderful men and women who have exemplified the greatest of human virtues but only Jesus of Nazareth exemplified this principle consistently in every situation. While he was always discerning and never permissive, he also prayed for the men who nailed his hands and feet to a cross. He uttered the infamous words, *"Father forgive them, they do not know what they are doing."* While he was hanging by the nails looking into the faces of the men that put him there he felt no malice towards them, only compassion. That is the Christian's example of character and justice. A Christian must pursue justice against the oppression of the innocent and yet, he cannot make the justice his own, but must always seek to preserve the justice of God for the sake of God's honor and glory. That is a world and life view most humans refuse to espouse. The more common human ethic encourages men to seek their own justice and demand their own rights. No wonder many find Christianity to be a mystery.

Scud alerts recurred several times in the following

weeks. In fact, every day at lunch, the Iraqis launched a scud. We surmised that Iraqi lacked any real offensive capability and their only victory came by ruining our lunch. They launched the scuds at night as well. The Brigade TOC had a television that was usually tuned to FOX news. We began to notice a pattern with the chemical alerts. When the news anchor stationed at Doha, put on his mask, we had less than 2 minutes until our alarm would sound. FOX became an early warning system for us. We would look over and see the anchor standing in a gas mask and someone would shout, *"Put your mask on"* and as sure as rain is wet, the alarm would sound and we would scramble to get our gear out and on.

My world changed again one night when I was awakened by a loud explosion. I sat up on my cot and looked around. Several of the others were moving around and then instinctively we grabbed our masks from beside our cots and began to put them on. There was no alert, no horn, and no siren. We heard a second explosion and we began to check on one another to make sure everyone was awake and putting on their gas (NBC) mask. We eventually learned that these were not scud attacks but an innovative use of the silkworm missile. The missiles were launched across the water towards Kuwait City and Camp Arifjan. Far inferior to the smart bombs used by the coalition, a silkworm is designed to skim across the water and lock onto the largest piece of metal it detects, presumably a ship. One of the silkworms launched by the Iraqis toward Camp Arifjan locked onto radars about 3 miles from away. A second missile locked onto the mall in Kuwait City. Besides the damage to the mall, neither missile had any real strategic effect.

They did score an emotional dividend however because we all realized that an attack is not always detected and announced. People that want to hurt or kill you will always seek to find a way. Even the most disadvantaged enemy can be creative and resourceful. Destruction requires far less resources and intelligence than construction. This realization causes your mind to be in a state of readiness that gradually wears you down. You can't stay in a state of constant alert for long before your mind and body simply begin to feel exhausted.

PATRIOTISM ON PARADE

Shortly after the war began, a humorous distraction came to us at the expense of Congressman Steve Buyer. He had issued a press release that claimed he had been called to serve as the 800th's Staff Judge Advocate. This was not true. Lieutenant Colonel James O'Hare filled the brigade's position. Major Garrity, an assistant S1, told O'Hare that she received a call during a scud attack requesting the information necessary to have orders issued to the Congressman. Major Garrity told the caller we were involved in a scud attack and the caller replied that she could not call back later. They wanted the line number immediately for O'Hare's position in order to create orders for Representative Buyer.

We all marveled at the nerve and total lack of empathy by someone sitting in the safety of an office in the United States, telling us they couldn't wait until after a scud attack to receive information. The Representative's plans fell thru when he discovered he would have to resign his congressional seat to go on an adventure with the Army. There was never a position for him and no one at the 800th MP Brigade ever considered asking him to come. We were more than adequately served by the JAG personnel we had and there were other assets available in Kuwait if we needed them.

MOVING FORWARD WITH THE MISSION

The pace of the ground war was remarkable. The 3rd Infantry Division moved rapidly across the desert floor towards Baghdad. The news reporters were amazed at how fast the 3rd Infantry Division juggernaut advanced. The Marines were doing almost as well but had slowed down due to resistance in their drive east of the 3rd ID. On the outskirts of Baghdad the commanders decided to pause and allow the supply trains to catch up. This also gave the soldiers a chance to catch their breath before the last victorious push into Baghdad.

The progress of the march to Baghdad moved our own operations forward as well. The 724th MP Battalion had been pre-positioned at Camp Coyote near the Iraqi border. All the supplies available for the first internment facility were located there in large steel containers. Life in the tent city of Camp Coyote had become manageable even if it wasn't comfortable. The MPs had a real sense of their role as our lead element responsible to establish a presence at Objective Freddie, the future Camp Bucca.

The location of the camp was at first planned for a position farther north than where it ended up. General Hill was concerned about intelligence indicating that remnants of the Iraqi Army still occupied positions at an airfield west of the proposed camp location. After consultations with the staff and the next higher command, the decision was made to move the EPW camp to a new location near the port city of Umm Qsar on the southern Iraqi boarder. The 724th assumed operational control over the camp and elements of the 800th MP Brigade (the deputy commander, the headquarters First Sergeant, and a representative from the S3 operations and the S2 intelligence sections) remained with the 724th to coordinate the efforts and keep the lines of communication open with the Brigade staff. This plan created better communication between the Brigade staff and the Camp Bucca but it outlived it's usefulness in the end and became a blight. The helpful coordination ended up in turf battles and confused roles.

In hindsight, the security risks for the first camp location were not as bad as they were reported to be and the location of the camp would have been far better in the original location, north of Umm Qsar. One of the challenges leaders face is to make the right decision at the right time. Often your decision can be second guessed by armchair quarterbacks, but when you have to make decisions that can save or lose American lives, you have to decide based on what information you have, not on what might develop in the future. Preplanning offers you the best scenario but when you are in the midst of operations and lives are at risk, you have to make decisions based on possibilities rather than absolutes. General Hill demonstrated he had the courage to change his plan when he felt the soldiers were at risk. If the situation was reversed and the threat had emerged as real and he pressed forward with the 724th, many American lives may have been lost as a result.

The Brigade began to occupy a position already secured by the British troops and affectionately dubbed, Camp Freddie. Transporting prisoners from forward holding areas in the north became more difficult as the coalitions main body consolidated around Iraq. Buses and trucks ferried Iraqi prisoners to Camp Bucca and eventually, they were transported back the same way.

On March 23rd, we learned that five soldiers were taken as POWs after they had gotten lost and captured. In comparison to the five captured by the Iraqis, the coalition had captured about 2000 prisoners. Among the US prisoners was a 30-year-old black female from Texas. At the shift change brief that night with Brigadier General Hill present, I suggested to the staff that if I were a POW, I wouldn't want them to recognize a moment of silence in my honor, but I would want them to be praying to God for my release. Among those captured were at least two females. We understood what to expect the treatment of females by Muslim soldiers to be. The theology of Islam promises faithful Muslim men a sexual paradise. Obviously, the conduct of Islamic militants shouldn't be expected to differ greatly from their theology. I am amazed at America's ability to so compartmentalize religion that belief and behavior are removed from one another. The rest of the world behaves as they believe. Only in America can such an inconsistency between thought and action be considered a virtue. I bowed my head and counted out thirty seconds for silent prayer and then prayed for the group. I feel this moved us all closer to together as a group and highlighted the importance of an active faith rather than private religious sentiments. To that point, I had led the Brigade staff in prayer some 8 or 10 times outside of any formal religious services. General Hill encouraged me to close our meetings in prayer and I thanked God for the opportunities I was offered. Even in private, General Hill was responsive to my request that we end our meetings in prayer. A significant division could be seen in the spiritual life of the soldiers on the brigade staff. Some were comfortable with prayer and requested it often while others shied away from it and even appeared awkward and uncomfortable when heads were bowed. Clearly, they didn't know what to do with themselves when people were praying.

Several days into the conflict, the evening briefings became less specific and informative. In fact, most of the information provided by the embedded media proved more up to date than the information transmitted through traditional intelligence venues. The intelligence assets in the field and in the air were not as successful in ascertaining the exact location and disposition of the Iraqi units. The rapid march of the 3rd ID and the obliteration of the Iraqi forces south of Baghdad made the most current information obsolete before it could be passed down to our brigade. The reports on Iraqi units and military strength were less certain in the north. No one seemed to understand why the Iraqi Guard positions remained occupied despite the pounding the Coalition Air Forces were giving them. Conventional wisdom suggested that the uncertainty of an invasion from the North through Turkey kept Iraqi units committed to the north of Baghdad while the 3rd Infantry Division and the Marine Expeditionary Forces sped across the Iraqi desert from the South toward the capital. Command and control had broken down for the Iraqi government and military. The lack of communication between the government and the army was a major Coalition goal, yet it also made the actions of the Iraqi field commanders less predictable. There wouldn't be any planned coordination between them and they became less predictable as well as less effective. Coalition forces blasted through Iraqi resistance and bypassed units that had surrendered. The focus of the coalition was on Baghdad. They rightly understood that breaking the back of the Iraqi regime was the key to limiting battlefield casualties on both sides. Coalition victories left broken Iraqi units scattered around the desert and towns of southern Iraq. We received reports of units that were not holding as many prisoners in the collection points as we had anticipated. The British and the U.S. Marines held some Iraqis at Camp Freddy near Umm Qsar. The 3rd Infantry Division had opened facilities further north and would eventually open one at the Baghdad airport.

On March 24th, I began to make plans to ride to our first Internment Facility (EPW camp). During Desert Storm, the 800th MP Brigade's assigned strength was over 7,300 personnel from 68 subordinate units. The Brigade was responsible for the command, control and accounting of over 70,000 Iraqi allied enemy prisoners of war. Camp Bucca was being built to accomplish the same mission. General Hill mentioned to the staff that the route to Camp Bucca was not as secure as we thought. The situation was less predictable than we would like due to the lack of uniforms in the Iraqi army.

I began to resent those who wanted to take my life. I had no personal grudge against the Iraqi people, in fact my hope was that they would be delivered from an oppressive and murderous regime. Now, tales surfaced describing a strategy of the Baath party. Members dressed like shepherds to get close to convoys and mortar teams set up positions to fire their anonymous rounds on American positions. These stories had begun to create apprehension and resentment. That night, I watched Ben Hurr with 1Lt Ken Rameriz on his laptop computer. One of the characters in the movie, Esther, said a rabbi named Jesus was teaching that love and forgiveness were stronger than hate. I reflected on the sermon I had delivered the previous week on loving our enemies. As all these strands of independent thoughts converged in my mind, a quiet peace settled on me. I wondered what God wanted me to learn from this situation. Beyond the fear that all soldiers experience at one level or another, I struggled with conflicting emotions about the Iraqi people themselves. I resented the threat they presented against my life. I resented coming half way around the world to liberate them from one of their own. I resented their extrapolations and exaggerations whenever you asked them for an answer. Yet, when one of the Iraqi children looked in our HUMVEE as we passed and made a sign asking for water and food, my heart went out to them. My affection for them was not limited to charity. I saw a dignity in them that inspired me. For years they have been held back and taken advantage of by their leadership but they retained an indomitable spirit and a will to survive. If there were ever a people that deserved our best efforts it is the Iraqi people. Clearly, I would not be in charge of the convoy I rode in. My fate was not left to my command. I wouldn't be able to control the Iraqis that may seek to harm us. So what choices did I have? How would I respond? Would I be able to endure it? That night when I called home, I didn't tell my wife about the next day's mission but in my heart I savored the call and wondered what the next day would bring.

The following day, a major sandstorm hit the area. The trip was cancelled and an airfield west of the internment facility was occupied by Iraqis. Large caches of weapons and a major network of tunnels had been discovered and while the Internment Facility did not appear to be in any immanent danger, it was lightly defended and there was concern about sabotage and snipers. Concern for compromising our position prompted General Hill to ask for a battalion of infantry from the National Guard and two MP Guard Companies to go in and clear the airport so that we could begin construction. The Marine Expeditionary Force was putting a good bit of pressure on us to take their prisoners from them. I was familiar with the National Guard Battalion that would take the mission. I had visited with them and I was concerned that this was a mission they simply were not ready to take. The Iraqi soldiers were dug in around the airfield and defended from tunnels underneath. Most of the young men in the infantry battalion had been living at home a month before and had never seen anything close to what they would be facing there.

Lieutenant General H. Steven Blum, National Guard Bureau Chief, described the dilemma faced by the nation's National Guard units in an August 2004 interview with National Guard Magazine. He said, "Nobody ever envisioned about 100,000 Army National Guard people being called to active duty in a shooting war short of World War III. When they called the Guard out they wanted it bad and that's the way they got it. It was kind of, 'pay me now' or 'pay me later.' They never equipped the Guard to be an operational force, yet they now want to use it as an operational force..."[5]

I wrestled all night with my responsibility to address this situation and I decided to ask General Hill to use the Guard soldiers to block any advance into the Internment Facility rather than to clear the Airfield in a search and destroy type mission. With the stakes so high, I had to lay aside my concerns for overstepping my professional boundaries and trust in the good graces of General Hill to allow me to voice my concern and opinion. I feel asleep repeating over and over in prayer, "God grant me wisdom and courage!"

On March 26th I decided to approach Lieutenant Colonel Cline, the Chief of Staff for the Brigade and address my concerns with him privately before asking to see the commander. I was relieved to discover that he shared my same concerns about the infantry battalion's limited capacity for offensive operations and he assured me that they were going into a defensive posture. I did not need to see the commander after all. This was an answered prayer. I learned a valuable lesson. War, like all of life, is a series of decisions that can result in life or death, success or failure. There are many options to any given scenario and leaders must be as careful as they are aggressive. In this case, General Hill made the best decision he could.

That evening I publicly thanked the brigade staff for slowing down and resisting the pressure that was being put on them to perform beyond the brigades ability. This marked a transition in thinking for the brigade. No one outside of the military can empathize with the pressure to always say yes to any mission. The military structure requires obedience and subordinate units depend on superior officers for wisdom in delegating tasks. When the assignments do come, sacrifice and personal risk are considered part of military life. Saying "no" is not an option. *"Doing more with less"* has become the unofficial Army motto. Leaders in the upper echelons of command sometimes lose a sense of a battalion's capability. They have a need and they determine that they have the means to accomplish their goals. Integrating the Reserves in the active duty missions further compounded the problem because Reserve forces need time to acclimate themselves to the heavier demands for mission accomplishment that the active army requires. The move from civilian life to Kuwait integrated the 800th immediately into the fast paced world of an active theater of war. The only remedy for this is an increased awareness by the active forces commanders that the reserves have certain personnel limitations and acclimation issues that are not readily apparent by appearances or paperwork. The National Guard and Reserves report for service and are willing to sacrifice everything for the sake of duty and country but not all sacrifices are necessary to accomplish the mission.

Reservists shouldn't be assigned tasks on a *"To do"* list without considering the particular dynamics of their units. Paperwork and performance ratings do not always tell the entire story. Abu Ghraib was a mission that the 800th appeared to be best suited to, on paper. Even on paper the 800th wasn't suited for the mission but they were the best option available. The attrition of key personnel and the lack of a military culture in the Reserves made the assignment a bad idea from the beginning. The difficulty with reassessing the decision to include the Reserves in such a prominent role is the lack of situational awareness the assessor has available. There is no way to recapture the urgency of the mission. There is no way to reconstruct the pressures brought to bear on the command from the political influences as well as the strategic. It is impossible to sense the affect years of constriction had on military budgets and personnel. The Army structure now depends on the Reserves as a vital part of the military since the active component manpower was reduced and bases were closed to help produce the budget surplus of the 1990's. Unless we are allowed to stand with Generals who look each other in the eye and ask one another to weigh the options and chose the best one, we can only second guess their decisions. War requires sacrifice and if there was a perfect answer our leaders would pick it every time. Unfortunately, there is only a best option and often the results are mixed. The 800th wasn't the perfect answer to Abu Ghraib but they were the best and perhaps the only option available to leaders working with smaller forces. They did more with less, but it came with a price tag the American public didn't want to pay.

MOVING INTO THE UNKNOWN

The brigade staff continued to follow the news briefs which were ordinarily more informative than our evening updates. The brigade intelligence officer was very good and resourceful but he was limited by the intelligence apparatus whereas the news reports were coming live from the field. The embedded media proved to be an invaluable source of information that helped us with planning. As the 3rd Infantry Division broke through the lines of defense around Baghdad and took the city, we began to make serious plans for a possible northern EPW camp. Several of the Republican Guard units remained in the north defending Saddam's hometown and, as tactically unsound as it seemed, some northern Coalition threat appeared to still be afraid of.

At some point, you would imagine that guarding against troops invading from the North would become a secondary priority to driving out the troops in your capital city, but the thought never seemed to occur to them. Fortunately, the northern camp was never necessary. Not only were there not enough prisoners taken in the north to warrant an additional camp, but the prisoners that were taken could be transported south to Camp Bucca where they were duly processed and released in a short amount of time. The brigade is not trained to build long term internment facilities. Their mission involves processing large numbers of prisoners for short term care and holding. In summary, Army Regulation (AR) 190-8 directs the Military Police to process the prisoners and create a record for them. They must provide them with food, adequate shelter, and medical support. Perhaps the most important distinction between their wartime function and their role as wardens in the Iraqi prison operations was that all the prisoners in an EPW camp are expected to be released as soon as the conflict is over. There is no place given for long term internment. The mission of the 800th MP Brigade was colossal, when the EPW camp was up and running it was nearly the size of a city.

- Construction costs 15 Million dollars in materials
- 115 Acres
- 8,000 Rolls of concertina wire
- 580 tents
- 31 Guard Towers
- 8' Berm around the entire facility's perimeter
- Semi-permanent sewage system
- 1.5 Megawatts of power generation
- 13,800 meals per day
- 50,000 gallons of water per day

Two days after the fall of Baghdad, I attended the bi-weekly command briefing with General Hill and the rest of the brigade staff. I usually used this time as an opportunity to encourage the leadership to break from the temptation to simply manage their soldiers and instead I pressed them to come along side of them as leaders to mentor them. After hearing a great deal of rancor and discontent between the staffs of Camp Bucca and Camp Arifjan, it was clear to me that some of the leadership saw war as an opportunity for personal advancement. This was evidenced in their frustrated attempts to receive more staff support and resources. At first glance this would appear to be a normal and in fact, responsible position for a leader to take. But in this case, the deputy commander pressed for resources that were committed to other missions. He of all people should be able to see the scope of the Brigade's responsibilities and worked to ensure all the resources were distributed where they were needed the most.

Since the mission of the 800th was to provide command and control to the separate MP battalions and to manage the construction of Camp Bucca, the demands by the deputy commander demonstrated his myopic view of the missions he was directly involved in. The irony of the situation was that a separate staff was supposed to take charge of Camp Bucca and act as a liaison for the Battalions working at Camp Bucca. In fact, a battalion commander was supposed to be in charge of Camp Bucca but the Brigade deputy commander refused to step down after his initial coordination was finished. Since every action causes a reaction, his decision to keep the reigns of Camp Bucca in his own hands caused a ripple affect down to the lowest ranks. When the Battalion commander is assigned the duty of an executive officer, the soldier's from the commander down all have to reconsider their own assignments. Even the 724th chaplain became distracted with the micromanagement of Camp Bucca. He began to complain that he should be in charge of the religious support mission for the prisoners rather than the brigade chaplain since his battalion was supposed to be in charge of Camp Bucca. The distraction and disruption caused by the self promoting motives of key leaders became the impetus for my discussion with the brigade staff. When I suggested that the conflict existing between key members of the staff was a result of false expectations constructed on selfish desires for self promotion and opportunism, I received a cold stare from the brigade commander and stifled approval from the staff.

Later, as if the hand of justice moved against him, the deputy commander lost his M-16 rifle with a 30 round magazine. While losing a weapon is serious on any occasion, this weapon was lost at Camp Bucca within a few hundred yards of the prisoner holding facilities. He claimed it had been stolen but even cadets are taught to keep up with their weapon and no excuse is ever accepted for misplacing it. I spent more than one night with an M-16 tied to my arm while I slept. A formal investigation was conducted but he was not held responsible for the loss until General Karpinski took command and required him to pay for it. The incident did spoil the Napoleonic image he had developed.

At the same briefing, Lieutenant Colonel Doyle, the commander of the 13th Psychological Operations Battalion invited me to go with him to visit his troops scattered from Camp Bucca in southern Iraq to Baghdad. I asked the Brigade commander for permission to accompany Lieutenant Colonel Doyle and it was granted to me but with reservations. One of the factors of war that is lost to the television audience is the feeling of uncertainty and vulnerability. The battlefield is a fluid and unpredictable environment where the use of chemical, biological, or nuclear weapons or the unexpected resurgence of an Iraqi resistance could suddenly alter the course of the war.

Before the war began, several soldiers were shot by anti-American terrorists while training in Kuwait. There is no rear area in the Middle East. Even when you are not involved on the leading edge of the battle, you are in enemy territory because terrorists are parasitic to every civilization. They blend in and lead outwardly acceptable lives until their objective is vulnerable and opportunity presents itself to them. Whenever General Hill had make a decision whether or not to send his soldiers into the unknown, I could tell his conservative instincts were to keep everyone as close as possible and take as few risks with his personnel as was necessary. I never doubted his personal courage, but he had great reservations about sending troops out of the secure areas. He even commented to me once that he was having trouble keeping me reigned in. Even with his reservations, he agreed that I should go forward to visit the soldiers of the

13th PSYOPS Battalion during Palm Sunday and provide services for them. This would be one of the more memorable experiences of my time in Iraq.

Our first stop was at Camp Bucca. Bucca was beginning to look more like an established EPW camp. The prisoners were still in unimproved holding areas separated from the soldiers by only a few strands of concertina wire. The detainees lived in modest tents, but frankly, the tents were in better condition than those the Americans first lived in. The 13th PSYOPS Battalion had a detachment at Bucca. A slice from the 800th MP Brigade and the entire 724th MP Battalion was also located at Bucca. The 724th had begun to relieve the British soldiers of guard duty and the transition from Camp Freddie to Camp Bucca was well under way. The British had a casual approach to the Iraqis. They would toss them cigarettes, candy, or anything else they wanted in an effort to keep the peace. They didn't require the Iraqis to observe any of the camp rules and procedures as long as they didn't cause trouble. The American approach was much more rigorous, and the Iraqis knew right away that a new sheriff was in town.

We stayed overnight at Bucca and I met with the soldiers and leaders of the PSYOPS battalion. Since the 724th MP Battalion and my own 800th MP Brigade staff were there, I took the opportunity to visit with them as well. When we went to bed at night, I placed liter sized water bottles in my boots to keep the scorpions and other creatures of the night from seeking shelter inside. In the morning, I carefully pulled my covers back to make sure that anything that had crawled on top of the covers didn't get tossed into my face.

Our convoy consisted of several soft skin HUMVEES. The MP Guard and Escort Company that chaperoned us provided the firepower for the convoy. Each HUMVEE carried three MPs equipped with heavy assault rifles and grenade launchers. None of the vehicles were up-armored, that is, none of them had a hard shell to protect the passengers from gunfire or shrapnel. At this point, there hadn't been any roadside bombs but the checkpoints had already been attacked several times. I carried my own personal GPS and began plotting our stops from Camp Bucca and I continued to do so at each stop along the way as we traveled north.

Our next stop was an airfield that was used as a detention facility. We found accommodations in a two story structure that was most likely barracks for Iraqi Air Force personnel. As we were driving in, we noticed a small fenced in compound with a guard post. The compound was deserted and we decided to look inside. It was a small outpost that couldn't have housed more than 50 Iraqi soldiers. I imagine it was some sort of military police or security outpost located just outside of the Air Base. Inside, we saw the evidence of the quick retreat of Iraqi soldiers. Uniforms were scattered around, many still in plastic bags. A barracks room had been ransacked by some opportunistic Bedouins who took advantage of the time between the Iraqi retreat and the American occupation of the airfield. Bedouins were nomadic and were adept at quick scavenger operations. There was more than one HUMVEE stripped to the bare metal by industrious Bedouins.

There were a couple of rooms that had been used for training as evidenced by several charts and diagrams hanging on the wall. Of particular interest were the displays used for their chemical training. Atropine injectors are issued to American military personnel as treatment for exposure to chemical agents in war. The injector has a spring-loaded needle inside that fires out and penetrates several layers of clothing to administer antidotes to the casualty. The Iraqis had an atropine injector broken down and attached to a wooden display board. This was their NBC (Nuclear, Biological, and Chemical) training area. In addition to the chemical suits and training aids, we also discovered a footlocker full of unexploded ordinance. None of the MPs were foolish enough to mess with the box. It contained an assortment of hand grenades, mortars, and bullets of every caliber imaginable. Several pictures of Saddam were painted on the walls and we posed by them for pictures before we left.

At the Air Base, soldiers labored to improve their living conditions. Some were beginning to wash clothes and others worked on their sleeping arrangements. Latrines was one area that no one seemed able to master. The Iraqi toilets didn't work. In fact, I never had the privilege of finding one that did the entire time I was in Iraq. The arrangement at Tallil Airfield was a hole that had been dug some fifty feet from a three story apartment complex. Plywood was arranged to create walls around it in a rectangular shape. It was divided in half, with a seat on each side situated over an open mouthed pit. The driveway into the facility passed right beside the makeshift toilet and when the refuse needed to be disposed of, kerosene was poured into the holes and burned. The smell of burning human waste was common to every consolidated troop location and it is one of the most putrid smells you will ever endure. There is nothing really like it and it burns all day long.

Chaplain (Lieutenant Colonel) Ellis was stationed here with the744th MP Battalion. I found him on the roof hanging up his laundry on a make-shift clothes line. When I approached him he was so startled that I was afraid he might jump off the roof. I asked him to give me an update on his morale, the battalion's morale, the leadership, and his religious support for the soldiers of the 744th and for the EPWs. He told me about the tremendous response of the soldiers to his ministry and their reliance upon him for spiritual encouragement. Then he began to relate to me a crisis in the detention facility. The guidance for chaplains always emphasized minimizing our contact with the Iraqi EPWs. There was a tremendous sensitivity to American Chaplains proselytizing Iraqis while they were detained in our facilities. Chaplain Ellis had been in frequent contact with the prisoners but only to observe their health and welfare.

One of the MPs approached him and asked him to get involved with an Imam in the holding area. The Imam claimed to be the second highest ranking Imam in Baghdad. He had been arrested and labeled as anti-American. He felt he had been handled roughly by the Marines and mentioned that one Marine and put his foot on him while he was being prepared for movement. I can see how a soldier or Marine might use a foot to help control a prisoner until the prisoner's hands were secured but the Imam was offended by this derogatory gesture. Chaplain Ellis then began to explain his actions toward the Imam. He left the Imam and obtained a standard issue Qur' an, the same one given to US Muslim soldiers. After he washed his hands, he presented the Qur' an to the Imam and asked for his forgiveness on behalf of the Marine that had inadvertently offended him. Chaplain Ellis also asked for the prisoner tag to be removed from the Imam that labeled him as anti-American. He said that the Imam looked at him in disbelief, tears welled up in his eyes and he said to Chaplain Ellis, *"This takes all the evil away!"* He asked Chaplain Ellis to write a note inside the Qur' an. Knowing that writing in a Qur' an is frowned upon, Chaplain Ellis recognized the significance of the request.

After telling me the story Chaplain Ellis sat still, staring at me. While I was two ranks his junior, he was accountable to me by virtue of my position as the brigade chaplain. I sat with my back against the wall and looked alternately from him to the sky. My choices were to condemn his interaction with the Imam or approve of his initiative. As a chaplain, he really had no business interacting on such a personal level with the detainees and he especially should not have been involved with reclassifying detainees. That is the job of the military intelligence personnel together with the MPs. Yet here we sat, on the roof of the Iraqi barracks, knowing that he had done more to promote diplomatic relations with this man and all who were under his influence than any other ambassador ever could.

I told him that I believed he had done the right thing and that in fact, I saw no other alternative to the actions he took. As a leader it was his responsibility to respond to the special nature of this crisis as only a chaplain could and that I believed he had handled it in an honest and forthright way. He in no way proselytized the Imam and in fact, guaranteed his freedom of religion while waiting at Tillil Airbase. I assured him that I would stand by him and support his decision if this ever became an issue. We embraced and prayed together. I promised to watch for the Imam when he appeared at Camp Bucca and to treat him with the same respect that Chaplain Ellis had. By the time the Imam reached Camp Bucca however, prisoners were being released too fast for me to be able to find him. He was repatriated to Baghdad.

That night was difficult. I first tried to sleep on the roof but in the middle of the night, nickel sized raindrops pelted my face and soaked my uniform. I grabbed my gear and rushed to the door leading downstairs. I didn't particularly want to stay inside the building. Not only was it dark but since most of the windows were busted out, sandstorms had deposited dust several inches thick on most of the floors. Higher was always better when sleeping in Iraq. I found a room and threw my gear down on the floor creating a small sandstorm of my own inside the room. I explored the room as best I could to make sure I wasn't sharing it with one of the many stray dogs that run around in the desert. Satisfied that I was alone in the room, I closed my eyes to capture a few hours of sleep.

Morning came quickly. One moment I was listening to dogs howling somewhere in the dark Iraqi desert and the next I was trying to breath through all the dust kicked up around me. I gathered my gear and packed it in the back of the HUMVEE.

I learned to travel light from my days with the 101st Airborne (Air Assault). While we were at Fort Bragg on Operation Purple Dragon, I was the only chaplain deployed with the 3rd Brigade task force. That made me, a junior chaplain, the acting brigade chaplain for the exercise. Fortunately I was given the Brigade Chaplain Assistant, Staff Sergeant Proctor. His soldier skills and motivation were really the key to my success in conducting ministry to the Brigade. As we prepared to accompany the infantry battalion on an Air Assault mission, I was tasked to accompany the PSYOPS team to a village and search for the political and religious leadership in the village. I gathered my gear, uniform, flashlight, poncho, gortex jacket, gloves, a number of Bibles, other religious hardware, and sleeping bag. I always carried a couple of MREs with me as well since I never knew when or where food was going to be supplied. Once packed, my rucksack towered over my head by a half foot. It should have been nearly level with my shoulders.

Late that night, we moved toward the pickup zone where the soldiers would load onto the Blackhawk helicopters to be carried to the Drop Zone and into the night for their mission. I looked at the soldiers that were to board with me and began to count them. I couldn't figure out how we were all going to get on the helicopter. Our bird moved into position and we all ran out from the cover of the wood line to board. Rucksacks were thrown on board and soldiers began to climb in. I watched as they boarded quickly and soon tossed my own bag in and jumped in with them. This was the first authentic sardine can I have ever been inside. I was literally sitting on top of a young man who was against the back wall of the Blackhawk with his feet drawn up under his chin. I sat on his knees and tried to keep my weight off of him by pulling on the airframe door. I thanked God that at least I could see out of the window even if it was pitch black outside.

The flight was at least 45 minutes and then hovering just a couple of feet off the ground the crew chiefs opened the doors to allow us to disembark. This was the first time that I realized I had packed too much for this trip. I grabbed my ruck and jumped off the helicopter. The bag dragged me to the ground. My legs were asleep from the awkward position I was in during the flight and I was having trouble clearing the rotor wash to move into a prone position in a perimeter defense. When the Blackhawk lifted off, the entire group rose from the ground and sprinted to the wood line. Most were wearing Night Vision Goggles (NVGs) but I was not. I ran straight ahead with the overloaded pack on my back. When I got into the wood line, it was clear that I was with the wrong group. Muttering to myself I turned in the direction I knew we were to travel and began making my way along the wood line in hopes of finding my patrol. Very quickly, I found them, or was found by them and we began our long nights walk to our objective. The bag weighed heavier and heavier on my back as the night stretched on and on. Every time we stopped to check our position, someone would help me to stand up again. I was careful not to complain since I had packed my own bags for this trip. In the days after our return, I could hardly walk. My thighs felt as if they had been run over by a truck. While word made it back to me that the infantry guys had been impressed with the pack mule chaplain's stamina and ability to keep up, I learned that packing less is better. That lesson served me well in Iraq.

After I loaded my bags on the HUMVEE, I began searching for Lieutenant Colonel Doyle. He was busy taking care of last minute coordination with the escort guard company that was our protection on the convoy. We left out soon after an MRE breakfast consisting of your choice of grill flavored beef, cheese tortellini, chicken breast, or some other delicacy rich in vitamins and calories. We checked our water, fuel, and provisions then left the small pocket of civilization and the security of the Air Base.

Traveling north toward Baghdad, I was taken aback by the abject poverty of the Iraqi people. Everywhere I looked, it seemed the houses only had two or three walls and the children were always running out toward the convoys. This became a real problem at the Iraqi/Kuwaiti boarder. The Iraqi children gathered at the crossing points and after learning that the Americans had no intention of harming them in any way, they aggressively approached the convoys. They ran next to the HUMVEEs reaching inside to strip whatever they could grab. They would eventually pick narrow passages to form human chains in an effort to stop the vehicles and solicit from the soldiers. This became increasingly dangerous for both the children and the soldiers. Moving vehicles are not the place for children to play for obvious reasons and additionally, stopping the convoys makes them vulnerable to roadside attacks from bombs, ambushes, or snipers. The soldiers would try to keep rolling at a snails pace, pressing through the masses of children calling out for water, food or money. Time and again, we would toss our MREs and water bottles to the children. I finally devised a plan to keep them away from the convoys. I would take all the candy sent to me from the states and when the children approached the vehicles, I would toss the candy as far over their heads as possible. They stopped in their tracks and turned to retrieve the candy. The convoy was able to clear the area in the meantime.

The trip north took over eight hours from the time we left the Air Base. In all of those miles, the desert scenery never changed. We traveled on major roadways that I considered to be in fairly good shape when they were visible under the sand. Finally, we arrived at Bushmaster. This was to have been a collection point for prisoners as well but it was soon to be closed since it turned out to be unnecessary. The soldiers at Bushmaster were living in a much more spartan environment than those at Bucca or at the Air Base. There were only rows of small hexagon shaped tents and some water containers here. The soldiers were tossing baseballs and trying to pass the time but the boredom was apparent. We stayed at Bushmaster for only an hour or so for refueling before moving on to the outskirts of Baghdad.

The carnage of war became more and more apparent the closer we got to Baghdad. Burned out vehicles dotted the desert, many were still on fire. I will never forget the first time I saw an American vehicle destroyed. Two sides of an armored personnel carrier was all that remained on the tracked foundation. Buses and trucks were overturned, burned, and looted. What was most striking however was the absence of any evidence besides the smoking vehicles that testified to the epic battle and drama that had occurred. The carnage of war was quickly swallowed by the cleansing sands of Iraq.

As we passed into the actual suburbs of Baghdad, we began to see the wrecked artillery and tanks of the Iraqi army. It appeared that Saddam had elected to defend Baghdad using small unit tactics. He recognized that the coalition couldn't be defeated by meeting them on the battlefield. So, he placed artillery and tank platoons in ditches, fields, and under trees next to homes. From those positions it seemed the tanks remained hidden until the last possible minute and then they pulled up from a ditch or out from behind a house to quickly fire into the approaching Americans. That firing position was where each of the now silent gladiators remained. They sat still beside the road in an attack position but no longer able to offer any resistance against the liberators. In each case, the tanks were charred and blackened hulks bearing silent testimony to the passing of the 3rd Infantry Division. What was most amazing is that the tanks next to homes were destroyed but the homes themselves were unscathed. I marveled at the precision of modern warfare and thanked God that the sheep grazing beside the tanks and the children now playing in the yards were not casualties of the war that visited their home. We considered stopping and looking closer at the tanks, but all of us decided against it. While security was a primary concern, none of us really wanted to look inside the wrecks. We knew that men had met sudden and violent deaths inside those machines and there was nothing about the death of any soldier that we considered a tourist attraction. Besides, we had a schedule to keep.

We arrived at the Airport and after passing through the check points, drove down the runway to the air terminal. That terminal was previously called the *Saddam International Airport* but had *recently* been renamed the *Baghdad International Airport*. We passed by the burned out wreckage of an Iraqi Airliner and by the rows of American Apache helicopters. We finally reached our destination which was the 3rd IDs prisoner holding facility. There were PSYOPS personnel here as well helping to translate for the Iraqis. Leaving the Airport, we drove into Baghdad. The signs of a battle were everywhere apparent, especially the burned and destroyed vehicles along the city streets. Only one HUMVEE caught my eye however. One building had a massive hole in it from some sort of blast. The architecture can best be described as late 70's American. Buildings were squared off and basic in design. Mechanical structures and air conditioners were all bulky and oversized, indicating that electronic modernization had not yet reached Baghdad. We continued through the city into a less populated area. There we found a compound that appeared to be a school with a picture of Saddam prominently displayed at the gate. We stopped and after determining that the compound was abandoned, we dismounted our vehicles to stretch and take a break. Several of us ventured into the school building. The facility had been vandalized. Books were thrown everywhere and glass littered the floor, crunching under our feet. We moved down one of the hallways and I became distracted by a room that had been burned. I walked inside, ever curious about the life of the Iraqis. I found the file cabinets overturned and drawers pulled out. The contents had been burned beyond any recovery. It became apparent that this was the records room for the school. I chuckled to myself at the thought of a few Iraqi students deciding the war was a great opportunity to get a fresh start for their academic careers. I only hoped it was as simple as that rather than records that were being destroyed to avoid detection by the Coalition. Numerous reports told of frantic Iraqi officials moving and destroying evidence. Other reports indicated that schools and hospitals were used by the government in an attempt to conceal their work.

As I left the room I heard movement down the hall. I moved in the direction of the sound and stopped at a door that had been busted out. As I peered through the jagged opening in the center of the door, I saw a puppy standing in the deserted room. He made no movement toward me, only stood looking at me. The room he was in had also seen its fair share of destruction. I took a picture of the dog through the door and decided to rejoin the others. I walked toward the location in which I saw them in and much to my chagrin, they were not there. I walked quickly further down the hall and called out quietly for them. There was no answer. I called a little louder. Again, I was greeted only by silence. I suddenly realized where I was. I was an American soldier, a Christian Chaplain, alone in Baghdad, Iraq. I didn't have any resources, no friends, no way home, and I was dressed like any other soldier that had rained destruction down on the city only two nights before with the notable exception of the cross displayed prominently on my Kevlar helmet and collar. I picked up my pace and decided to move quickly to where the convoy was parked just outside the gate.

As I emerged from the school and looked at the gate, my heart sank. The convoy was gone. I glanced around the courtyard of the walled enclosure. I appeared to be alone in the deserted schoolyard. My thoughts began to race, "Do I hide and hope that some Americans come by, should I look for a friendly Iraqi face and try to get them to take me to the Americans, should I run out into the street and try to search for the convoy myself?" As I stood there paralyzed with indecision, the convoy pulled back up. Apparently they had just been turning around, and were about to form a search for me if I didn't emerge from the building. I decided right then that I loved those guys and I would never take a walk alone again. This served as a lesson for me that when you are in war, you can never forget where you are and who you are because the enemy is always watching and in a moment, you can find yourself isolated and alone (1 Peter 5:8). At home in America, we are free to explore and assuage our curiosities, but in a war zone, curiosity must take a back seat to wisdom.

As we headed south from Baghdad, we were forced to slow down when we encountered civilian traffic. The gunners perched on top of the HUMVEEs scanned across the car tops and into the windows of buses as they passed by, looking for any sign of aggression from the Iraqis. What we received back were smiles and waves. Suddenly, a small passenger car with three Iraqi men sitting together in the back seat pulled up beside our vehicle and stopped. Our convoy was struggling to move together through the congested Baghdad traffic and was nearly stopped waiting for an opening to move. The man sitting in the center of the back seat was obviously struggling to get to the window closest to me. Already rattled from my experience at the school, I sat staring at him as the window opened up and I wondered what he planned to do. Again, there was nowhere for me to go, nowhere to run except into the arms of other Iraqis that were packed around our vehicle.

The window was completely down and his face was four feet from the side of our HUMVEE. He looked at me and in broken English said, *"Thank you for downing Saddam!"* *"You're welcome"* was all I could say.

That night we stayed at Dogwood, a military post just on the southern side of Baghdad. The PSYOPS platoon that was stationed there was glad to see us and I was happy to perform the Palm Sunday service that evening. After the service, I explored the Iraqi military base on foot careful to remain well within areas clearly under the watchful eyes of American sentries. As the sun set, the PSYOPS soldiers pulled out horseshoes and started a tournament. My quick elimination served to inflate the ego of at least one of the Non-commissioned officers that advanced in the tournament. As I scrambled up a ladder to sleep on the roof, I was more than happy to talk to any and all of the soldiers already perched on top. I sat on my cot and looked around. There was nothing to obstruct my vision as far as the horizon. There is a real beauty in the desert as the sun sets. The beauty was scarred by pillars of black smoke rolling up into the clouds at different intervals all around us. The putrid smell of burning waste continued to drift past from time to time. Even through the destruction that man brings to his world, you can still see the beauty of God's creation breaking through. It gave me a sense of peace to know that one day the fire producing the pillars of smoke would be extinguished and the smell of burning waste would be replaced by the sound of flushing toilets and God's world would once again occupy the canvas alone in all of its majestic wonder.

One particular NCO that was bunked next to me sat

listening to his CDs through headphones. There was one selection from a group named *Three Doors Down* that he thought I really needed to listen to. He sat patiently with a smile that wouldn't go away while I sat listening to the music through his headphones. He pulled out one selection after another asking if I had heard of this group or song. Then he pulled out a song titled, *"I'm Already There"* by a country music band named *Lonestar*. I told him I wasn't familiar with that song and he warned me that I would cry if I listened to it. Again, curiosity drove me to put the headphones on my head and listen to the words. He was right. This song is about a man who was away from home. His message to his children and wife was that while physically apart, his love was all around them. Those lyrics proved more than a match for me that day. I remembered some of the e-mails my family had been sending me. They were having a pretty rough time of it without me. After they left the church in New Jersey, Bevalie had sold our home because of our heavy financial burden and was living with her parents. They had welcomed her into their home without hesitation when I left for the war. They weren't used to having houseguests for an extended time however, and as with any family forced to live together under difficult circumstances, the tensions were running high.

My wife and children were living virtually out of their suitcases. Our cat lived in the family van for two weeks, litter box and all until a friend from church offered to adopt her until we had a home again. My son's performance in school had deteriorated significantly and he expressed his frustration by hitting a locker and nearly lost the use of his finger. Twelve stitches were required to patch him up. My two youngest were still being home-schooled by my wife and Lydia, my 8 year old daughter had a significant strep infection. My oldest daughter Tiffany, known for her Christian convictions, was eventually accused of not even having a relationship with Christ by a friend of the family that couldn't understand the stress they were all under. After losing our home, our church, and the security of our family, the family van became "home". It was their sanctuary from an uniformed and impatient world. An air freshener was hung from the rear view mirror that said *"Home Sweet Home"* just to complete the picture. My wife stayed in it from 7:30 in the morning when she took my son to school until she came back to her parent's home at night to put the kids to bed. Then she would leave again the first thing in the morning and start the cycle all over again. Her place of refuge and support was a Bible study group that we had been a part of nine years before. They welcomed her, embraced her, cried with her, and most importantly they prayed with her. I will never be able to adequately express my gratefulness to those friends and realatives who opened their lives and homes to my family. I so wanted to be there for them myself and take away the hardship and stress they were under. Not only was their father and husband not there, but the uncertainty of my return was always in the back of their minds as well as mine. I dropped to my cot helpless to make my family's suffering any easier. Tears filled my eyes and I turned over to try and find sleep.

The next morning our adventure began again only in reverse. The long ride home was made more miserable by having sandbags in the floorboards forcing my knees up into my chest. I appreciated the protection they provided against landmines but they cultivated a sour attitude in me within a few hours. We also drove smack into a ferocious sandstorm. I wrapped a scarf tightly around my face but nothing would keep the dust out of my mouth. I repeatedly wiped my glasses in an effort to keep my vision clear. The storm was so bad that our convoy was forced to stop at two different points. We couldn't see the vehicles in front of us and feared hitting a stopped vehicle or becoming disoriented and getting lost.

Occasionally, the wind would slow just enough to see 50 feet or so. Once during a pause in the sandblasting, I noticed a herd of camels passing slowly by on our right. They are a lonely looking creature and I wondered how they were able to survive with nothing but sand as far as the eye can see.

Once the storm abated, we drove directly to the Air Base and after spending another night just like the first we had spent there, we headed to Bucca and then back to Camp Arifjan. I finished the trip with a tremendous respect for the younger and lower ranking soldiers in the Army. While some in senior leadership positions do become infected with some sort of a career progression bug, the soldiers that make our Army great are there because they believe in what they are doing. Sure, some join to get money for college and are shocked when they are called upon to go to war but there are others, and there are many of them, that believe they have an opportunity to make a difference in the world. There are others in this world not as blessed as we are. They have a deep respect for the people and want to be used for their good. They want to go home believing they were heroes, at least to some small Iraqi child that looked up at them with brown eyes and gestured with their thumb that they were thirsty or hungry. These soldiers are liberators and understand they have removed the fear of repression from an entire civilization by their selfless service and sacrifice. I will continue to serve only because I am able to serve with soldiers like these.

FORGOTTEN MOMENTS OF AMERICAN BENEVOLENCE

As Camp Bucca began to develop and the EPW population rose, several incidents occurred that demonstrated the heart and compassion of the American soldiers. The news reported that Saddam had opened up the asylums and the prisons before the ground war began. Those patients and criminals were often caught on the battlefield and eventually brought to Camp Bucca for processing and evaluation. A lack of medication, and language barriers often slowed the proper treatment of the mentally unstable. One such man worked a piece of metal loose from the concertina wire surrounding his holding area. He took the metal piece and began to cut himself on the chest from his left shoulder to the bottom of his right-hand ribcage. He cut deeper and deeper even through the muscle at points. Ken, the Brigade Physicians assistant was at Camp Bucca when the injured Iraqi man was discovered and brought in for treatment. Ken was moved with compassion and worked diligently to clean and suture the wounds. Over and again the doctors would move from compound to compound treating skin ailments and broken bones. Working with whatever instruments and medicine available, they worked patiently with the Iraqis and listened to every complaint.

One other extraordinary event took place when a family approached the compound gates with their sick daughter who was around ten years old. They were brought in and presented to the Doctors. They determined that she needed immediate medical treatment. She was loaded on board a helicopter and eventually underwent heart surgery to save her life. Her parents remained at Camp Bucca and were hired to help with preparing food for the prisoners until they were reunited with their daughter who had successfully recovered from her surgery. When the helicopter landed to bring her home, the family rushed out to her and they embraced. This was one of the moments that will always be remembered by those who were there.

These are only a token sample of the remarkable compassion shown by Americans to the Iraqis. Every day soldiers are interacting with the people of Iraq and every day the relationships grow stronger. The charitable deeds of Americans in Iraq is taking away the suspicion and the injuries of living under a brutal dictator.

AFTER THE DUST HAS SETTLED

Once the major conflict had ended, the routine of day to day life began to wear everyone down. We tried working out in the physical fitness tent but even that became routine. The briefings turned into nothing more than discussion on supplies for Camp Bucca and the anticipation of releasing prisoners. It wasn't long before thoughts began to turn toward home. We all felt that the war had all but ended, prisoners were being released at a phenomenal rate thanks to the hard work and efforts of the Brigade JAG officer and his staff. Out of approximately 10,000 Iraqi EPW's that processed through Camp Bucca, all but 600 were released by the end of June 2003. Additionally, the email traffic and rumor mill was suggesting that without prisoners, the 800th had no mission.

Going home was all that soldiers began to talk about. The chaplain community began to press homecoming and reunion issues. Everyone was talking about going home. After all, after Desert Storm the soldiers returned home quickly. When the World Wars were over, the ships disembarked thousands of troops into the streets of New York for the victory celebrations that followed the war. We were all ready for ours. Whether you had been in the country two days or one year, it felt like an eternity. We were tired and homesick. There was a collective sigh of relief as the last of the Iraqi Army evaporated and disappeared. Sure the search for Saddam and his political henchmen would continue, but that belonged to the CIA or someone else, we thought.

I began working on my redeployment briefing that was to help soldiers transition back to their normal lives and families. Words can not explain how focused soldiers are on returning home. Even with the excitement, the transition is difficult. Spouses back home had to learn to get along in life without their soldier. Sometimes it is hard to reassimilate the soldier into the family. Romance has to be rekindled even in the strongest of marriages because love has been waiting in such uncertainty. Bills often are piled up and waiting and sometimes, the financial burden overcame a bewildered spouse who may have never been forced to manage all of life alone before. The first few days back home are critical for the peace and happiness of the following months. When I suggested to General Hill that we should plan and schedule the redeployment briefs, he was evasive. I didn't understand his resistance to planning for our return since it seemed immanent. After all, we were running out of work! His only comment was, you never know when we are going until we get the word. I polled the staff and they all suggested to me that they didn't understand his hesitancy either. One after another, the battalions under our command began to be picked up by other commands. Now we were not only running out of EPWs but troops to command as well.

It was during this time of anticipation that I received an e-mail from a friend in Georgia, a pastor in my denomination. He asked if I would be interested in accepting a position as a church planter in Georgia. The opportunity had been suggested to me before the war but I was not in a position to take the job while the church I pastored in New Jersey was in the midst of a major transition from the Dark Ages into the light. Now however, I found myself unemployed when I returned home. My quick mobilization had cost me not only my job but the opportunity to make a living after I returned. This seemed like God's providential hand of opportunity. I wasn't sure when we were set to leave however since General Hill was not talking about the matter. In fact, he suggested we make plans for his change of command with Colonel Karpenski in June 2004. Changing command in the midst of a deployment in wartime seemed ludicrous to everyone on the staff, especially when we were expecting the order to pack up and go home anytime. We had completed our mission and had done it well.

I mentioned to the Chief of staff the opportunity I had and asked when I might expect to hear about our return. He said that we would have at least 6 more weeks in Kuwait just to clear Bucca and pack up. I groaned inside, but he saw the expression on my face. The S1, MAJ Hinzman was there as well and said I should ask to be released for demobilization. I looked at him as if he were speaking in Swahili. He reasoned that since I had not been a part of the 800th MP Brigade prior to the war, I should receive some consideration due to my short notice deployment, loss of a job, and dislocation of my family. I asked him if he thought that was fair for the rest of the troops and he pointed out that the permission had been granted for commanders to individually demobilize and that we had sent several people home already. Sergeant Major Dunbar, the senior active duty Sergeant Major in the Brigade was even being allowed to retire from Kuwait in the next week. He pressed me to create a memorandum asking permission to demobilize. A week after I wrote the memorandum, General Hill met with the staff and with their support of my request, he signed and I was on my way home. I flew home alone and wandered into the Philadelphia Airport to find my family waiting for me with balloons, hugs and tears. I was sure the rest of the Brigade was right behind me. In fact, in the report prepared by Army Maj. Gen. Antonio M. Taguba he stated:

"Prior to BG (Janis) Karpinski taking command, members of the 800th MP Brigade believed they would be allowed to go home when all the detainees were released from the Camp Bucca Theater Internment Facility following the cessation of major ground combat on 1 May 2003. At one point, approximately 7,000 to 8,000 detainees were held at Camp

Bucca. Through Article-5 Tribunals and a screening process, several thousand detainees were released. Many in the command believed they would go home when the detainees were released. In late May-early June 2003 the 800th MP Brigade was given a new mission to manage the Iraqi penal system and several detention centers. This new mission meant Soldiers would not redeploy to CONUS (Continental United States) 37 when anticipated. Morale suffered, and over the next few months there did not appear to have been any attempt by the Command to mitigate this morale problem".

One reason the command may not have been quick to help soldiers adjust to the news that they would not be going home could be that General Karpinski took command on June 29, 2003 just as the change in mission was handed down. She inherited a depleted staff. The Chaplain, Doctor, Physician's Assistant, Chief of Staff, NCOIC of operations (S3), and many other key personnel both enlisted and commissioned officer had been redeployed to the United States. Taguba's report accurately observed that *"Reserve Component units do not have an individual personnel replacement system to mitigate medical losses or the departure of individual Soldiers that have reached 24 months of Federal active duty in a five-year period."* Therefore, the slow attrition of personnel created a handicap virtually invisible to higher commands.

With her new command understrengthed, battalions being assigned and reassigned, no institutional history or experience with the remaining personnel, and a new mission that would stretch her soldiers out from Kuwait City to Baghdad engaged in a work without precedent, General Karpinski could not recognize the change in the Brigades mental preparedness to take this mission. When the mission was announced, Major Cavallaro suggested that he was not aware of any unit that had ever been tasked to do this mission before. The 800th had conducted interment and resettlement operations since establishing Camp Bucca and often they had to rewrite doctrine or reconcile Army policy with the international community. None of that could prepare them for taking over the responsibility to establish, man, and subsequently train Iraqis to run the nations prison system. The 800th MP Brigade was responsible for all of the fourteen operational prisons, small police station jails, and the four Detention Camps. They were tasked to escort hundreds of contractors and workers to and from Abu Ghraib every single day, except Fridays. The 800th was responsible to secure the MEK (the Iranians) at a compound all the way out near the Iranian border. There were no air assets to help with covering the expanse between the compounds.

It was a twelve-hour drive to camp Bucca and three hours more to Basra. The Brigade had seven facilities in Baghdad but could not visit or inspect all of them in one day because the roads were so dangerous. The brigade provided their own security and Force Protection which further depleted the soldiers. The shortage was particularly pronounced at Abu Ghraib because it was under constant mortar attack every night. The Army was faced with a mission no one had trained for nor anticipated and the 800th seemed the best fit despite their inexperience and lack of doctrinal guidance.

The next 9 months I remained psychologically on deployment. The 800th MP Brigade received a follow-on mission, one they were not trained, staffed, or equipped for. A recently published book, *"The Abu Graib Investigations,* includes the final report of the Independent Panel to Review Department of Defense Detention Operations. That report erroneously concludes:

"Problems at Abu Ghraib are traceable in part to the nature and recent history of the military police and military intelligence units at Abu Ghraib. The 800th Military Police Brigade had one year of notice to plan for detention operations in Iraq. Original projections called for approximately 12 detention facilities in non-hostile, rear areas with a projection of 30,000 to 100,000 Enemy prisoners of War."[6]

This report is confusing the anticipated mission to create three Enemy Prisoner of War encampments using twelve battalions to staff them with the civilian prison mission that came to the 800th as a follow on mission to the original EPW mission. No one had projected that the Coalition would take over the civilian prison system in Iraq.

The 800th took over a wrecked prison system for Iraq. They had to rebuild the prisons and staff them. Already missing a number of key personnel and with others such as the experienced Chief of Staff, the retired operations NCO Sergeant Major Dunbar, the deputy commander, the Headquarters First Sergeant, myself and many others, the 800th MP Brigade took the mission with a new commander and performed admirably.

In June 2003, Janis Karpinski, an Army reserve brigadier general, took command of the 800th Military Police Brigade and was given charge of military prisons in Iraq. General Karpinski was an experienced operations and intelligence officer who had served in the 1991 Gulf War, but she had never supervised a prison system. Now she was in charge of three large jails, eight battalions, and thirty-four hundred Army reservists, most of whom, like her, had no training in handling prisoners and had not anticipated this sort of mission. In a December 2003 interview with the St.

Petersburg Times, she said that, for many of the Iraqi inmates at Abu Ghraib, *"living conditions now are better in prison than at home. At one point we were concerned that they wouldn't want to leave."*

A month later, General Karpinski was formally admonished, and quietly suspended while a formal investigation began.

Brigadier General Janis Karpinski wrote, *"The MP (Military Police) units were deployed for one mission and performed it successfully. They were given a new mission and their deployment was extended in Theater. New missions are assigned all the time, yet in this case, the new mission was more demanding, more dangerous, required no additional equipment and more soldiers. The Brigade received additional equipment nor additional soldiers and no support from either of the two, three star headquarters, because the Commanders seemed to be bickering about who had to support the Brigade. CFLCC (Coalition Forces Land Component Command) wanted to wash their hands of the Brigade because they wanted to redeploy their own soldiers back to the US, and they did just as soon as the Brigade was assigned to Iraq. The CJTF7 refused to take on the responsibility of supporting the Brigade because we were still assigned to CFLCC. This essentially placed our soldiers at great risk because two, three star GOs (General Officers) were at odds with each other."*

Eventually the embattled and maligned 800th MP Brigade returned home to their families; dishonored. The actions of a few isolated soldiers in a subordinate battalion soiled the reputation of the 800th and spoiled months of sacrifice, courage, and hard work. The Brigades awards were delayed and many were downgraded. General Karpinski wouldn't have an opportunity to celebrate a mission accomplished with her command. Many soldiers would transfer or leave the unit and recruiting suffered. The

800th will most likely be called upon to return to Iraq. Their past will be behind them and new faces will take charge of a new mission.

Despite the tragic reputation the 800th has been given, families of soldiers returning home embraced them as heroes. The months of separation created a hunger for reunion that cut through any controversy. The sentiments of my daughter represent every little girl waiting for her daddy to return home from war.

"Dear Daddy,

You are finally home. I missed you so much but I knew you were coming home soon and that everything would be fun again. (We will be) singing songs, reading books, and playing games. You are finally home! You and me (will be) together forever and ever and everything will be fun again day and night. The stars of the night and the sun of the day. You were gone for a very long time and now you are home again! Love your daughter, Lydia"

PART II

FROM THE WAR ROOM TO THE LIVING ROOM

AN ANATOMY OF AMERICA'S RESPONSE TO ABU GHRAIB

"The purpose in a man's heart is like deep water,
but a man of understanding will draw it out."
Proverbs 20:5

"The unexamined life is not worth living"
Socrates

"Sometimes I've believed as many as six impossible
things before breakfast."
*Lewis Carroll,
THROUGH THE LOOKING GLASS*

Most children have seen some adaptation of Lewis Carroll's *Alice in Wonderland.* In his novel, Carroll takes Alice, who desperately wants to grow up, down a hole to an underground world of strange and unusual characters while illustrating his masterful ability to weave logic with nonsense. Each one that Alice meets consistently turns everything upside-down with mind-boggling logic, word play, and incredible parodies. Once Alice manages to escape from Wonderland, however, she comes to realize she is trapped on the wrong side of a mirror [looking glass]. Alice can see her parents on the other side, but they cannot see her and after reading a scary poem, her nightmares come true.

The reader at once notices that Alice's reactions to the strange events around her are not normal. She doesn't think twice about a talking rabbit and without a thought follows him into his hole. She falls into darkness but doesn't panic or become afraid. Further and further down she goes, falling away from everything she knows and into the unknown. The passing of time during her fall serves only to increase her boredom and she begins to daydream while she falls. Once down the hole, Alice begins to live in the world of her imagination and loses a context for understanding the events or people that surrounded her. What seemed thrilling in her imagination became frightening and unpredictable in reality. Every association with her world, to the real world, became blurred and the surreal became her reality. The imaginary became the ordinary. Without a context for interpreting meaning, she lost hope and had no answers to her questions. This loss of context is illustrated in her conversation with the Cheshire Cat.

> *"'Cheshire Puss,' she began, 'Would you tell me, please, which way I ought to go from here?' 'That depends a good deal on where you want to get to,' said the Cat. 'I don't much care where' said Alice. 'Then it doesn't matter which way you go,' said the Cat."*
>
> *Alice had no direction, no purpose in traveling, and in the end she didn't even have a question. Our context is the lens through which we are able to make sense of our world. Our present reality may be the nightmare of our founding fathers imaginations."*

CONTEXT IS KING

"Context is King." Any reputable seminary teaches students of the scriptures that a proper interpretation of a biblical passage must consider the historical, cultural, and linguistic context of the passage. That same rule for interpretation applies to world affairs. Therein lies one of the problems in understanding the prisoner abuse at Abu Ghraib.

American's have been looking at the world *"through a looking glass"*, or out of context, for nearly a generation. The video monitors permanently fixed in front of us and the channels on our television sets limit our field of vision and perception of our world. The result is an unusual view of reality. The world has become something like the Mad Hatter's tea party and the guests all seem to turn reality and truth on its head as the world makes less and less sense. It is not because the world is more complex or harder to understand. We have numerous tools at our disposal to help us gather and organize information on any subject we desire. The problem is not the availability of information; it is our ability to assimilate it. Americans have lost the cognitive structures to see world events within the context of history, politics, and morality.

According to the U.S. Department of Education, thirty-three percent of 4th grade students perform at or below the basic level in their knowledge of U.S. History. Fifty-seven percent of high school seniors perform at or below the basic level in U.S. History. We no longer know our own history, much less the history of South Africa, Russia, France, the Balkans, or the Middle East. Yet, we demonstrate confidence in forming strong opinions about world affairs despite our historical ineptitude.

To understand the prisoner abuse in Iraq, we have to place the incident in context. In the following analysis the Iraqi prisoner abuse and Americans watching the drama unfold are placed in the context of history, politics, and moral thought. A careful and systematic analysis of the events, media coverage, the war, and the soldiers involved will reveal disturbing truths about America. To really understand Abu Ghraib and learn from it, we will have to take a look at ourselves as well. We need to know why we interpret events the way we do and what motivates us to wage war.

SEARCHING FOR STARS BEHIND BARS

Since The People's Court first aired in 1981, the American public has been treated to a steady fare of court cases. Whether it is petty theft, broken promises, or multiple homicides, the television treats them all the same. The networks have created a public courtroom to broadcast a trial before a national jury. The criminal justice system is on par with *Jeopardy, Wheel of Fortune* and *Who Wants to Be A Millionaire*. There are winners and losers, all for the entertainment of the public and ratings for the networks.

One of the most infamous cases broadcast to the public was the O.J. Simpson trial. He faced charges alleging that he killed Ron Goldman and Nicole Brown Simpson. From the moment the helicopters caught up with his slow moving SUV, Simpson's case seemed too strange to be true. American's were riveted to their screens as broadcasters took five minutes to discuss every minute of the trial.

Never before have so many people in America been so thoroughly acquainted with and involved in a trial. Viewers were given the facts, theories, and police failures in the case. The trial was broadcast live from coast to coast. No matter what background a person may come from or what civic group or religious affiliation a person might claim the O.J. trial became a part of America's common culture. His case took on the air of a soap opera drama as T.V. experts discussed celebrity justice and the legal prejudice against black men in America. When a verdict was announced, the country convulsed with either jubilation or rage.

The networks had discovered a silver bullet to boost ratings. Real life drama was an unexplored territory that promised to yield a faithful and ever expanding audience.

Now, judicial cases are routinely discussed in the sterile environment of a television studio. Panels of experts convene to discuss the legal strategies and the details of the case. Social and moral angles are discussed such as prejudice and sexual fidelity. Before the trial begins, the experts have briefed their audience on every detail of the case and examined every possible outcome. The public verdict is determined long before the prosecution calls the first witness.

Crime has not always enjoyed such prestige and popularity. Criminals haven't always been celebrities and local crimes were once considered a matter of local concern. Now bad news and crime are prime time entertainment. *Cops, American Justice, Judge Judy,* and *America's Most Wanted* have created a new genre in entertainment.

Turning crime into family entertainment was bound to have some dangerous side effects. Criminals sense their public forum and the exposure appeals to their carnal desire for attention and influence. Ordinary people in safe neighborhoods feel less assured of their safety since the crimes of the nation are beamed into their living rooms and presented to make the most remote news seem relevant and intensely personal to every viewer. Perhaps most dangerous of all is the new American paradigm of journalistic justice. Rather than waiting for the court to adjourn or reading an opinion of the justices, Americans are content to allow newscasters to read and interpret the news for them.

IN OUR NEXT SEGMENT YOU WILL DECIDE...

Before the days of exhibitionist trials that turn real life tragedy into a game of Trivial Pursuit, the public was granted a much longer time to consider the facts of a case.

Only those in the affected families and local communities felt an investment in the outcome of the trial. The information was kept in perspective by the rest of the nation and some objectivity was retained. When someone distant from the case was asked an opinion, their response was, "I don't know because I wasn't there."

Initial responses that were more emotional than rational abated over time and a search for truth and justice emerged as the common goal. The presentation of cases on television today tends to draw the viewers into it in such a personal way that they feel they have an investment in everything. The viewer feels compelled to make a quick decision of guilty or not guilty before the next segment. Unfortunately, time to consider the evidence is limited to the evening broadcast. Viewers are not able to grasp the real context of the case. Conclusions are made quickly in a rush to judgment based on the information the media provides and the commentary of the experts assembled in the television studios. Each criminal case becomes a personal issue to the increasingly voyeuristic public.

This type of coverage is an injustice to the criminal justice system and the person accused of a crime. Lawyers and judges become too aware of the power of public opinion and purposefully work to manipulate public opinion to bring pressure on the court instead of seeking justice. Cases are made more difficult to handle as untainted juries become harder to find. Before a jurist is interviewed to serve, they have already been inundated with the media's opinion on the case. They have heard the experts opinions and the defendant doesn't have a chance. Crimes have never been kept secret and the public has always known about notorious criminals. But, like a good novel, the facts used to be presented slowly in a process of discovery rather than speculation stated as if it were fact. This newest trend has been the case with Abu Ghraib. Since the verdict on Abu Ghraib was rendered long before the investigations were finished, we must work diligently to re-examine the context of the abuse and the source of our bias in judging it as evil.

A PICTURE IS WORTH A THOUSAND WORDS

There has been no lack of news coverage or opinions about the prisoner abuses at Abu Ghraib. Commentators have not lacked for words to describe their shock and outrage over what they see in the infamous Abu Ghraib abuse pictures. Unfortunately, from the very first showing of the pictures opinions were offered without the benefit of context. The public outcry was heard in the halls of Congress, the offices of the Pentagon, and at the White House. The President addressed the Arab world and assured them that Americans did not approve of the treatment of the Iraqi prisoners. Investigations were launched and the 800th MP Brigade commander was suspended from her command in May of 2004. The awards for the Brigade were downgraded. Was this the best way to seek truth and justice at Abu Ghraib? What standard can we apply to measure the degree of guilt the 800th MP Brigade should shoulder for the isolated and non-systemic crimes at Abu Ghraib? The pictures and information came to the public like a tsunami and overwhelmed viewers by the sheer volume of information and the contemptuous comments made by broadcasters and political pundits. No point of reference was ever offered to understand the events that took place within the prison walls. The only option for the public to choose was guilty, guilty, guilty! But who is guilty and why did it happen?

As news of the prison scandal in Iraq spread through the airwaves of America, the first incongruence emerged. The hometowns, families, and neighbors of those accused of crimes were shocked. Neighbors of the Reserve and National Guard soldiers from West Virginia and Pennsylvania were interviewed and one after another expressed their disbelief that the young man or woman they had known for their entire lives could have ever perpetrated such crimes. The character witnesses could not agree with the presentation given by the media. Unfortunately, the verdict was already in.

WHY DOES ABU GHRAIB BOTHER US?

The pictures have been on the news and on the internet adnauseam. We grimace each time we see them again and wonder why the media seems to be fixated on this tragedy. Why does the press have such an insatiable addiction to exploit any misstep taken in the war against terror? It seems that reporters play the role of the prosecution in the world's court of opinion rather than American journalists working to bring us the news of the day.

Americans have expressed a collective sense of shame over Abu Ghraib. We cannot deny that a tragedy occurred there. Unfortunately, before we closed the book on Abu Ghraib, we did not take the opportunity to properly understand it. We cannot just move on without addressing the critical questions Abu Ghraib has brought to the surface. Why do we feel a collective shame? Perhaps the answer to this is more important than the justice meted out on the perpetrators themselves.

Christian apologist David Wells has defined *shame* as, *"the sense that we have been exposed and uncovered. We know ourselves to be something other than what we hoped [we were]. And this revelation often comes when others come to see, accidentally and without warning, a side to us about which we feel vulnerable and embarrassed."*[7] Has the press unwittingly exposed our shame? Most will balk at the suggestion that we all feel some shame as a result of the Abu Ghraib prisoner humiliation and abuse but yet there is an uneasiness felt by many. We know the individual soldiers must shoulder individual responsibility for their abuse. Yet, something inside of us warns that there is more to be concerned about than the law. We all feel the chill of the shadow of immorality that extends beyond Abu Ghraib. Why do some of us feel a collective sense of guilt even though we do not condone the abuse nor were we involved in it? Where is our shame coming from?

At the trial of Adolph Eichman, the butcher of Auschwitz, a Jewish man who identified him broke down and wept. He even fainted when he recognized Eichman. When he asked if lingering fear of Eichman caused him to faint, he denied that he was still afraid of him. It was not because he feared the man, but because he saw that he was just a man. He imagined that he was a monster or a god, but when he discovered he was just a man, he realized that he too could be just as evil as Eichman. He glimpsed the reality of human nature, the cause of our shame. Would a different group of soldiers have behaved differently?

There are two questions that remain unanswered. The most obvious is, *"Why did the soldiers abuse the prisoners?"* The second is *"What would have been different if I had been there?"* The first question has not been addressed to my satisfaction and the second question has not been addressed at all. While the courts move to quickly punish those who were involved and assign blame to several levels of leadership, there is something that Americans must consider that involves much more than justice. How did normal young people become comfortable treating other human beings the way they did? Do the soldiers of Abu Ghraib represent a new American ethic or were they directed to do this by some sinister and sadistic mind? Were they trained to do this by the military? Has something sinister been added to the American ethic or has something noble been lost?

Perhaps we are most disturbed because these young soldiers come from small towns across America rather than from a secret Army lab that creates monsters for war. We want to believe that there was something in their upbringing, culture, or environment that caused their behavior.

EVERY JOURNEY BEGINS AT THE START

Is the 800th MP Brigade a cancer or blight that needs to be removed from the Army? When the leadership has been punished and the culprits have been brought to justice, has the problem been fixed? Can we assume that the circumstances that allowed this travesty to occur were isolated to this maverick brigade, or, do conditions exist in other units of the Army that would allow this to happen again? And even further, are they a part of the moral fabric of America?

Some basic facts must be established before we begin to analyze the different parts of Abu Ghraib. We must keep in mind that the soldiers in the 800th MP Brigade are reservists. They are accustomed to being in the Army two days of the month and the balance of their time is spent in civilian occupations working and living like any other American. They are a cross section of America's civilian population much more than they represent the military or a governmental agency. Since these soldiers were coming more from the civilian fabric of our nation, we must all take a long and honest look at ourselves and wonder why these individuals acted the way they did.

Introspection is one of the most important tasks a person can undertake. Socrates taught that, *"The unexamined life is not worth living."* We are quick to blame our misconduct on everything from our environment to government and if that doesn't explain our trouble we will blame God too. It is rare to find an individual that commits an offense and stands to take responsibility for it. *"Human beings have a limitless capacity to raise the question of the problem of evil as we see it outside of ourselves, but a disproportionate willingness to raise the question of evil within us."*[8]

Confession is never popular. Confession requires conviction that a wrong has been committed. It requires a commitment to reform and an attempt to make amends. Americans feel ashamed about the prisoner abuse at Abu Ghraib and that shame is appropriate. The problem is that we don't know why we feel ashamed. After all, we weren't there and we didn't condone the behavior. Despite all the reasons why we should feel free from guilt, we still feel that somehow, we ought to be ashamed. Shame is not always something to dread. It can serve us well.

Shame has been described as the central nervous system of the conscience. It is our early warning system alerting us that we are doing something seriously wrong. In the last century, our sense of shame has been dulled by displacing responsibility and consuming ourselves with our own affairs. Like a horse with blinders, we have resisted taking action against the downward spiral of our ethical standards and now find ourselves in moral chaos. Our collective and individual conscience cries out for us to maintain our integrity and live a life without shame. Unfortunately, for some, shame is something that has been lost. Freed from the shackles of conscience, they have learned to act in any way and at any time without regard for others and without shame.

THE BLINDING INFLUENCE OF EVIL

In the 1960's Charles Manson convinced a number of people that he was Jesus Christ or the "fifth angel". He also convinced them that Armageddon (Helter Skelter) would begin in 1969. On August 9, 1969, twenty-six-year old actress Sharon Tate was entertaining her friends, 25-year-old coffee heiress Abigail Folger and Folger's 32-year-old boyfriend Voytek Frykowski and 36-year-old internationally famous hair stylist Jay Sebring.

The evening ended brutally. Charles Manson, Susan Atkins, Leslie Van Houten, and Patricia Krenwinklebegan began a two-day killing spree that would claim the lives of seven people. The crime was horrible enough, but the public was unprepared for what they discovered after the arrests. Many people have wondered how these apparently "normal" people commit such morbid crimes and yet, show no signs of regret or remorse. Did Charles Manson use threats, guilt, and terrorism to seduce these people into doing his will. No, Manson's followers were devoted to him, doing whatever he wanted them to do.

We can except that he used force and brainwashing but there are other cases where force was not a factor. In 1997, thirty-nine men and women died in a mass suicide believing that the Hale-Bopp comet was their passage to heaven. How did reasonable and intelligent adults come to believe and take such decisive action on something so bizarre? We cannot tell just from the facts. We have to inquire deeper into their lives and backgrounds. Unless we know those who made the decisions, we can only observe the action and guess at the motive.

PEERING INTO THE DARKNESS

Whereas seeking justice only requires us to know the letter of the law and the nature of the offense, an anatomy is much more complex and frightening. An anatomy is a careful and thorough science of observation. To understand what happened in Iraq, we have to look at the soldiers of the 800th MP Brigade and their experiences, as they were mobilized from the civilian world and sent to war as soldiers. We have to consider what actions are common in war and why the press has covered Abu Ghraib the way it has. We must analyze the factors that created an environment for the events at Abu Ghraib to occur. "As we have no immediate experience of what other men feel, we can form no idea of the manner in which they are affected, but by conceiving what we ourselves should feel in the like situation".[9] We have to consider why we perceive and judge the images we see the way that we do. This is frightening because we may learn more about ourselves than we learn about the subject studied.

Rather than seeking to judge those involved in a legal or forensic sense, this book is an anatomy of America's response to the events at Abu Ghraib. Urban legend suggests that in medical school, the first day of anatomy class is often the last day of school for students that do not have the stomach to look closely at a dissected body. Likewise, many Americans will occupy themselves with entertainment or activities and avoid ever thinking about their own character. The unfortunate events at Abu Ghraib give us an opportunity to examine the soldiers involved and ourselves as well. Each of the essential areas for understanding Abu Ghraib will be carefully laid out for inspection. First, we will examine the justification for the war. To determine the nature of the crime, we have to consider the circumstances surrounding it. When a soldier shoots at a charging enemy his action is not considered a homicide because it is in the context of war.

We must first decide whether or not we accept the premise that America is at war. Second, we will journey with the 800th MP Brigade. The 800th is a collection of individuals. Little is known about them beyond the comments they have made in response to the accusations against them. You will need to make careful observations regarding the personalities, stresses, fears, and the moral climate of the brigade. Third, we will place the events at Abu Ghraib in the context of war. Viewing the pictures in the safety of our living rooms places the events in the wrong context. We must consider what our expectations for soldier's behavior should be in a time of war. Fourth, we will examine the media's coverage of Abu Ghraib. Have they presented the facts of the case reasonably without commercial or political bias? Finally, we will reflect on the lessons learned and ask ourselves if we could have been the guards in the pictures at Abu Ghraib.

Presenting the issues, much like an anatomy, will be a significant contribution to understanding why we have reacted to Abu Ghraib the way we have and why the soldiers there behaved without shame. Is the shame we feel now due to their treatment of the prisoners, or has the press taken hold of this unfortunate situation and manipulated it to score political points?

This book will demonstrate that the incident at Abu Ghraib is not typical of the 800th Military Police Brigade; while at the same time, it isn't something we should be surprised about either. In fact, we should have anticipated that this or something worse would eventually occur. I hope that by providing the details of the struggles, fears, short-comings, and victories of the 800th you will gain insight into these citizen soldiers that are your neighbors and friends.

The 800th MP Brigade is not a cancer that needs to be cut out of an otherwise healthy society. It is the expression of the current moral and social climate of America. While the press expressed their shock and outrage over the sexual perver-sions of the soldiers at Abu Ghraib, the Supreme Court quietly decided on behalf of the ACLU July 29, 2004 by a 5 to 4 vote to block a law limiting children's access to porn sites on the internet. Months before, entertainer Janet Jackson exposed her breast on national television to the entire world as part of an erotic halftime show, and pop star Britney Spears shared a moment of sexual perversion with Madonna before the world during the MTV music awards. We live in a society with a conflicted and even schizophrenic morality. How can we be so outraged at the behavior that reflects a morality we so religiously protect.

The Reservists of the 800th MP Brigade come from every sort of neighborhood and walk of life. Some are doctors, ministers, lawyers, firefighters, police officers, professional cooks, college students, active duty military, and a host of other backgrounds. They live in New York, New Jersey, Pennsylvania, Arkansas, Georgia, and several other states as well. Some are husbands and fathers, others are mothers and daughters. How are we to condemn such an eclectic group of individuals that are representative of all of America?

Studies on the effects of war have long instructed us about the psychological effects of battle and fatigue on soldiers. Living under constant threat from an unseen enemy wears down even those with incredible mental toughness and resilience. History has shown us how unpredictable and unmanageable war is. The effect of killing on soldiers and the stress of never knowing when death will visit you have a profound affect on the mind.

Movies have portrayed Vietnam as nothing but an experience in depravity. We are supposed to believe that young men went into battle virtuous and emerged as baby killers and war criminals. Most of what is portrayed by Hollywood is an exaggeration or has zero basis in truth. We are often shown the sensational images of criminal behavior with any and all of the good that happens being ignored by the media and moviemakers.

In the weeks directly following the release of pictures portraying prisoners being victimized by American soldiers, an American was beheaded by Muslim extremists, a car bomb exploded killing a high ranking official in the emerging Iraqi government, and chemical agents were detonated in Iraqi field artillery rounds. When you turn on the news however, the top billing remains committed to pictures of naked men stacked in a pyramid. Sitting and looking at those pictures I wonder if that is the work of soldiers that hate their enemy, or if it is a juvenile, albeit inexcusable, attempt at humor.

What is the root of our desire for the exploitation of Americans who have erred? Why turn an American tragedy into nightly entertainment? A week after the news of the prison pictures broke, an American was beheaded and it was broadcast on the internet for all to see. Yet, two days later, the pictures of naked men in a pyramid are back on the top of the news. Another week passes and a car bomb blows up killing one of the heads of the emerging Iraqi governing council, yet what remains on the news? Pictures of naked men stacked in a pyramid and now added to it, a small-framed woman holding a dog leash with a naked Iraqi man at the other end. News programs haul in experts from nearly every field to discuss the political, social, and military ramifications of stripping Iraqi criminals as an aid to interrogations. We discover that the prison guards may have stood on the hands of the Iraqis and that on occasion some may have been struck by the guards as well.

There is a battle being waged for the soul of America. It has moved from the halls of Congress which has made itself nearly irrelevant due to partisan bickering, to the halls of academia, to the airwaves, to the streets of urban and rural America. Statesmanship has given way to showmanship. Radio talk shows and twenty-four hour news channels are commonly turned on in public places like airports, malls, and restaurants. People watch the so-called, "reality" TV shows that are no closer to reality than a comic book. Bookshelves are lined with books on why we should hate or love the President and how he has saved or destroyed the country. Oddly, we can't even agree on whether our country is lost or saved! The war against good and evil waged in the desert of Iraq is mirrored by the war going on in the collective conscience of our American psyche as well. Real life has become less a tragedy as it has prime time entertainment.

America is on the verge of a significant shift in our national character. Whether it is collapse or renewal remains to be seen. I do not believe the die is cast "yet" and I hope our momentum can be redirected. We are standing at some crossroads. I word it ambiguously because I do not think we even know what decisions lay before us. There is not a lack of voices but most are simply commenting on individual situations they find appalling. America needs to recover her lost vision for the republic. We need to be reminded that liberty and personal rights are not necessarily the same thing. We have to understand the crisis of faith and integrity our nation is facing.

The tragedy of the 800th MP Brigade is an American tragedy. Despite what the movies portray about the military, soldiers are not created in a lab and sent to war; they are our sons and daughters, our neighbors and friends, our classmates and scholars, our mothers and fathers. When we speak of our soldiers, sailors, and airmen, we are speaking about ourselves. They were made in the workshops of America. They were educated in our schools, learned right from wrong in our homes, worshipped in our churches, voted in our elections, served on church boards and preached in our pulpits. They are in every sense of the word "us". Are these soldiers more than criminals? Are they representative of all of us? The answers to these questions will determine how we are supposed to interpret Abu Ghraib. Rather than simply being a sad page in America's history book, perhaps the soldiers of Abu Ghraib are a prophetic warning against the decline of virtue and moral sense in America. What then are we to make of our behavior?

PHOTOS

Last family picture made before deploying with the 800th
MP Brigade

Headquarters Company formation in the snow at
Ft. Dix, NJ

800th MP Brigade enjoys a farewell dinner hosted by the
Ft. Dix mess hall staff

Chaplain Cannon leads the staff in prayer before boarding
the plane for Kuwait

Brigade Chaplain, Surgeon, and Public Affairs officer in
NBC suit at Camp Arifjan chow hall

Suiting up during an inbound Scud alert

Chaplain Cannon with convoy returning from Baghdad

Chaplain leads services on Palm Sunday just South-West of Baghdad

Iraqi tank stopped before it could attack during the 3rd ID
march to Baghdad

Killed tank in an unscarred field bear testimony to the lack
of collateral damage during US attack.

Hallway in Baghdad school

Chaplain's flag marking the location of the worship
service at Camp Arifjan, Kuwait

Drawing by Iraqi child celebrating the defeat of Saddam
Hussein and showing that they understand the contrast
between totalitarianism and liberty.

Drawing by an Iraqi child demonstrating the good will and
hope for peace in a post Saddam environment.
The children represent the future and an opportunity for
real peace in the Middle East.

LOST IN A LOOKING GLASS

AN ANATOMY OF WAR

"For some minutes [the Caterpillar] puffed away
without speaking, but at last it unfolded its arms,
took the hookah out of its mouth again and said, 'So
you think you're changed, do you?' 'I'm afraid I
am, sir,' said Alice: 'I can't remember things as I
used - and I don't keep the same size for ten
minutes together!' 'Can't remember what things?'
said the Caterpillar."
Lewis Carroll: Alice's Adventures in Wonderland

"What experience and history teach is this — That
people and government never have learned anything
from history, or acted on the principles deduced
from it."
G.W.F. Hegel, Philosophy of History

"A few months ago, and again this week, bin Laden
publicly vowed to publicly wage a terrorist war
against America, saying, and I quote, "We do not

differentiate between those dressed in military uniforms and civilians. They're all targets." Their mission is murder, and their history is bloody".

President Bill Clinton, August 20, 1998

"Peace if possible, but truth at any rate."

Martin Luther

"The table was a large one, but the three were all crowded together at one corner of it: 'No room! No room!' they cried out when they saw Alice coming. 'There's *plenty* of room!' said Alice indignantly, and she sat down in a large arm-chair at one end of the table.

'Have some wine,' the March Hare said in an encouraging tone.

Alice looked all round the table, but there was nothing on it but tea. 'I don't see any wine,' she remarked.

'There isn't any,' said the March Hare.

'Then it wasn't very civil of you to offer it,' said Alice angrily.

'It wasn't very civil of you to sit down without being invited,' said the March Hare.

'I didn't know it was *your* table,' said Alice; 'it's laid for a great many more than three.'"

[From Alice in Wonderland chapter 7]

IT AIN'T A WAR UNTIL WE SAY IT'S A WAR!

How can we make sense of the situation we find ourselves in? Much of that will depend on what the situation actually is. A fight on the school playground results in detention. A fight at Madison Square Garden can be worth several million dollars to the fighters. A bacteria growing in your body can make you sick. A bacteria growing in a Petri dish can result in cures that save lives. To interpret the actions at Abu Ghraib and in the War against Terrorism, we need to decide if we are at war or not.

On September 14, 2001 President George Bush speaking at the National Cathedral said, "War has been waged against us by stealth and deceit and murder. This nation is peaceful, but fierce when stirred to anger. This conflict was begun on the timing and terms of others. It will end in a way, and at an hour, of our choosing." In the last quarter of 2004, the United States Army coordinated more then 330 ship movements in the largest schedule of shipments the Department of Defense has undertaken since World War II. Reserves and National Guard soldiers were called up for deployment in record numbers and the military budget continued to grow to support the increased military commitments. Every day, the news broadcasters reported the number of American casualties. Still, several years after the attacks in Manhattan a true consensus on the war eludes America. Is America at war?

Many are not convinced that America is in a real war as they prefer to consider the deployment of the military a police action against international criminals.

"The war on terrorism cannot be won by waging war. . . . Crime requires police work, not military action. Some of us have always held that there was no 'war' on Iraq; it was a 'military engagement' perhaps, but with no worthy adversary, a 'war' it was not. And nowadays it's all-too-clear that if U.S. troops knew how to act more like cops instead of soldiers, they'd be doing a much better job at security." [10]

Unfortunately, ours is not the only opinion to consider. Just as it takes two to tango, it takes at least two for war. If the Coalition of nations against terrorism is one of the dancers, whom can we name as the second?

The following is a translation of a terrorist's statement made just prior to the decapitation of Nicholas Berg. Since identifying the belligerents in a war is so important, the entire translation is provided here.

"Praise to Allah who honored Islam with his support, humiliated the infidels with his power, controlled everything with his Command, and tricked the infidels. Prayers and peace be upon the one that raised the banner of Islam with his sword.

Nation of Islam, Great news! The signs of dawn have begun and the winds of victory are blowing. Allah has granted us a great victory, in one of his battles in Fallujah. Thanks to Allah alone.

Nation of Islam, Is there any excuse left to sit idly by? How can a free Muslim sleep soundly while Islam is being slaughtered, its honor bleeding and the images of shame in the news of the satanic abuse of the Muslim men and women in the prison of Abu Ghraib. Where is your zeal and where is the anger for the religion of Allah? And where is the jealousy over the honor of the Muslims and where is the revenge for the honor of the Muslim men and women in the prisons of the Crusaders?

As for you, scholars of Islam, it is to Allah that we complain about you. Don't you see that Allah has established the evidence against you by the youth of Islam, who have humiliated the greatest power in history and broken its nose and destroyed its arrogance?

Hasn't the time come for you to learn from them the meaning of reliance on God and to learn from their actions the lessons of sacrifice and forbearance? How long will you remain like the women, knowing no better than to wail, scream and cry?

One scholar appeals to the free people of this world, another begs Kofi Annan, a third seeks help from 'Amr Musa and a fourth calls for peaceful demonstrations as if they did not hear the words of Allah "O Messenger, rally the believers to fight!'

Aren't you fed up with the jihad of conferences and the battles of sermons? Has the time not come for you to lift the sword, which the master of the Messengers was sent with?

And we hope that you will not intervene as usual by denouncing what we do to please the Americans. The Prophet, the master of the merciful has ordered to cut off the heads of some of the prisoners of Badr in patience. He is our example and a good role model.

As for you, Bush dog of the Christians, we promise you things that will displease you. With Allah's assistance, hard days are coming to you. You and your soldiers are going to regret the day that you stepped foot in Iraq and dared to violate the Muslims.

Another message for the collaborator and traitor Pervez Musharraf; we say to you, we can not wait to welcome your soldiers. By Allah, we will target them before the Americans and will avenge the blood of our brothers in Wana and others.

As for you, mothers and wives of the American soldiers, we say to you that we offered the American Administration the chance to exchange this prisoner for some of the prisoners in Abu Ghraib, but they refused. We say to you, the dignity of the Muslim men and women in the prison of Abu Ghraib and others will be redeemed by blood and souls. You will see nothing from us except corpse after corpse and casket after casket of those slaughtered in this fashion.

> *'So kill the infidels wherever you see them, take them, sanction them, and await them in every place'"*

This diatribe delivered by the murdering terrorists was meant to incite moderate Muslims around the world and bring a revival of fidelity to the Qur'an. The terrorists hoped to incite widespread violence against the Coalition and America in particular. Roughly fifty-seven nations in the world support Islam as the foundation of their dictatorship or theocratic government. It is considered to be the world's second-largest and fastest-growing religion among the oppressed and disenfranchised. If the radical and violent Jihadist message were to convince the majority of Muslims residing in every corner of the world that they were in danger, there would be a hemorrhage of violence around the globe. America has always been able to declare when we were or when we were not at war. If we did not want to be at war then we might engage in a conflict or operation. Now, war has been declared on America and the larger community of Christians and Western nations specifically. In Islamic theology there are only two places to be, the House of Islam and The House of War. We have to keep in mind that any people of any nation that are not Muslim are considered infidels and enemies of Islam. Jihad is waged against all who are outside the House of Islam.

Muhammad called Muslims to Jihad when he said, "We must fight and slay the Pagans wherever we find them, and lie in wait for them in every stratagem of war." JIHAD is an Arabic word that literally means "combat" or "striving". Jihad and allegiance to the Imam is sometimes regarded as the violent Sixth Pillar of Islam. Orthodox Islam only recognizes Five Pillars or fundamental practices of the Islamic faith. The idea of jihad as the violent Sixth Pillar comes from the Khawarij sect. This sect was part of the fundamentalist Islamic movement that started in the early 20th Century. The

Khawarij sect is named after Dhul-Khuwaysarah, a man that Muhammad prophesied would have an overprotective love of religion. The Khawariji and the Salafist differ greatly in their interpretations of key Islamic doctrines. Salafism is more restrictive than the Khawariji about who should be declared an infidel and excommunicated from Islam. The Jihadists who are followers of the Khawariji interpretation see few if any restrictions on who can be declared an infidel. This justifies an unrestricted warfare or terrorism against infidels.[11]

We cannot overstate just how important it is to answer this question concerning the nature of this conflict. If we are involved in a police action, then our expectations should be fundamentally different than they will be if we are at war with Islamic Jihadists.

Consider these universally accepted principles of a Just War:

- A war can only be just if it is fought with a reasonable chance of success. Deaths and injury incurred in a hopeless cause are not morally justifiable.
- The ultimate goal of a just war is to re-establish peace. More specifically, the peace established after the war must be preferable to the peace that would have prevailed if the war had not been fought.

As Americans considered war against the Taliban and then continued to pursue Al-Qaida, we had to consider whether the war was winnable and whether our goal was to re-establish peace. President Bush determined that there would never be peace until we destroyed the blood lust of these terrorist cults. Since the overthrow of the Islamic theocracy in Afghanistan, the US has waged a deliberate and largely successful war against terrorism. Military forces swarmed into Iraq and ran roughshod over the Iraqi forces.

Coalition forces continued the battle against immigrant terrorists after they won the war against the organized Iraqi military. The terrorist will ultimately lose a war of attrition. Now we must wonder if America will have the will to finish the conflict that was begun.

General Vo Nguyen Giap possessed one of the finest strategic minds of the twentieth century. His struggle againt America in 1968 was not won on the battlefield. His strategy was to undermine American resolve by inflicting demoralizing political defeats. On Christmas Eve in 1954 he lured the French into a battle and won a stunning victory at Dien Bien Phu, Giap. That victory turned the will of the French against the war in Vietnam and ultimately the French Army left the battlefield and returned to France. In 1968, on the eve of the lunar New Year celebrations, the General launched a major surprise offensive against American and South Vietnamese forces. The cost in North Vietnamese casualties was tremendous; his daring gambit produced a pivotal media disaster for the American White House and President Lyndon Johnson. Johnson became a casualty of the Tet Offensive and refused to run for a second term. The Tet Offensive turned the tide of the war and destroyed any remaining American resolve to continue the war against communism in Vietnam. We now wonder if America will have the will to finish what we have begun after the shock of Abu Ghraib. Despite the remarkable victory of American forces in March and April 2003 and the apprehension of nearly every wanted criminal in the Iraqi government, Abu Ghraib caused Americans to wonder if we should be there at all. Americans need to re-evaluate our interpretation of Abu Ghraib and think of it in perspective of a global war.

EXPECTATIONS CAN DETERMINE INTERPRETATIONS

As an elementary school child, my wife would often

carry her own lunch to school. After arranging everything carefully for her picnic, she would place each item in its proper position to determine which food groups received the priority of effort. On one such day, she noticed a slice of pound cake, neatly wrapped in clear wrapping. She decided that the pound cake certainly deserved a priority effort for lunch and quickly unwrapped it. After she took her first bite, she began choking and gagging on it. This was the worst pound cake she had ever tasted. She threw the piece down and spit out the remainder from her mouth. It was so dry and coarse that she could hardly imagine it had ever been cake. She picked up the discarded cake and inspected it further. Cautiously she smelled it. Cornbread! It was not cake at all; it was cornbread. She loved both cake and cornbread; but to this day, she can hardly eat either one. Had she known she was eating cornbread then she would have had a great lunch. But expecting cake and getting cornbread destroyed her desire for either one. Expectations often determine interpretations.

In a May 2004 interview with radio host Don Imus, Republican senator John McCain suggested that the guards at Abu Ghraib acted like the German Gestapo of WWII. To be fair, McCain seemed to be using exaggerated terms to voice his concern that America should not tolerate this type of abuse lest we end up like the Gestapo. Nevertheless, such incendiary commentary produces a ripple affect and clouds the real issues. Did American soldiers act like the legendary Gestapo? The Gestapo was responsible for establishing concentration camps. They sent racial and political undesirables to concentration and annihilation camps for slave labor and mass murder. "In 1936, under the command of *Heinrich Himmler*, who also was given charge of the German SS, the Gestapo was merged with the *Kriminalpolizei* (or "Kripo," German for Criminal Police). The newly integrated unit was then called the *Sicherheitspolizei* (or "Sipo," German for

Secret Police).

The law granted the Gestapo responsibility for administering the concentration camps. During World War II, the *Einsatzgruppen* (Task Force) was formed, and came to be an integral part of the Gestapo. They were responsible for rounding up communists, partisans and Jews and others considered a threat to German rule. The Gestapo soon developed a reputation for using brutal interrogation methods to obtain confessions. The army units within the Gestapo were taught many torture techniques, and were taught many of the practices that German doctors in *Dachau* tested on the inmates of concentration camps. The Gestapo, during its tenure, operated without any restrictions by civil authority. This meant that soldiers and officers of the Gestapo could not be tried for any of their brutal police and interrogation procedures. This unconditional and blind authority created an elitist element to the Gestapo. The Gestapo police knew that whatever actions they took, no consequences would arise."[12] At the *Nuremberg War Crimes Trial,* the Gestapo was indicted for crimes against humanity.

Certainly, Senator McCain does not mean his comments to be taken literally. Yet, when such allegations are made, a characterization of the 800th MP Brigade is created not only in the press but also in the public minds of Americans. The Senator's call is more likely a prophetic call for America to be careful lest we end up like the Gestapo. His inadvertent comments charge that the 800th MP Brigade was a rouge and lawless Brigade that routinely practiced the techniques employed by the German Gestapo.

McCain's historical perspective does make a positive contribution. A close examination of the history of war and of the expected and usual conduct of the overwhelming majority of our soldiers during war reveals that on balance we ought to be celebrating the virtuous behavior of our soldiers rather than focusing solely on the incidents at Abu Ghraib. The senator's comments demonstrate just how confused we are about the nature of the conflict. More than any senator serving in the United States Senate today, Senator John McCain knows firsthand how brutal war can be.

Americans have become adept at assimilating information at lightning speed. Sorting and compiling data has evolved into an art form. Daily progress in electronic media and medical science make living in the present an exciting vocation. The past is all but irrelevant in a fast-changing world. Unfortunately, the irrelevance of yesterday's technology does not make yesterday's human history irrelevant as well. On April 11, 2003, the Washington Times published an article by George Archibald. The article titled, "Ignorance of US History Called a Threat to Security". He wrote, "Widespread ignorance of American history among students and teachers at high schools and colleges is a major threat to the nation's security, Pulitzer Prize-winning historian and author David McCullough told a Senate panel yesterday. 'We are raising a generation of people who are historically illiterate'. Eugene W. Hickok, undersecretary of education, said only 10 percent of high school students scored at the "proficient" level on the history test administered in 2001 by the National Assessment of Educational Progress." Since a war is based on historical ideas and issues, a fundamental misunderstanding of history will confuse any ideas about the nature of the present conflict. To determine whether we are at war or not, we will have to review the actions taken against America by our enemies in the recent past to help us put the conflict in context. As you read through the following accounts, ask yourself, "What was the intention of the belligerents?" Was it peace or harm? Was it an act of passion or premeditation? Did the crisis pass or is it still ongoing? Answering these questions will give us an indication what to expect in the future.

In 1992, Ramzi Yousef entered the United States with a

false *Iraqi* passport. Instructions for making a bomb were found in the luggage of his compainon, Abu Barra, which was an alias of Mohammed Jamal Khalifa. Traveling with a false passport is against the law and thus, Abu Barra was arrested. The INS holding cells were overcrowded however; so, the authorities told Yousef to come back in one month. Yousef moved to Jersey City, New Jersey, and traveled freely around New York and New Jersey. He called Sheikh Omar Abdel Rahman, a controversial Muslim preacher, via cell phone and worked to aquire chemicals for making a bomb.

Eventually when he was prepared to carry out his attack, Yousef stole or rented a Ryder van that was to use as the delivery system for his bomb. Yousef created a 600 kilogram bomb made of nitroglycerin, aluminum azide, urea pellets, sulfuric acid, bottled hydrogen, and magnesium azide. Sodium cyanide was added to the bomb to to create toxic vapors that would travel through the ventilation shafts and elevators of the towers. On February 26, 1993, the bomb exploded in the underground garage of the World Trade Center at 12:17 P.M. It created a 30 meter wide hole through 4 sublevels of concrete. Thankfully, the cyanide gas that Yousef put in the bomb was destroyed in the explosion. Only six people were killed and around 1,040 were injured. The towers were not destroyed as Yousef had hoped. He fled to Pakistan several hours later.

In September, 1995, the US Embassy in Moscow was attacked with Rocket Propelled Grenades. The attackers were not apprehended.

In November, 1995, U.S. military headquarters in Riyadh, Saudi Arabia was bombed killing 7 Americans.

In February, 1996, the US Embassy in Athens was bombed using an anti-tank missile.

In June, 1996, the Khobar Towers in Dhahran, Saudi Arabia were bombed, killing 19 US servicemen.

In November, 1997, 5 American oil-company employees were killed in Karachi, Pakistan.

In June, 1998, the US Embassy in Lebanon was attacked with rocket-propelled grenades.

In August, 1998, U.S. embassies in Nairobi, Kenya, and Dar es Salaam, Tanzania were attacked in a coordinated effort killing 263, and injuring 5000. It is suspected that this attack was financed by Usama bin Laden.

In October, 2000, The American Destroyer USS Cole was bombed in the Yemeni port of Aden killing 17 US Sailors.

In September, 2001, coordinated attacks were carried out against World Trade Center in New York City, the Pentagon in Washington DC, and an airline loaded with passengers crashing in Pennsylvania. Over 6000 people were killed and thousands more were injured.

Since the United States defeated the Army of Iraq, terrorists have targeted additional US interests in Iraq as well as abroad. American lives have been saved since September 2001 only by the grace of God and the diligent work of the Homeland Security and local law enforcement.

Considering this list of attacks against the United States and her people, it would appear that we are indeed at war.

In Secretary of State, Condoleezza Rice's opening statements to the 9-11 commission in April 2004 she said,

"The terrorists were at war with us, but we were not yet at war with them. For more than 20 years the terrorist threat gathered, and America's response across several administrations of both parties was insufficient. . . . The U.S. government did not act against the growing threat from Imperial Japan until the threat became all too evident at Pearl Harbor. And, tragically, for all the language of war spoken before September 11th, this country simply was not on a war footing. . . . Because of these briefings and

because we had watched the rise of Al-Qaida over many years, we understood that the network posed a serious threat to the United States. . . . President Bush understood the threat, and he understood its importance. He made clear to us that he did not want to respond to Al-Qaida one attack at a time. He told me he was "tired of swatting flies."[13]

Perhaps one of the reasons there is so little agreement on the weight of actions by Americans such as those at Abu Ghraib is that we are divided on the issue of war. While our troops are engaged with forces around the world, we are grappling the most basic question of whether or not we are in a war. There is no doubt that our enemies imagine they are at war with us and they will continue to kill Americans whenever and wherever they have an opportunity.

If we are in a war, then the behavior of our troops must be considered in a light of the life and death struggle that occurs in war. Wars are savage and brutal. Individual rights are not considered as they are in the streets of a major American city. How this conflict has been presented to us by the press and our lack of historical perspective has shaped the opinion of Americans about the nature of the conflict.

Americans are blessed with one of the most efficient news networks in the world. Reporters and anchors of news programs travel everywhere there is news to bring the facts, and often viewpoints, to the American people. They keep us among the most informed people in the world. We have a sense of omnipresence in the world.

On April 29, 2004, the CBS broadcast 60 Minutes II posted their story on the prisoner abuse at Abu Ghraib. Throughout the war members of the press corps courageously embedded themselves in military units often at the cost of their own lives. Reporters frequently put themselves in harms way to discover truth and bring a reliable report to the people. The morning that CBS planned to air their report on Abu Ghraib, Radio talk show host Michael Regan asked his callers if they thought the show should be aired. His issue seemed to be that there was such a lack of positive coverage on the rebuilding of Iraq that it was unfair to pick the actions of so few soldiers and impugn the rest.

The United States has in fact rebuilt the infrastructure of Iraq. Engineers have labored to fix or construct everything from schools to hospitals. They have brought in experts to bring utilities and public transportation back on line. Much of the work has gone unnoticed by the press who choose to focus instead on the more sensationalistic stories. The World Press, particularly the American press, has nearly exhausted the American public's attention with their fascination of the events at the Iraqi prison, Abu Ghraib.

While Americans have always held ourselves to a higher standard than our enemies, it is difficult to understand the fascination the American press has with the incidents at Abu Ghraib when it is placed in the context of a World War. The treatment of prisoners in the same location by their own people operating under the direction (sometimes direct orders) of Saddam Hussein and the growing list of war crimes perpetrated by radical Muslims makes the misbehavior and humiliation of prisoners at Abu Ghraib seem like a misdemeanor in comparison.

This present conflict with terrorism has left most Americans unaffected. In fact, while Korea was called the forgotten war, the war against terrorism might be called the invisible war. Rising gas prices in 2004 was about the most dramatic affect of the war on most households. The tremendous loss of life on September 11, 2001, and the deployment of American service members to the Middle East has been a television experience for the majority of Americans. Couples and families gathered around the TV to watch the drama unfold as American forces marched across the desert of Iraq to depose a ruthless dictator. There have been upwards of 130,000 soldiers in Iraq at any given time. The United States population is estimated at 290,342,554 in 2003. Less than 1% (0.045%) of our population has walked in the sands of Iraq and our economy has insulated the continental United States from any real or protracted suffering.

The result is a war that seems more like a police action. The anti-terrorism efforts of the Bush administration and the work of the FBI, CIA, and local law enforcement authorities has been so effective that we no longer feel any real threat. Therefore, the actions of war seem unreasonable and inexcusable to a nation that feels at peace even while soldiers, sailors, airmen, and marines are fighting for their life in the streets and deserts of the Middle East.

To understand our preoccupation with events such as Abu Ghraib we have to free ourselves from the safety of our insulated world and venture out into the violence or war. Man's thinking in war is far less civilized than it is in peacetime. Survival rather than civility is the law and otherwise decent people sometimes commit savage acts when they lose themselves in the violence of war.

TOURING THE BATTLEFIELD

My wife was nearly a triple major in college. She graduated with honors in psychology and sociology from Wesleyan College in Macon, Georgia. She was only one course short of a religion major as well. She related a bizarre experience from her psychology class. She entered the classroom and took her seat as usual. The professor began the class by introducing a black and white picture they were to examine. The picture was of a man, a blue collar worker outside in a working environment. It was a close-up of his face only. He was expressionless, maybe a little tired from the physical labor, and his eyes were fixed on what was most likely his work. All in all, there was nothing particularly outstanding or unusual about the picture or the man.

The next picture was of the same man, in fact it was the same picture but this time, the perspective was from a greater distance. Now you could make out a piece of heavy equipment. He was on some sort of tractor or bulldozer. He was engaged in some sort of work, similar to what you can see road crews or landscapers involved in today. Handling a piece of heavy machinery like a bulldozer requires great attention lest it get away from you and do more damage than you were planning on. Again, nothing really made this any more remarkable than a picture of a man on a tractor you might find in a children's book of trucks and tractors. The man could have been anyone's father or grandfather. He was heavy built, a little older than middle aged and had a serious countenance.

The third and last picture was of the entire scene. The tractor now occupied only a third of the picture and the man not clearly discernable unless you moved closer to the picture. The tractor was indeed a bulldozer at work pushing something around. The students peered at the picture trying to make out the object of the mans work. He was filling a hole. Their minds worked feverishly to make sense of what their eyes were telling them. Slowly, the truth began to sink in, the bulldozer was filling the hole with bodies. These were the bodies of Jews, killed in one of Hitler's concentration camps. The driver of the bulldozer remains unknown. He was just one of the many that worked in this environment, just doing a days work for a days wages in order to feed his family in the difficult times that war often brings.

What are we to make of scenes like this? Was the man devoid of a conscience? We always talk about Adolph Hitler as the killer of Nazi Germany but he really did not do the killing. Thousands of ordinary Germans did the killing, the disposing of bodies, and living the lie, pretending to be normal.

By the end of the Second World War, the Germans had annihilated over 6 million Jews and countless others from surrounding nations and the United States on the fields of battle. Intellectual, historical, and military analysis abound treating each facet of the war and examining the leaders both in their genius and in their folly. What philosophers, historians, and soldiers can't explain is how an entire nation either actively participated or passively ignored the mass extermination of an entire race of people right in their own backyards.

While I was stationed in Wiesbaden, Germany, I took advantage of a USO tour going to Konzentrationslager Buchenwald, or simply *Buchenwald* (initially named Ettersberg) concentration camp near Weimar, the capital of Thuringia. In 1938, the Gestapo took more than 13,000 Jews from Germany and Austria to Buchenwald. In January 1945 there were 110,000 prisoners in the camp. 13,000 prisoners died in those early days of 1945. The fame of Buchenwald is overshadowed only by the notorious Dachau or Auschwitz. The prisoners of Buchenwald were liberated by the 3rd US Army on April 11, 1945. on April 19, 1945 a memorial service was held for the survivors to honor the 51,000 people who died at Buchenwald.

When we arrived we received a short introduction by a staff member at the site. He discussed the camp conditions, the guard posts, and the camp commander. The tenants of the camp were subjected to a lack of sanitary facilities, a lack of water and long days of fourteen to sixteen hours of labor. Insufficient clothing led to frostbite in the winter and amputation of limbs.

The Camp Commandant, Karl Koch had a zoo just outside the fence of Buchenwald that the commander's wife used to enjoy with her children. Only the bear-garden and the water fountain remain today. The shed where dead bodies were stored was located just east of the zoo. It is alleged that she would inspect the inmates of the camp and any that had tattoos she would have skinned and use the skin for lamp shades. She would have their thumbs mummified and use them as light switches. All this while raising a family and doting over her children.

We entered through the front gate and stopped to examine the prison cells along the front wall. This prison bunker was the worst place of torture in the entire camp. The SS and the Gestapo used any number of torture techniques and instruments to torment the prisoners. There purpose in torture was not to extract information but simply to torture in order to break the will of prisoners. One Martin Sommer was a particular sadistic torturer and over 160 people died under his ministries. Over the Gate are the words *"EACH TO HIS OWN"*. The words can only be read from the inside of the camp. Dank cells but not so unlike what you would imagine a cell to look like. These were holding cells for those about to be executed. The actual barracks had long since been burned down by the nearby community seeking to remove evidence of the horrors of Buchenwald.

Leaving the front gate we explored the three-story museum. There we found relics that had been removed from the Jews by prison guards: buttons, letters, teeth, and other items of interest. It appeared that the captors might allow you to pack a few things when you were arrested and then deliver them to the prison guards. You would never again see your belongings. Prisoners lost everything that gave them any individuality or personal distinctions including their hair. They were given a number for identification. Their names, professional occupations and social status were made a fact of the past. They were no longer people, only something less than human in the eyes of their captors.

From the museum we moved to the infirmary and crematorium. This is where the doctor worked. This doctor didn't heal; however, he butchered. The Camp Commandant is quoted saying, "There are no sick people in my camp. There are only those who are dead or alive!" Approximately 1,100 people were strangled to death on wall hooks in the body storage cellar. Ivan Belevzev from Kharkov is believed to be the youngest victim to die by strangulation. He was eight years old.

The practice of murdering Soviet prisoners and those sick with tuberculosis began with lethal injections at Buchenwald. There was a deep sink and a table. After we entered the room, I stood there for a moment wondering what suffering and abuse took place there. I wondered how a man with the power to heal could either take delight in causing suffering or be so indifferent to it that he was unmoved. How could a man so intimately acquainted with human anatomy lose any sense of the dignity of man. When did the Jews cease to be human? There is a picture on the infirmary wall of the victims of Buchenwald. They were piled like a cord of wood covered with nothing but tight skin over their bones. I was revolted by the picture and confused as to whether I should be sad they died or relieved that their suffering had ended. Who should I feel the most sorrow for, those that suffered or those that lost their humanity in causing their death?

Moving past the examination room I entered the crematorium where the ovens were. These were used to cremate the bodies of those already dead to keep diseases from breaking out in the camp. I only wish that was all they were used for. An elevator at the end of the room led down to the storage room. We descended by the stairs and saw a white room with hooks on the walls. We learned that this was the room the Jews were brought to when it was time for them to be prepared, that is strangled, for the ovens. They were hanged on the hooks like sides of beef and left to die. I looked around the room and this time my minds eye saw blood on the walls and I could almost hear the screams of living men and women; naked, and hanging on hooks till their breath was gone and their life's blood ran out onto the floor.

This was one of the most necessary and tragic tours that I took while I was in Germany. I left with more questions than I had answers. I had read about the holocaust in history books for most of my life. But standing there in the very place the Germans stood who committed this crime, I wondered how they could do it. Why doesn't the mind react normally to the suffering of people? Why was I horrified seeing only the echo of violence while the prison guards and Nazi doctors just walked by without a thought?

Regrettably, it wasn't just the prisons of Buchenwald, Aushwitz, and Dachau that hosted horrible scenes of human degradation.

"Some figures on the institutions of killing and their personnel, incomplete as they are, convey the magnitude of the German 'camps' (including ghettos) has identified a total of 10,005 positively, with the full knowledge that many more existed which have not yet been uncovered. Among the ten thousand camps (not all of which housed Jews), 941 forced labor camps designated specially for Jews were within the borders of just (today's) Poland. An additional 230 special camps for Hungarian Jews were set up on the Austrian border. The Germans created 399 ghettos in Poland, 34 in East Galicia, 16 in small Lithuania. So just the known forced labor camps and ghettos reserved for Jews totaled over 1,600. In addition to these, there were 52 main concentration camps, which had a total of 1,202 satellite camps (Aussenlager). It is not known how many Germans staffed each of these camps and ghettos. Auschwitz, by itself, with its 50 satellite camps, had 7,000 guards among its personnel at various times. In April 1945,

4,100 guards and administrators were stationed in Dachau alone. At the same time, the Germans had over 5,700 people staffing Mauthausen and its satellite camps. One estimate concludes that 50 guards were necessary for every 500 prisoners in a satellite camp, a ratio of one to ten. If anything resembling this ratio is applied to the more than 10,000 German camps with its millions of prisoners, or even to the smaller number of these camps which housed Jews, it becomes obvious that the number of people manning the system of destruction was enormous."[14]

These numbers are staggering. Rather than just a few immature prison guards acting up for their own egos, this represents an entire nation willingly going along with the destruction of a race of people. It wasn't just the prison guards however.

"The men of Police Battalion 101 were now ready to enter into the climactic stage of their first genocidal enterprise. New assignments were given to the men, and so they were set to begin the systematic slaughter. They had already been instructed in the recommended shooting technique during the initial assemblage around (Major) Trapp. 'About Dr. Schoenfelder I recall with certainty... we stood, as I said, in a semicircle round Dr. Schoenfelder and the other officers. Dr. Schoenfelder sketched on the ground so that we could all see the outline of the upper part of a human body and marked on the neck the spot at which we should fire. This picture stands clearly before my eyes. Of one thing I am not sure, whether in drawing on the ground, he used a stick or something else.' The battalion's doctor, their healer, who tutored the men on the best way to kill, obviously

did not deem his Hippocratic oath to apply to Jews.

A squad would approach the group of Jews who had just arrived, from which each member would choose his victim, a man, a woman, or a child. The Jews and Germans would then walk in parallel single file so that each killer moved in step with his victim, until they reached a clearing for the killing where they would position themselves and await the firing order from their squad leader. The walk into the woods afforded each perpetrator an opportunity for reflection. Walking side by side with his victim, he was able to imbue the human form beside him with the projections of his mind. Some of the Germans, of course, had children walking beside them. It is highly likely that, back in Germany, these men had previously walked through woods with their own children by their sides, marching gaily and inquisitively along. The Germans had to remain hardened to the crying of the victims, the crying of women, to the whimpering of children. At such close range, the Germans often became spattered with human gore. Although this is obviously viscerally unsettling, capable of disturbing even the most hardened of executioners, these German initiates returned to fetch new victims, new little girls, and to begin the journey back into the woods."[15]

The lasting power and force of this institutionalized hatred of the Jewish people cannot be underestimated. My first tour of military service was with the US Air Force. I attended a rather long electronics training course in Biloxi, Mississippi and then it continued at Tinker AFB, Oklahoma. After two years of schooling I felt obligated to search for employment in electronics or electrical work. The only job available when I transitioned from active duty to the Air

National Guard was home security system installations. I actually enjoyed the work and learned a great deal in the process.

When your job routinely takes you into people's homes, you learn a great deal about how people view life. There is so much variety in the way people keep house and greet visitors. Some talk to you without ceasing and others pretend you are not even there. One particular job has remained fresh in my mind though it has now been many years since it occurred. One man living alone taught me that hatred once learned is not easily discarded. Hatred cannot be turned on and off. It consumes you and you become your hatred.

I went into the apartment of a retired German man in the summer of 1988. He was pleasant and we spoke about his love for Germany and about how he had gotten along well in the US. He informed me that he was a veteran and received a pension from Germany for his military service. He had small models of World War II combat vehicles, all of German war machines, sitting around his apartment. It was meticulously kept and everything was neat and in place, which is typical of German housekeeping as I later learned.

As our conversation developed, I asked him about the Jews and whether or not he thought the whole affair was a great mistake. His eyes changed completely and rage filled his voice. I wish I could quote him exactly but he informed me that not only was it not a mistake but that the Jews are the most vile of all peoples and they were responsible for all of the suffering Germany had experienced in two World Wars. He labored to settle down and I did not continue with the conversation.

To become so personally acquainted with the victims of the Holocaust and kill them at close range, even after talking to them moments before they were executed the hatred had to run deep.

"Jewish survivors report with virtual unanimity German cruelties and killings until the very end. They leave no doubt that the Germans were seething with hatred for their victims; the Germans were not emotionally neutral executors of superior orders, or cognitively and emotionally neutral bureaucrats indifferent to the nature of their deeds. The Germans chose to act as they did with no effectual supervision, guided only by their own comprehension of the world, by their own notions of justice, and in contradistinction to their own interests in avoiding capture with blood on their hands. Their trueness to meting out suffering and death was not an imposed behavior; it came from within, an expression of their innermost selves."[16]

Are we in danger of learning to hate so much that we have to dehumanize our enemies? If we do, our victory will cost us our own humanity. Not only can war dehumanize an entire culture, but the disorientation and isolation associated with killing another human being can dehumanize the individual soldier as well.

On the morning of March 16, 1968, elements of Task Force Barker moved into a small group of hamlets known collectedly as My Lai in the Quang Ngai province of South Vietnam. It was intended to be a typical "search and destroy" mission, that is, the American troops were searching for Vietcong soldiers so as to destroy them.

Relative to other units operating in Vietnam, the troops of Task Force Barker had been somewhat hastily trained and thrown together. In the previous month they had achieved no military success. Unable to engage the enemy, they had themselves sustained a number of casualties from mines and booby traps. The province was considered to be a Vietcong stronghold, in which the civilian population was largely controlled and influenced by the Communist guerrillas. It was generally felt that the civilians aided and abetted the guerrillas to such a degree that it was often difficult to distinguish the combatants from the noncombatants. Hence the Americans tended to hate and distrust all Vietnamese in the area.

Army intelligence had indicated that the Vietcong were being harbored by the villagers of My Lai. The task force expected to find combatants there. On the eve of the operation there seemed to be a mood of anticipation. They would finally engage the enemy and succeed in doing what they were there for.

The nature of the instructions given to the enlisted men and the junior officers that evening by the senior officers was at best ambiguous in regard to the distinction between combatant and noncombatants. All troops were supposed to be familiar with the Geneva Convention, which makes it a crime to harm any noncombatant or, for that matter, even a combatant who has laid down his arms because of wounds or sickness. Whether they were, in fact, familiar with the convention is another matter. It is probable, however, that at least some of the troops were not familiar with the Law of Land Warfare from the U.S. Army Field Manual, which specifies that orders in violation of the Geneva Convention are illegal and not to be obeyed.

Although essentially all elements of Task Force Barker were involved one way or another in the operation, the primary element of ground troops directly involved was C Company, 1st Battalion, 20th Infantry of the 11th Light Brigade. When "Charlie" Company moved into the hamlets of My Lai they discovered not a single combatant. None of the Vietnamese was armed. No one fired on them. They found only unarmed women, children, and old men.

Some of what happened from that point is unclear. What is clear, however, is that the troops of C Company killed at least somewhere between five and six hundred of those unarmed villagers. These people were killed in a variety of ways. In some instances troops would simply stand at the door of a village hut and spray into it with rifle fire, blindly killing those inside. In other instances villagers, including children, were shot down as they attempted to run away. The most large-scale killings occurred in the particular hamlet of My Lai. There the first platoon of Charlie Company, under the command of Lieutenant William L. Calley, Jr., herded villagers into groups of twenty to forty or more, who were then slaughtered by rifle fire, machine gun fire, or grenades. It is important to remember, however, that substantial numbers of unarmed civilians also were murdered in the other hamlets of My Lai that day by the troops of other platoons under the command of other officers.

The killing took a long time. It went on throughout the morning. Only one person tried to stop it. He was a helicopter pilot, a warrant officer, flying in support of the search-and-destroy mission. Even from the air he could see what was happening. He landed on the ground and attempted to talk to the troops, to no avail. Back in the air again, he radioed to headquarters and superior officers, who seemed unconcerned. He gave up and went about his business.

The number of soldiers involved can only be estimated. Perhaps only about fifty actually pulled triggers. Approximately two hundred directly witnessed the killings. We might suppose that within the week at least five hundred men in Task Force Barker knew that war crimes had been committed.

The failure to report a crime is itself a crime. In the year that followed, no one in Task Force Barker attempted to report the atrocities that had occurred at My Lai. This crime is referred to as the "cover-up".[17]

Americans are not the only ones capable of violence in war. The most casual look at the history of war demonstrates that humans of any kilt are capable of extraordinary acts of barbarity and uncivilized treatment of human beings, especially non-combatants.

The battlefields of Europe are not the only place we can find inhumanity in war. The wars that involved Japan and China also reveal that brutality and inhumanity are not an Anglo European monopoly. A Japanese Army physician, Yuasa Ken, was imprisoned in China for crimes to which he confessed after the war. He returned to Japan after his release in 1956. This was taken from his confession.

"The hospital building adjoined a courtyard and a requisitioned middle-school building. Our patients were in there. There were nearly a hundred employees. Ten nurses, fifty to sixty technicians, some noncoms, too. I'm the kind of man who usually agrees to whatever I'm told to do. A 'yes man,' you could say. I remember that first time clearly. I arrived a little late; my excuse was that I had some other duties. ...

A solitary sentry stood guard. He saluted me the moment I opened the door. I then saw Medical Service Colonel Kotake and Hospital Director Nishimura, so I snapped to attention and saluted. They returned my salute calmly. I approached Hirano, my direct superior. That's when I noticed two Chinese close to the director. One was a sturdy, broad cheeked man, about thirty, calm and apparently fearless, standing immobile. I thought immediately, that man's a Communist. Next to him was a farmer about forty years old. He was dressed as if he were dragged from his field. His eyes raced desperately about the room. Three medics were there, holding rifles. Nurses were adjusting the surgical instruments by the autopsy tables. There were some fifteen or sixteen doctors present.

You might imagine this as a ghastly or gruesome scene, but that is not how it was. It was just the same as any other routine operation. I was still new to it. I thought there must be a reason for killing those people. I asked Hirano, but he just answered, 'We're going to kill the whole Eighth Route Army.' I pretended to know what he meant. The nurses were all smiling. They were from the Japanese Red Cross.

The director said, 'Let's begin.' A medic pushed the steadfast man forward. He lay down calmly. I thought he'd resigned himself to it. That was completely wrong. As a rule, Chinese don't glare at you. He had come prepared to die, confident in China's ultimate victory and revenge over a cruel, unjust Japan. He didn't say that aloud, but going to his death as he did spoke for itself. I didn't see that back then.

I was in the group assigned to the other fellow. A medic ordered him forward. He shouted, 'No! No!' and tried to flee. The medic, who was holding a rifle, couldn't move as fast as the farmer, and I was a new officer, just arrived in the command. I was very conscious of my dignity as a military man. The hospital director was watching. I never really thought, if this man dies, what will happen to his family? All I thought was, it will be terribly embarrassing if I end up in a brawl, this man in farmer's rags and me dressed so correctly. I wanted to show off. I pushed that farmer and said, "Go forward!" He seemed to lose heart, maybe because I'd spoken up. I was very proud of myself. Yet when he sat on the table, he refused to lie down. He shouted "Ai-ya-a! Ai-ya-a!" as if he knew that if he lay down he was going to be murdered. But a nurse then said, in Chinese, 'Sleep,

sleep.' She went on, 'Sleep, sleep. Drug give' in a Japanese style of Chinese. The Chinese of the oppressor always bears that tone, as if to say, 'There's no possibility you will fail to understand what I'm saying.' He lay down. She was even prouder than me. She giggled. The demon's face is not a fearful face. It's a face wreathed in smiles.

I asked the doctor who was about to administer lumbar anesthesia if he wasn't going to disinfect the point of injection. 'What are you talking about? We're going to kill him,' he replied. After a while, a nurse struck the man's legs and asked him if it hurt. He said it didn't, but when they tried to get him to inhale chloroform, he began to struggle. We all had to hold him down.

First, was practice in removing an appendix. That was carried out by two doctors. When a man has appendicitis, his appendix swells and grows very hard. But there was nothing wrong with this man, so it was hard to locate. They made an incision, but had to cut in another place and search until they finally found it. I remember that.

Next a doctor removed one of his arms. You must know how to do this when a man has shrapnel imbedded in his arm. You have to apply a tourniquet, to stanch the flow of blood. Then two doctors practiced sewing the intestines. If the intestine or stomach is pierced by bullets, that kind of surgery is a necessity. Next was the opening of the pharynx. When soldiers are wounded in the throat, blood gathers there and blocks the trachea, so you need to open it up. There is a special hook-shaped instrument for field use for cutting into the trachea. You drive it in, hook it open, then remove it, leaving only a tube behind. The blood drains out. It all took almost two hours. You remember the first time.

Eventually, all the doctors from the divisions left. Then the nurses departed. Only the director, the medics, and those of us from the hospital remained. The one I did, small-framed and old, was already dead. But from the sturdy man's mouth came, 'Heh. Heh. Heh.' One's last gasps are still strong. It gave us pause to think of throwing him, still breathing, into the hole out back, so the director injected air into his heart with a syringe. Another doctor-he is alive today-and I then had to try to strangle him with string. Still he wouldn't die. Finally, an old noncom said, 'Honorable Doctor, he'll die if you give him a shot of anesthesia.' Afterwards we threw him into the hole. This was the first time. Another time they sent us two for educational purposes. We did not have many doctors at the time, so we were able to do all we had to do on just one of them. But we really couldn't send the other one back. The director chopped his head off. He wanted to test the strength of his sword." [18]

The Japanese occupation of Nanking, the capital of the Republic of China, lead to one of the greatest war horrors of the 20th century .

"In 1928, the Chinese Nationalist Government moved the capital of China from Peking to Nanking. The city normally held about 250,000 people, but by the mid-1930's its population had swollen to more than 1 million. Many of them were refugees, fleeing from the Japanese armies which had invaded China since 1931. On November 11, 1937, after securing control of Shanghai, the Japanese army advanced towards Nanking from different directions. In early

December, the Japanese troops were already in the proximity of Nanking.

On December 9, after unsuccessfully demanding the defending Chinese troops in Nanking to surrender, the Japanese troops launched a massive attack upon the city. On the 12th, the defending Chinese troops decided to retreat to the other side of Yangtze River. On December 13, the 6th and the 116th Divisions of the Japanese Army first entered the city. At the same time, the 9th Division entered Guang Hua Gate, and the 16th Division entered Zhong Shan Gate and the Tai Ping Gate. In the afternoon, two Japanese Navy fleets arrived on both sides of the Yangtze River. On the same day, December 13th, 1937, Nanking fell to the Japanese. In the next six weeks, the Japanese committed the infamous Nanking Massacre, or the Rape of Nanking, during which an estimated 300,000 Chinese soldiers and civilians were killed, and 20,000 women were raped.

During the Nanking Massacre, the Japanese committed a litany of atrocities against innocent civilians, including mass execution, raping, looting, and burning. It is impossible to keep a detailed account of all of these crimes. However, from the scale and the nature of these crimes as documented by survivors and the diaries of the Japanese militarists, the chilling evidence of this historical tragedy is indisputable

From 1937 to 1990, the Japanese militarists, the government and the public dealt with the undeniable atrocities committed by the Japanese troops in Nanking and the rest of Asia in a number of ways. The major waves of Japanese treatment of this dark historical tragedy ranged from total cover-up during the war, confessions and documentation by the

Japanese soldiers during the 1950's and 60's, denial of the extent of the Nanking Massacre during the 70's and 80's, official distortion and rewriting of history during the 80's, and total denial of the occurrence of the Nanking Massacre by government officials in 1990."

Aleksandr Solzhenitsyn, a Russian author and historian, who was awarded the Nobel Prize for Literature in 1970; was exiled for many years after being expelled from the Soviet Union in 1974. His accounts of tyranny under Stalin's communist regime led to his being exiled from his homeland. He documented the arrest, enslavement, torture, and murder of an estimated 65 million in Soviet labor camps. He spent 11 years in Soviet prison camps. He writes from first-hand experience of what wicked people in a putrid system can do to people. [19]

His assessment of the state of our world is penetrating, even though it was printed 25 years ago:

If only there were evil people somewhere insidiously committing evil deeds, and it were necessary only to separate them from the rest of us and destroy them. But the line dividing good and evil cuts through the heart of every human being. And who is willing to destroy a piece of his own heart?[20]

He explained how human beings can waiver between doing the good and reverting to the bad.

During the life of any heart, this line keeps changing place; sometimes it is squeezed one way by exuberant evil and sometimes it shifts to allow enough space for good to flourish... At times, he is close to being a devil, at times to sainthood. . . From good to evil is one quaver, says the proverb.[21]

Solzhenitsyn's view of human nature has a strong biblical ring. Jesus Christ knew human nature and cultures thoroughly. Jesus declared:

What comes out of a man is what makes him unclean. For from within, out of men's hearts, come evil thoughts, sexual immorality, theft, murder, adultery, greed, malice, deceit, lewdness, envy, slander, arrogance, and folly. All these evils come from inside and make a man unclean."[22]

It was Solzhenitsyn, raised in an atheistic, communist society, who reached his conclusions after observing what the tyrants of his society did to people. Of course, he also was informed by a Christian world view.

Charles Colson, of Watergate fame, visited the Soviet Union and its prisons. He found himself at a negotiating table with Vadim Viktorovich Bakatin, the Minister of Internal Affairs and the fourth highest ranking official in the Communist Government.

Bakatin candidly told Colson of the increasing crime problem the Soviet Union faced in 1989. Colson's candor was as devastating as Bakatin's admission of the crime situation:

I told him that crime is not caused by economic or political or ethnic factors. It is caused by sin — by the fundamental evil in the human heart.

In a system that rejects God, there can be no transcendent values or authority to which people are accountable — so one can only reasonably expect unfettered human behavior. And that means crime.[23]

This message was similar to that of another Russian

philosopher and writer, Fyodor Dostoyevski. Dostoyevski is best known for his portrayal of the solitary, alienated individual. He reflected the despair of alienation from God in The Brothers Karamazov, *"... they have already proclaimed that there is no crime, that there is no sin. And that's consistent, for if you have no God what is the meaning of crime?"* As Colson paraphrased it, *"When there is no God, everything is permitted. Crime becomes inevitable."* [24]

Since this is the case, R. C. Sproul's assessment is not that shocking after all: "If you think about it, we are all really more like Adolph Hitler than like Jesus Christ."[25] Christopher Browning wrote a disturbing book, Ordinary Men, in which he "conveys to us that it was not a few brutes, but many good and ordinary men, who committed murder for Hitler."[26]

Modern day citizens of Iraq have experienced all of the horrors of war but not from the hands of foreign invaders. Their horror came from the very government that should have protected them.

"THE GREAT TERROR"

A number of anti-war voices have suggested that the Iraqis were actually better off when Saddam Hussein was President of Iraq. They argue that the influx of terrorists and the battles in the streets of Baghdad and Falujah are a greater evil than the rule of Saddam. This argument not only lacks any understanding of our purposes in Iraq in the larger struggle with terrorism but also lacks historical perspective. Putting aside the larger war against global terrorism currently fought in the sands of Iraq, were the people of Iraq better off under Saddam Hussein?

There is no way to actually experience life under the brutal hand of Saddam Hussein. Historians and researchers will always be handicapped by historical and experiential distance. Perhaps by immersing ourselves in the drama of only one Kurdish family, we can begin to sympathize with their horror.

Jeffery Goldberg wrote an article for the New Yorker capturing the essence of the war Saddam waged against his own people.

"In northern Iraq, late in the morning of March 16, 1988, an Iraqi Air Force helicopter appeared over the city of Halabja, which is about fifteen miles from the border with Iran. At the time, the city was home to roughly eighty thousand Kurds, who were well accustomed to the proximity of violence to ordinary life.

A young woman named Nasreen Abdel Qadir Muhammad was outside her family's house, preparing food, when she saw the helicopter. The Iranians and the peshmerga had just attacked Iraqi military outposts around Halabja, forcing Saddam's soldiers to retreat. Iranian Revolutionary Guards then infiltrated the city, and the residents assumed that an Iraqi counterattack was imminent. Nasreen and her family expected to spend yet another day in their cellar, which was crude and dark but solid enough to withstand artillery shelling, and even napalm.

'At about ten o'clock, maybe closer to ten-thirty, I saw the helicopter,' Nasreen told Goldberg. 'It was not attacking, though. There were men inside it, taking pictures. One had a regular camera, and the other held what looked like a video camera. They were coming very close. Then they went away.'

Nasreen thought that the sight was strange, but she was preoccupied with lunch; she and her sister Rangeen were preparing rice, bread, and beans for the thirty or forty relatives who were taking shelter in the cellar. Rangeen was fifteen at the time. Nasreen was just sixteen, but her father had married her off several months earlier, to a cousin, a thirty-year-old physician's assistant named Bakhtiar Abdul Aziz.

The bombardment began shortly before eleven. The Iraqi Army, positioned on the main road from the nearby town of Sayid Sadiq, fired artillery shells into Halabja, and the Air Force began dropping what is thought to have been napalm on the town, especially the northern area. Nasreen and Rangeen rushed to the cellar. Nasreen prayed that Bakhtiar, who was then outside the city, would find shelter.

The attack had ebbed by about two o'clock, and Nasreen made her way carefully upstairs to the kitchen, to get the food for the family. 'At the end of the bombing, the sound changed,' she said. 'It wasn't so loud. It was like pieces of metal just dropping without exploding. We didn't know why it was so quiet.'

A short distance away, in a neighborhood still called the Julakan, or Jewish quarter, even though Halabja's Jews left for Israel in the nineteen-fifties, a middle-aged man named Muhammad came up from his own cellar and saw an unusual sight: 'A helicopter had come back to the town, and the soldiers were throwing white pieces of paper out the side.' In retrospect, he understood that they were measuring wind speed and direction. Nearby, a man named Awat Omer, who was twenty at the time, was overwhelmed by a smell of garlic and apples.

Nasreen gathered the food quickly, but she, too, noticed a series of odd smells carried into the house by the wind. 'At first, it smelled bad, like garbage,' she said. 'And then it was a good smell, like sweet apples. Then like eggs.' She looked out the window. 'It was very quiet, but the animals were dying. The sheep and goats were dying.' Nasreen ran to the *cellar. 'I told everybody there was something wrong. There was something wrong with the air.'*

The people in the cellar were panicked. They had fled downstairs to escape the bombardment, and it was difficult to abandon their shelter. Only splinters of light penetrated the basement, but the dark provided a strange comfort. 'We wanted to stay in hiding, even though we were getting sick,' Nasreen said. She felt a sharp pain in her eyes, like stabbing needles. 'My sister came close to my face and said, 'Your eyes are very red.' Then the children started throwing up. They kept throwing up. They were in so much pain, and crying so much. They were crying all the time. My mother was crying. Then the old people started throwing up.'

Chemical weapons had been dropped on Halabja by the Iraqi Air Force, which understood that any underground shelter would become a gas chamber. 'My uncle said we should go outside,' Nasreen said. 'We knew there were chemicals in the air. We decided to run.' Nasreen and her relatives stepped outside gingerly. 'Our cow was lying on its side,' she recalled. 'It was breathing very fast, as if it had been running. The leaves were falling off the trees, even though it was spring. The partridge was dead. There were smoke clouds around, clinging to the ground.'

The family judged the direction of the wind, and decided to run the opposite way. Running proved difficult. 'The children couldn't walk, they were so sick,' Nasreen said. 'They were exhausted from throwing up. We carried them in our arms.'

Across the city, other families were making similar decisions. Nouri Hama Ali, who lived in the northern part of town, decided to lead his family in the direction of Anab, a collective settlement on the outskirts of Halabja that housed Kurds displaced when the Iraqi Army destroyed their villages. 'On the road to Anab, many of the women and children began to die,' Nouri told Goldberg. 'The chemical clouds were on the ground. They were heavy. We could see them.' People were dying all around, he said. When a child could not go on, the parents, becoming hysterical with fear, abandoned him. 'Many children were left on the ground, by the side of the road. Old people as well. They were running, then they would stop breathing and die.'

Nasreen's family did not move quickly. 'We wanted to wash ourselves off and find water to drink,' she said. 'We wanted to wash the faces of the children who were vomiting. The children were crying for water. There was powder on the ground, white. We couldn't decide whether to drink the water or not, but some people drank the water from the well they were so thirsty.'

They ran in a panic through the city, Nasreen recalled, in the direction of Anab. The bombardment continued intermittently, Air Force planes circling overhead. 'People were showing different symptoms. One person touched some of the powder, and her skin started bubbling.'

A truck came by, driven by a neighbor. People threw themselves aboard. 'We saw people lying frozen on the ground,' Nasreen told Goldberg. 'There was a small baby on the ground, away from her mother. I thought they were both sleeping. But she had dropped the baby and then died. And I think the baby tried to crawl away, but it died, too. It looked like everyone was sleeping.'

At that moment, Nasreen believed that she and

her family would make it to high ground and live. Then the truck stopped. 'The driver said he couldn't go on, and he wandered away. He left his wife in the back of the truck. He told us to flee if we could.'

As heavy clouds of gas smothered the city, people became sick and confused. Awat Omer was trapped in his cellar with his family; he said that his brother began laughing uncontrollably and then stripped off his clothes, and soon afterward he died. As night fell, the family's children grew sicker—too sick to move.

Nasreen said that on the road to Anab all was confusion. She and the children were running toward the hills, but they were going blind. 'The children were crying, 'We can't see! My eyes are bleeding!' ' In the chaos, the family got separated. Nasreen's mother and father were both lost. Nasreen and several of her cousins and siblings inadvertently led the younger children in a circle, back into the city. Someone—she doesn't know who—led them away from the city again and up a hill, to a small mosque, where they sought shelter. 'But we didn't stay in the mosque, because we thought it would be a target,' Nasreen said. They went to a small house nearby, and Nasreen scrambled to find food and water for the children. By then, it was night, and she was exhausted.

Bakhtiar, Nasreen's husband, was frantic. Outside the city when the attacks started, he had spent much of the day searching for his wife and the rest of his family. He had acquired from a clinic two syringes of atropine, a drug that helps to counter the effects of nerve agents. He injected himself with one of the syringes, and set out to find Nasreen. He had no hope. 'My plan was to bury her,' he said. 'At least

I should bury my new wife.'

After hours of searching, Bakhtiar met some neighbors, who remembered seeing Nasreen and the children moving toward the mosque on the hill. 'I called out the name Nasreen,' he said. 'I heard crying, and I went inside the house. When I got there, I found that Nasreen was alive but blind. Everybody was blind.'

Nasreen had lost her sight about an hour or two before Bakhtiar found her. She had been searching the house for food, so that she could feed the children, when her eyesight failed. 'I found some milk and I felt my way to them and then I found their mouths and gave them milk,' she said.

Bakhtiar organized the children. 'I wanted to bring them to the well. I washed their heads. I took them two by two and washed their heads. Some of them couldn't come. They couldn't control their muscles.'

Bakhtiar still had one syringe of atropine, but he did not inject his wife; she was not the worst off in the group. 'There was a woman named Asme, who was my neighbor,' Bakhtiar recalled. 'She was not able to breathe. She was yelling and she was running into a wall, crashing her head into a wall. I gave the atropine to this woman.' Asme died soon afterward. 'I could have used it for Nasreen,' Bakhtiar said. 'I could have.'

After the Iraqi bombardment subsided, the Iranians managed to retake Halabja, and they evacuated many of the sick, including Nasreen and the others in her family, to hospitals in Tehran.

The Iranian Red Crescent Society, the equivalent of the Red Cross, began compiling books of photographs, pictures of the dead in Halabja. 'The

Red Crescent has an album of the people who were buried in Iran,' Nasreen said. 'And we found my mother in one of the albums.' Her father, she discovered, was alive but permanently blinded. Five of her siblings, including Rangeen, had died.

Nasreen lived but she kept a secret from Bakhtiar: 'When I was in the hospital, I started menstruating. It wouldn't stop. I kept bleeding. We don't talk about this in our society, but eventually a lot of women in the hospital confessed they were also menstruating and couldn't stop.' Doctors gave her drugs that stopped the bleeding, but they told her that she would be unable to bear children.

Nasreen stayed in Iran for several months, but eventually she and Bakhtiar returned to Kurdistan. She didn't believe the doctors who told her that she would be infertile, and in 1991 she gave birth to a boy. 'We named him Arazoo,' she said. Arazoo means hope in Kurdish. 'He was healthy at first, but he had a hole in his heart. He died at the age of three months.'

Saddam's cousin Ali Hassan al-Majid, who led the campaigns against the Kurds in the late eighties, was heard on a tape captured by rebels, and later obtained by Human Rights Watch, addressing members of Iraq's ruling Baath Party on the subject of the Kurds. *"I will kill them all with chemical weapons!" he said. "Who is going to say anything? The international community?"*

Iraqi Medical geneticist Christine Gosden, said, "Please understand, the Kurds were for practice."[27]

WHERE DO WE STAND NOW?

If we continue to delude ourselves about the true nature of the present world conflict and focus on trivial misdeeds rather than the larger moral and political issues, we may succumb to the same degenerated thinking that other nations and individuals have experienced in all of human history.

Most Americans that experienced WWII are no longer with us. That is our loss. They knew what it was like to live in a country at war. They understood personal sacrifice when they were issued coupon books for everything from tires to sugar. They knew that they were doing their part to ensure success for the national objectives in a time of war. American industrial production of war machines in large part paved the way to a successful conclusion of the war in Europe. The sacrifices of Americans provided the industry with the surplus of materials to manufacture the needed supplies for the war. What do Americans sacrifice today in the war against Terrorism? Why do we fail to grasp the violent and threatening nature of this present conflict? Why are we so intent on insulating ourselves from associating with this war? Is it fear or simply a commitment to self-serving causes?

On the evening of September 20, 2001 President Bush stepped up to the podium to address the American people after the attacks on the World Trade Center and the Pentagon. In just these few excerpts from that historic speech, he clearly outlined the nature of our present conflict, the tremendous loss of life we have already experienced, and his resolve to see it through to the end. How much of this speech frames the current debate over the war on terrorism?

"We are a country awakened to danger and called to defend freedom. Our grief has turned to anger and anger to resolution. Whether we bring our enemies to justice or bring justice to our enemies, justice will be done. We will not forget the citizens of 80 other nations who died with our own. Dozens of Pakistanis, more than 130 Israelis, more

than 250 citizens of India, men and women from El Salvador, Iran, Mexico and Japan, and hundreds of British citizens. On September the 11th, enemies of freedom committed an act of war against our country. Americans have known wars, but for the past 136 years they have been wars on foreign soil, except for one Sunday in 1941. Americans have known the casualties of war, but not at the center of a great city on a peaceful morning.

Americans have known surprise attacks, but never before on thousands of civilians. All of this was brought upon us in a single day, and night fell on a different world, a world where freedom itself is under attack.

The evidence we have gathered all points to a collection of loosely affiliated terrorist organizations known as Al-Qaida. They are some of the murderers indicted for bombing American embassies in Tanzania and Kenya and responsible for bombing the USS Cole.

Al-Qaida is to terror what the Mafia is to crime. But its goal is not financial. Their goal is to reshape the world to impose their radical beliefs on all people everywhere.

The terrorists' directive commands them to kill Christians and Jews, to kill all Americans and make no distinctions among military and civilians, including women and children. This group and its leader, a person named Usama bin Laden, is linked to many other organizations in different countries, including the Egyptian Islamic Jihad, the Islamic Movement of Uzbekistan.

The enemy of America is not our many Muslim friends. It is not our many Arab friends. Our enemy is a radical network of terrorists and every govern-

ment that supports them.

Our war on terror begins with Al-Qaida, but it does not end there.

It will not end until every terrorist group of global reach has been found, stopped and defeated.

We have seen their kind before. They're the heirs of all the murderous ideologies of the 20th century. By sacrificing human life to serve their radical visions, by abandoning every value except the will to power, they follow in the path of fascism, Nazism and totalitarianism. And they will follow that path all the way to where it ends in history's unmarked grave of discarded lies.

A great harm has been done to us. We have suffered great loss. And in our grief and anger we have found our mission and our moment. Freedom and fear are at war. The advance of human freedom, the great achievement of our time and the great hope of every time, now depends on us.

Our nation, this generation, will lift the dark threat of violence from our people and our future. We will rally the world to this cause by our efforts and by our courage. We will not tire, we will not falter and we will not fail.

I will not forget the wound to our country and those who inflicted it. I will not yield, I will not rest, I will not relent in waging this struggle for freedom and security for the American people. The course of this conflict is not known, yet its outcome is certain. Freedom and fear, justice and cruelty, have always been at war, and we know that God is not neutral between them."

Almost immediately, the howls of protest against the war found forums for discussion. The internet sprang to life as a place for malcontents to gather and feed on one another's fear and anxiety. Shortly after I deployed to Iraq, I found a discussion page linked to my hometown newspaper. I expected to read comments that reflected the patriotism and confidence I experienced before I left home. Cars were adorned with flags and yellow ribbons. The National Anthem was played at little league games and local ministers were called upon to give invocations before the kickoff. What I read was less than encouraging. I was able to post messages to the discussion group page. These are some of the extracts from that message.

"I am disappointed that the readers of the State [sic] lack a vision for justice. War with Iraqi is just that, a quest for justice, not only for ourselves but for the people of Iraq. One only has to visit the CIA official web site to read of the CONFIRMED uses of VX gas, mustard gas, and other agents used by Iraq against Iran and against the citizens of Iraq, especially the Kurds. Thousand have been killed. Let that sink in, THOUSANDS. A further search on the web and you may find a picture of children, laying in the streets dead after being gassed by Saddam's government.

Without a doubt, war with Iraq will be inconvenient. Gas prices may climb a little higher, stocks may take a beating too. Obviously, the charge that Americans can only recall what happened the last 60 minutes but can't explain anything from the last 60 years is proven in our focus on the price of our current tank of gas.

I am currently in Kuwait. Yesterday I traveled for two hours on the roads and saw the people of Kuwait. They rejoice that we are here and hope that many of their missing loved one who were abducted by Iraq twelve years ago will be returned home. Iraqi's that are here describe the horror of living in Iraq. They talk about relatives being taken in the night and never returning home. Suspicion is guilt in Iraq.

Do we owe it to the people of Iraq to free them from this oppression? No more than we did to the Jews of the 1940's and no more than the Northern states owed to the slaves of the south in the 1860's. No, we can continue to allow the Kurds to be gassed and killed. We can pump our gas at the cost of countless lives in Iraq and in the region once he is finally turned loose again. We can tell the people of Kuwait, "You're on your own, hope your family returns and you are not invaded again." We can ask all terrorist not to shop in Iraq for the parts to weapons of mass destruction but instead to do all their own research and create their own weapons.

I have lived in Columbia, SC for many years and it is a wonderful place. It feels safe and is a long way from Iraq, and a long way from lower Manhattan. Terror has never really visited us, not since Sherman.

Putting our head in the sand is a comfortable place to be sure. Complaining about the gas prices is certainly a favorite pastime. I encourage you to reconsider the cost of our ease. War is tragic. Justice and right requires it. We are at a crossroads of history in America. We have always hesitated to put self-interest ahead of a sense of right. Will evil be allowed to have the day? Will we shirk from the responsibility God has given us. Our blessings come to us not just for our pleasure, but for us to be faithful stewards of. A quick and decisive war against the regime of Saddam Hussein is the surest way to deliver a just decision for the innocent people of Iraq, and all the world.

LIFE IN A LOOKING GLASS

AN ANATOMY OF THE MEDIA AT WAR

-OR-

SELECTIVE MORAL OUTRAGE IN THE AMERICAN PRESS

> "Let me hear you make decisions without
> your televisions"
>
> *Depeche Mode*

The news media has to make decisions every day. There is no possible way they can present every bit of news in the world day in and day out. The weather in Beijing, the financial markets in Mexico, the birth of twins in Romania, and the melting of glaciers at the polar ice cap are all news items but they are not all equally valuable for broadcast. For one thing, the accumulation and presentation of the material is impossible. For another, the public isn't interested in everything that happens in every corner of the globe. How do they decide what they want to present and what they allow to disappear into history and fade from memory?

Media executives are not so different from people working in any other line of business. They have interests and they want to make a living. They want to be the best at what they do and yet they are bound by whatever constraints are placed upon them either by themselves, the industry, or the government. When they choose to cover a story, especially when they choose to cover it exhaustively, their motivations should be determined to help us understand how we should interpret their presentation. They are either moved by public safety, humanitarian concerns and compassion, profit potential, or political agendas. They often work sacrificially to get the best perspective they can on their subject. Dan Rather visited the 800th MP Brigade while he was touring Camp Arifjan, Kuwait after the end of the war with Saddams military. As he shook my hand, I noticed how tired he looked. He seemed to genuinely appreciate our service and sacrifice. After a quick picture under the Brigade sign, he was gone. That would not be the last word Mr. Rather would have on the war, soldiers, our Commander in Chief, or the 800th MP Brigade.

In late September of 2004, the presidential campaign appeared to be too close to call. Senator John Kerry had seemed a good contender for the Presidential election but a series of adds questioning his Vietnam record had damaged his campaign. Suddenly, official looking memorandums appeared purportedly typed by then Lieutenant Bush's squadron commander, Lieutenant Colonel Jerry Killian. Despite the concerns of LTC Killian's surviving family about the character of the memorandums and the lack of guarantees about their authenticity, CBS presented them to the public as genuine Air Force documents questioning President Bush's service record in the Air National Guard.

Almost immediately radio and television commentators alike began to question the evidence linked to the memorandums. Despite the growing evidence against the legitimacy of the memos, CBS insisted they were real and kept them in the news cycle. The story originally aired on September 8th and CBS waited until September 20th to retract the story. That unprofessional and frankly untrustworthy reporting leaves Americans to wonder, "Why"? If a major news outlet is willing to air such a dubious story that could potentially alter the political landscape of America, shouldn't we question their motivations? Now, we need to reflect back on the war coverage of CBS and other news outlets. Has their coverage been honest or has it been purposefully crafted to focus and manipulate public opinion? What motivated the coverage of Abu Ghraib? There was no threat to Americans so it couldn't have been public safety. Humanitarian, political, and financial concerns are all possible motivations for CBS. Taken together with the later memorandum story, I believe their purpose emerges frighteningly clear.

Like most Americans I sat staring at the television screen as images displayed the humiliating abuses at Abu Ghraib. I was filled with anger and shame for my association with the unit that had come under fire as being responsible for the abuse. I shared the concerns of Dan Rather as he presented this embarrassing international incident and I thought that this must be the lowest form of sexual deviance and misconduct I had seen on public display in my life. Then a commercial break began to discuss erectile dysfunction. A woman discussed how her man was having a much faster and more satisfying response in their intimate encounters. The hypocrisy was obvious. How can we be so concerned with young soldiers putting women's panties on a man's head when our children are being taught about erectile dysfunctions every night? Americans have lost the ability to discern truth for themselves. Instead, they adopt the views that their favorite TV host espouses. In an environment tainted by newscaster's opinion, truth will become lost in the storm of controversy created for program ratings.

When Spec. Jeremy Sivits (24 years old) was brought forward for trial, Capt. Scott Dunn, Sivits's lawyer, entered the plea of guilty on Sivit's behalf and then expressed his concern about the extent of media coverage of the trial. He asked the judge, "can you make a fair decision?"

The judge in the trial, Col. James Pohl, replied: "Just because it's on TV, it doesn't mean it's true." This short answer to a complex question betrays a general distrust of the media that has begun to emerge since the 1990s. America's marriage to the media has sometimes been for the better but just as often it has been for the worse. To say that it has emerged in the 1990s is a misstatement. It has re-emerged in the 1990s. Since print and broadcast media assumed the role of the world's *looking glass,* distrust of the media has been a recurring historic problem. In the late 1800s a brand of reporting that was more opinion than fact was labeled Yellow Journalism. Competition between newspapers for readership gave rise to more sensationalistic reporting. Serious national issues were turned into soap opera presentations meant to draw the readers into the story as if it were literature rather than news. Readers lacked any device to corroborate the stories presented to them by the mainstream press. The opinions of the journalists were injected into the news reports without apology.

In Neil Postman's *Amusing Ourselves to Death*, he first describes and then warns against *Huxleyanism*. Huxleyanism is a spiritual devastation that results from our infatuation with technology. It affects people as individuals and it has a subtle but dangerous affect on society in general. The danger manifests in our love affair with self-indulgence and entertainment. Life becomes trivialized and culture is *"redefined as a perpetual round of entertainments, when serious public conversation becomes a form of baby-talk, when in short, a people become an audience and their public business a vaudeville act, then a nation finds itself at risk; culture-death is a clear possibility."*

Because American's love to be entertained, there are few voices that challenge the open door granted to every form of electronic and print from PacMan to Playboy. The thirty-second sound bite and the two-second image have challenged retailers to acquire and retain consumer's attention. Detailed information about a product has become far less important than the image presented on the television screen. Hence the saying, *"Image is everything."* The press faces many of the same challenges as retailers for the attention of readers and viewers. Twenty-four hour a day news broadcasts leave the evening news fighting for an audience. After all, the news has been reported all day in short segments for anyone interested before the traditional anchors sit down to host the evening news. The only way to stay viable in such a competitive market is to be creative and sensational with the presentation of the news. Creativity does not necessarily imply that anything false is being published or reported. However, it may imply that the facts are being sensationalized or presented in a way to make the ordinary news seem like the extraordinary story of our time.

Postman prophetically points out that *"Television... serves us most usefully when presenting junk-entertainment; it serves us most ill when it co-opts serious modes of discourse-news, politics, science, education, commerce, religion-and turns them into entertainment packages."*[28]

A good example is the report of Vice-President Dick Cheney's cursing at Senator Patrick Leahy in June 2004. With soldiers deployed to Iraq, the economy at a twenty-years high, and two political conventions approaching, the news media spent days interviewing experts to solicit their professional opinion about the vice-President's curse word spoken directly to Leahy. It did not matter if the comment was related to public discourse and debate or that is was not a matter of presidential policy. The comment was made spontaneously in a moment of passion and personal confrontation. Was it uncalled for? Perhaps. Was it worthy of national news? Hardly. Yet, it was treated with the same weight as announcement of grave importance and national security.

Journalism, according to G.K. Chesterton, "largely consists of saying 'Lord Jones is Dead' to people who never knew that Lord Jones was alive." And *"it was (Thomas) Jefferson who wrote John Norvell (in a letter he insisted not get into the press) that newspapers could be divided into four chapters — truths, probabilities, possibilities, and lies — the first chapter being very short and the second not much longer."*[29]

There is a saying among the press corps that they are journalists first and Americans second. It appears that often they are not able to balance their two loyalties and many are simply journalists first and Americans rarely. Bernard Shaw of CNN, who received high praises for his reporting during the 1991 Gulf War, refused to be debriefed by the military because he considered it a compromise to his neutrality as a reporter. Shaw defined himself as a part of the larger community of humanity rather than as a US citizen. As his view is stated here, we have to assume that he is convinced his reporting is a greater service for mankind than any information he could share even if it would save American lives. After September 11, 2001, ABC News forbid it's journalists from wearing flags on the lapels of their suits. Host Barbara Walters explained on "The View" that wearing an American flag is discouraged because it may confuse the audience." Loren Jenkins, a senior foreign editor of NPR, told the Chicago Tribune on October 12, 2001, that his job was to "get a story, not worry about American lives."[30] To prove their loyalty and objectivity, media personalities seem pressed to be anti-American in their coverage of the news. This certainly does not mean that the majority of the members in the press corps are not patriotic nor that they do not have a love for their country. It does mean that there is an institutional paradigm that normalizes an anti-American bias in the news. In other words, Americans, particularly those considered to be conservative (backwards in the eyes of the liberal media), are guilty until proven innocent.

L. Brent Bozell II describes anti-American bias evidenced during ABCs coverage of the humanitarian aid sent from the United States to the Afghan civilians. The aid was given while the U.S. Military was conducting operations against the Taliban. During Peter Jennings' broadcast to America, he reported that everyone in Afghanistan was not thrilled about the food and medicine being delivered by America to the destitute Afghans. The effort was described as military propaganda meant to justify the bombing taking place against the Taliban. After the terrorists attacks against the Trade Center and Pentagon, America did not need further justification for bombing. The following night, ABC reporter Dan Harris continued to downplay the humanitarian effort as being little more than propaganda that actually was doing more harm than good.

Americans were delivering food and medicine to the people of a nation whos government sponsored and gave safe haven for terrorists. But Jennings and Harris cannot seem to find anything good about American benevolence to report on. The media's bias is evident when they report on crimes against Americans by criminals and terrorists in the international community. They allow nations and individuals hostile to the United States a great deal of latitude whereas they spare no criticism for the slightest misstep by their fellow Americans. Whether they hold to some romantic idea that America should play the suffering servant of the world or whether they actually harbor a deep resentment against Americas contribution to the world, crimes against Americans are portrayed as justifiable simply because they are against Americans.

In a very real sense, the media appears to harbor a deep resentment against America or the role America is destined to play in world history. For example, CNN reported on their web site that the beheadings of Nick Berg and Paul Johnson would inevitably result in more bad American behavior. "The murders of Paul Johnson and Nicholas Berg triggered hate mail, verbal attacks and anti-Muslim signs. Muslims received death threats and their mosques were vandalized. Al-Qaeda-linked militants in Saudi Arabia decapitated Johnson, an American engineer, after warning that they would kill him if the Saudi government did not release jailed comrades. Berg, a businessman, met a similar fate last month (June 2003) in Iraq.

Following Johnson's death, anti-Islam signs surfaced around the rural New Jersey neighborhood where he once lived. One read 'Stamp Out Islam' next to a drawing of a boot over a crescent and star. Another, hung on a mailbox next door to Johnson's sister's home, was more detailed."[31] American reaction to the murder of an innocent man is characterized as a hate crime. When Islamic radicals cut the head off of an unarmed and innocent American, it is considered revolutionary! Putting anti-Islam signs on par with sawing a living man's head off seems out of touch with reality. Is this reporting the news or influencing public opinion?

When the press began to report on the prisoner abuse at Abu Ghraib on April 29, 2004, I was initially impressed with their restraint. The Pentagon exerted pressure and influence on CBS to avoid sensationalizing the story for the sake of our soldier's safety. Eventually, the prize of viewership relevance proved too much of a temptation for the networks to resist. The images began to occupy every newscast as if it were the first time they had been shown. Almost as an apology, Dan Rather confessed that CBS aired their version of the story because other networks were going to air their versions soon. CBS wouldn't lose the privilege of airing it first no matter what the dangers were to Americans battling in Fallujah.

Like synchronized swimmers, the press grabbed hold of the reports of prisoner abuse in Iraq and with an inexplicable obsession, and continued to hold it before the American public. The pictures they presented showed Iraqi prisoners stripped of their clothes with their heads covered in most cases. Those prisoners were more often than not placed in either sexually suggestive positions, some ridiculous posture such as those piled into a pyramid, or simply subjected to being exposed to American females that seemed to be mocking and making fun of the prisoners' genitals.

The nature of media today does not lend itself to sustained objectivity. Audiences must not only be attracted but retained. The reports that followed the initial 60 Minutes II presentation were not necessarily false but the cumulative affect of the myopic coverage portrayed the events as something far worse than they were. Repeated and consistent descriptions of the humiliated Iraqi prisoners with terms like, "Abuse" and "torture" create an image in the public's mind that is skewed from reality. CBS further spiced the story by insinuating that the details had been kept secret until April 2004. In fact, the investigations were available for public scrutiny but there was little interest in them until the pictures emerged from Abu Ghraib. The only influence the Department of Defense exercised was to request that CBS delay showing the pictures until the violence in Fallujah had passed. But nothing catches a nation's attention like exposing government secrets. If this were the only case of prisoner abuse ever reported, their reactions might well be warranted.

There are numerous cases of prisoner abuse in American

prisons that make Abu Ghraib seem like a misdemeanor in comparison. These abuses are largely ignored by the media leaving us to wonder if the their fascination with Abu Ghraib is representative of American's public interests or whether it is an indication of political and philosophical bias against the mission in Iraq? Bernard Goldberg, a winner of seven Emmy Awards and long-time reporter and producer for CBS News discussed the bias of the press in his book titled, "Bias". While the media elite champion humanistic social causes, they often spend exorbant amounts of time attacking causes associated with morality, freedom, and justice. The republic which is of the people and for the people is suspect while the agendas of the minority voices that oppose the representative will of the people are championed.

Goldberg says, "These are people who love to take on politicians and businessmen and lawyers and Christians and the military and athletes and all sorts of other Americans..."[32]

On May 4, 2004, radio talk-show host Rush Limbaugh commented on the media's treatment of the prisoner abuse.

"Now, don't misunderstand, I'm not suggesting that the torture is okay, because I don't think it is. I'm not suggesting it's not a big deal. I'm not suggesting anything of the sort. I'm trying to say we are in a war, and there are bad guys from our perspective, and there are good guys from our perspective, and we are it; and amongst both groups you've got some factions who don't qualify. There are probably some good people in the bad guys and some rotten apples in the good guys, and these people that did this so-called torture may in fact be the rotten apples of the good guy group. But it's like I said: it doesn't taint the whole military effort and it doesn't taint us, but the world is joining in now

trying to taint us as a nation, as a people, and as a culture by virtue of these pictures on the basis that we have humiliated these people. What is hijacking our own airplanes and flying them into the World Trade Center and the Pentagon? How humiliating is it to blow up American civilians in a convoy and have their charred bodies dragged from the car and dragged through the streets? [As in Falujah] There seems to be no sensitivity, concern or outrage for any of this anywhere in the world.

There is such an overreaction to this torture business. Again' don't misunderstand me. I am not condoning it, and I am not suggesting that it's something we ought to engage in routinely because we're not that kind of a people. But that's the point, we don't do this. This is an isolated incident or two. This is not how we can be and are defined, and everybody is having too good a time overreacting"

Limbaugh referred to both the nature of the humiliation as well as the exaggerated media coverage of it. Some commentators referred to the abuse as nothing more than college-style pranks growing out of minds molded and confused by the hypersexual society we live in while others portrayed it as possibly the worst war crimes ever committed against mankind. Limbaugh also defines the essence of character judgment in his explanation. America's character is not found in the isolated incidents of her citizens but in the corporate vision for liberty and justice. America must be reminded over and again by our elected representatives and local religious and civic leaders that our nation is founded on the rule of law, respect for the dignity of man as created by God, and the pursuit of mature spirituality and conformity to the character of God. When this vision is lost, people begin to fragment and divide setting up different and arbitrary criteria for finding meaning and purpose in life. Abu Ghraib and the media reaction to it are evidence of the moral wandering that has taken root in America. Like the Hebrews that wandered in the wilderness, America's collective soul is wandering in a moral abyss in search of some firm foundation and common purpose. Truth has been made optional and now there are so many voices claiming their vision is right for America that America is beginning to show signs of stress fractures and balkanization. The media has become a voice for one of those views.

Perhaps the media's preoccupation with Abu Ghraib in the network news can be understood by considering where the template is set for news coverage. According to Goldberg, "One thing to remember about network news is that it steals just about everything from print. So if the New York Times is against the flat tax, and the Washington Post is against the flat tax, the networks can't and won't be far behind."[33] To understand the networks interest in Abu Ghraib we will have to consider the written press' interest and if Goldberg is correct, the disposition of the New York Times in particular. From April 29 through June 2, 2004 the New York Times published 32 successive front page articles on Abu Ghraib.[34]

This coverage seems to go beyond comprehensive. It rises even beyond a fixation or preoccupation. This boarders on an institutional compulsive disorder. The New York Times seems to have enjoyed taking advantage of the rich target of opportunity that Abu Ghraib presented and wanted to make the most of it. They worked to link Abu Ghriab to more horrific events in America's history such as My-Lai. On May 11, Columnist Paul Krugman wrote in the Times, "Just trust us, Donald Rumsfeld said early in 2002, when he declared that *'enemy combatants'*—a term that turned out to mean anyone, including American citizens, the administration chose to so designate—don't have rights under the

Geneva Convention. Now people around the world talk of an *'American gulag,'* and Seymour Hersh is exposing My Lai all over again."

Seeking to prove that you may indeed be able to get blood out of a turnip, the visual media followed suit and in the process demonstrated not only their journalistic bias but their intellectual ineptitude. While they focused exclusively on the half dozen soldiers that posed with naked Iraqis and put women's panties on prisoners heads, they failed to make their coverage comprehensive on the subject of prisoner abuse and also failed to make it intellectually honest by asking the question, "Why?". They chose instead to stand in judgment against the military leadership and even promoted the idea that the Secretary of Defense and the President himself may be culpable. They also fostered the idea that American's are doing more harm than good because of this isolated incident. Every day, American soldiers are interacting with Iraqis. Every day, soldiers are restoring public services such as power, phone, schools, and hospitals to the Iraqi people. Every day, an Iraqi citizen is able to stay with his family who would have been arrested and tortured in Abu Ghraib by Saddam's agents in the Baath party. Every day, Americans are bring more hope and enlightenment to the Iraqi people and in an historic sense, we are altering the course of history to bring the light of liberty to an oppressed people in the entire region. Every day, the media seems to prefer an isolationist policy that will deprive the Iraqi people of the liberty that is within their grasp. Isolationists policies also allow terrorists now displaced by our military to return to places of safety to train and prepare for another attack on America. And what evidence does the media present in its case? Abu Ghraib.

What is the alternative perspective the media could have adopted? Instead of acting like the prosecution in a court case, could they have presented information that would have enlightened instead of misled America?

The psychology of prisoner abuse should be nothing new to Americans. I can remember as a youth watching a report on television of a study conducted by Stanford University in 1971. They created a prison environment in the basement of a campus building and students were randomly assigned as either prisoners or the prison guards. For two weeks each group played their roles, complete with the appropriate uniforms. Within a few days, the guards began to show disturbing behavioral trends. They put bags over the prisoners' heads, striped them naked and encouraged them to perform sexual acts for the guards amusement and as an act of humiliation. The actions of the guards is disturbing enough without even considering that they understood that the prisoners in the study weren't really criminals doing time but their peers. They were abusing their fellow students and it was only an act of providence rather than merit of their own that earned them the position of a prison guard rather than a prisoner. This 1971 study should have alerted America to the dangers of absolute power. Edmund Burke is reported as saying, "The greater the power the more dangerous the abuse."[35]

The Americans in the high security Green Zone were under considerable stress and actual life threatening attacks from an enemy that was elusive and lethal. Bullets whizzed over their heads almost continually, medivac helicopters were called in almost daily to take wounded American soldiers out of the Green Zone in Baghdad and into a safer area for treatment. Rocket Propelled Grenades (RPGs) were fired routinely into the Green Zone. Iraqis were being arrested in the area carrying weapons and often caught participating in attacks against American forces in Baghdad. They were taken to Abu Ghraib as felons. They resisted giving any information to the Americans that might help the coalition fend off the attacks and save coalition lives.

Interrogators came under increasing pressure to produce results. Every day that passed more Americans were being attacked. Every day more roadside bombs were exploding, killing and maiming Americans for the rest of their lives. Everyday, the Iraqis that had the answers refused to divulge the locations of anti-coalition forces in Iraq. What would you do if you were the commander of the American forces in the Green Zone? What would you do if you had to write another letter to grieving parents about the efforts given to protect their son or daughter and your sorrow for their loss? What would you do if you stood in front of a formation of young soldiers that depended on you for their lives?

According to the Boston Herald on May 6, 2004, more than 24 investigations were launched seeking the answers. Criminal charges have been filed against a number of soldiers from the lowest enlisted ranks to the highest commissioned officer. If a picture is worth a thousand words, "The photographs tell it all. In one, Private England, a cigarette dangling from her mouth, is giving a jaunty thumbs-up sign and pointing at the genitals of a young Iraqi, who is naked except for a sandbag over his head, as he masturbates. Three other hooded and naked Iraqi prisoners are shown, hands reflexively crossed over their genitals. A fifth prisoner has his hands at his sides. In another, England stands arm in arm with Specialist Graner; both are grinning and giving the thumbs-up behind a cluster of perhaps seven naked Iraqis, knees bent, piled clumsily on top of each other in a pyramid. There is another photograph of a cluster of naked prisoners, again piled in a pyramid. Near them stands Graner, smiling, his arms crossed; a woman soldier stands in front of him, bending over, and she, too, is smiling. Then, there is another cluster of hooded bodies, with a female soldier standing in front, taking photographs. Yet another photograph shows a kneeling, naked, unhooded male prisoner, head momentarily turned away from the camera, posed to make it appear that he is performing oral sex on another male prisoner, who is naked and hooded.

Such dehumanization is unacceptable in any culture, but it is especially so in the Arab world. Homosexual acts are against Islamic law and it is humiliating for men to be naked in front of other men, Bernard Haykel, a professor of Middle Eastern studies at New York University, explained. 'Being put on top of each other and forced to masturbate, being naked in front of each other—it's all a form of torture,' Haykel said."[36]

Beyond the cultural and personal humiliation, there is a deeply theological reason this was so offensive to the prisoners. These men are Muslims and their view of women was what made this form of abuse even more severe.

Muslim culture, ordered by the teachings of the Qur'an, allows for polygamy, slave holding, near instant divorce for men but not for women, and is an almost impossible system for any woman to receive justice even in crimes such as rape. Not every Islamic nation enforces the most oppressive social system on women. In fact, nations such as Jordan and Kuwait have granted women a considerable degree of freedom and personal rights. Those are not considered strict Islamic cultures however. The society established by the Taliban in Afghanistan is the model many Muslim men long to see established in societies around the world. That system would disenfranchise women from the political and educational system. They would be forced to wear veils or to stay at home. They would be subject to public beatings according to the Qur'an.

In his revealing book, *Islam Unveiled*, Robert Spencer describes the thinking of Muslim men regarding women: "...in its instructions about legal testimony (the Qur'an teaches): *'Call in two male witnesses from among you, but if two men cannot be found, then one man and two women whom you judge fit to act as witnesses; so that if either of them commit an error, the other will remember'* (Sura 2:282). That is, one female witness is worth half as much as a man."[37]

Roberts goes on to note that husbands that complain about their wives are given permission to beat them in the Hadiths while complaining wives just get criticized for complaining. In the "Narrated Umar ibn al-Khattab: The Prophet said: A man will not be asked as to why he beat his wife."[38]

Overall, women are viewed as being a creation with lesser dignity and as the legal testimony laws above demonstrate, of lesser intelligence than men. Women are considered objects for men's pleasure. "When they deal with women, they are dealing with a group believed to suffer from severe moral and intellectual shortcomings, not to mention all sorts of physical impurities in a religion obsessed with ritual cleanliness. Women are, moreover, in extra jeopardy of winding up in hell."[39] Women who are made slaves in an Islamic society can be pressed into prostitution for the profit of their male heads of house. "If anyone (ie. Slave owner) compels them (female slaves), God will be forgiving and merciful to them. Qur'an, Sura 24:33. There is no concept of "mutual love and affection" to be found in the Qur'anic law or the Hadiths. "The Qur'an commands a man not to take more than one wife unless he can treat all of them equally, but Muslims have generally understood this to mean equal economic support."[40] This doesn't mean that a Muslim home may be devoid of any mutual respect but that is an infusion of western values rather than Qur'anic teaching.

When American women, even in the context of a prison, exercised power of Muslim men and humiliated them by exposing and then making fun of their genitals, this was indeed striking at the heart of Islam. The thinking of the Islamic male is oriented towards the eternal reward of 70 perpetual virgins there for his pleasure in all eternity and yet here he is being overcome and humiliated by this lesser person, a woman.

The humiliation of the Iraqi prisoners was wrong. The creator endows every human being with dignity. No one can make a reasonable defense for taking advantage of the prisoners at Abu Ghraib. But, does the story of prisoner abuse really deserve the intensity of coverage it is getting in the Western media? On the one hand, yes it does. The story should be covered and discussed for two reasons. The first is that we must be held to a higher level of accountability and demonstrate that our standards for conduct and our respect for the individual, no matter their sex at birth, is based on the inherent dignity of every living person. Second, this should be used to demonstrate the thinking of the Muslim male and the Islamic culture in general.

We continue to present Islamic society through a western filter. When we are told that women will be voting in Afghanistan, we take it as a matter of fact, as if it was legislation that was long overdue. We have to understand that this represents an upheaval in Islamic culture and goes against the grain of religious practices begun in the first century.

On the other hand, it seems the press has abandoned any attempt at a proper perspective related to the prisoner abuse in Iraq. If their concern for human rights was authentic, they would cover the stories in Sudan, China, and many other nations with the same zeal that they covered Abu Ghraib. If their purpose is to discredit the military or the mission in Iraq, then Abu Ghraib is honey for the bees. For the sake of argument, let's assume that the press has an interest in human rights and that any prisoner abuse offends their sense of right and wrong. If anyone was to counter that assumption by suggesting the press is indifferent to right and wrong then we should expect all prisoner abuse everywhere to receive equal treatment. Let's further assume that members of the media consider all men to be equal whether they are prisoners or guards, presidents or peasants. If we make those assumptions, we can expect equal coverage for all prisoner abuse cases. The following stories are a catalog of prisoner abuse. The stories are true. The volume of accounts related here serves to demonstrate just how many prison scandals could be covered if the media was actually outraged by prisoner abuse. Remarkably, most of these will be "news" to you. Keep in mind, these are only a sampling of the prison abuse that occurs every day. Compare these stories to the Abu Ghraib guards actions in Iraq.

Human Rights Watch submitted an extensive report on prison abuse that contained the following excerpt:

> *"California has a history of inappropriate sexual contact between male officers and female prisoners in its women's prisons. In July 1990 the* Orange County Register *ran a series of investigative articles on CIW alleging rape, corruption, and negligent medical care and documenting retaliation against women and correctional employees who spoke out about such practices. According to the* Register, *Harold Delon Anderson, the son of the former CIW warden, Kathleen Anderson, was dismissed in October 1987 amid allegations that he had forced ten incarcerated women to submit to sexual relations with him. Internal investigations and other documentation obtained by the* Register *indicated that Anderson forced some of the women into sexual relations repeatedly, over a period of months or years. Corrections staff reportedly discovered him on three separate instances in 'compromising positions' with prisoners before any disciplinary action was taken. One female corrections officer who exposed Anderson's actions was allegedly threatened and harassed by coworkers. At the time*

the article ran in the Register, *the CDC had treated Anderson's behavior as a personnel matter and had not referred the case to the county prosecutor for a criminal investigation.*

In addition to the cases of rape and attempted rape, we also learned of cases involving sexual assault of prisoners by corrections staff."

In California:

"Corcoran State Prison was being investigated by the FBI because numerous corrections officers — prison guards — were accused of staging inmate fights, sometimes wagering on the outcome and then, when those fights got out of control, of shooting the inmates involved.

The original report in 1997 found a shocking state of affairs. Since Corcoran opened 12 years ago, more than 30 inmates had been shot — eight of them killed — during these fights.

A corps of prison guards wearing black masks were said to often abuse inmates during routine searches. One former officer was convicted of taking a Taser gun to the genitals of a prisoner.

Since 1988, Corcoran Prison's guards have killed eight inmates and wounded scores of others, more than any other prison in the country.

According to both prison guards and inmates, staged battles, commonly known as gladiator fights, became a regular entertainment at Corcoran. Matches were set up as guards selected inmates from rival gangs, and released them one by one into the SHU yard. At least one Corcoran supervisor reportedly amused himself by calling the fights like a ring announcer, and many guards gambled on the bouts."[41]

In India:

"India has the largest population of street children in the world. At least eighteen million children live or work on the streets of urban India, laboring as porters at bus or railway terminals; as mechanics in informal auto-repair shops; as vendors of food, tea, or handmade articles; as street tailors; or as ragpickers, picking through garbage and selling usable materials to local buyers.

Indian street children are routinely detained illegally, beaten and tortured and sometimes killed by police. While it is true that street children are sometimes involved in petty theft, drug trafficking, prostitution and other criminal activities, the police tend to assume that whenever a crime is committed on the street, street children are either involved themselves or know the culprit. Their proximity to a crime is considered reason enough to detain them. This abuse violates both Indian domestic law and international human rights standards." [42]

In a prison in Tennessee:

"Jailers told an inmate, [Mr.]Gooch, it was time for him to be moved from his usual cell to a cell in the jail's booking area. The move was intended as punishment for failing to comply with an officer's orders, according to the government's statement of facts.

Gooch refused to cooperate.
The officers attempted to force Gooch to move.
He still refused.

'One officer held Gooch as another repeatedly and forcefully struck Gooch in his head and upper body in an effort to punish Gooch. The assault continued until Gooch ceased resisting and was

placed into a holding cell,"[43]

In Florida:

"Between July and October, 1999 the Florida correctional medical authority conducted a survey of female prisoners in Florida. Some of the results of that survey include:

More than a third of the female prisoners surveyed reported inappropriate sexual, verbal or physical behavior by male and female staff.

Over half of those surveyed reported having experienced sexual abuse before coming to prison.

More than one third reported that male guards are present when they are in various stages of undress.

More that one third reported that male guards are present when they are showering or using the toilet.[44]

In Colombia:

On April 27, 2000, in what was described as the bloodiest prison conflict in Colombian history, at least twenty-five inmates were killed in Bogotá's Modelo prison. The incident, which pitted rival inmate groups against each other, was sparked by the discovery of a mutilated body stuffed in a sewer pipe.

While the body count from this incident was exceptional, the violence itself was not. As evidenced by a subsequent prison search that resulted in the discovery of two AK-47 assault rifles, eight grenades, dozens of firearms, and several thousand knives, Modelo prison was a mini-arsenal, and violence was frequent. Indeed, some 1,200 Colombian inmates were killed over the past decade, a disproportionate number of them in Modelo prison. "In the four years that I've been in the Modelo I've seen more blood and more death than in all my life of crime," said an inmate there.[45]

In Michigan:

"Two guards at the Macomb County Correctional Facility (Michigan) are facing criminal charges for allowing six inmates to go into the cell of another prisoner, strip him and force him into the hallway." [46]

And finally, at Abu Ghraib, before the Americans arrived, this was the experience of many prisoners.

"Saddam Kamal (who was head of the Special Security Organization) oversaw the torture and execution of thousands of political prisoners. The prison was under the control of the Directorate of General Security (DGS) also known as the Amn al-Amm.

As many as 4000 prisoners were executed at Abu Ghraib Prison in 1984. At least 122 male prisoners were executed at Abu Ghraib prison in February/ March 2000. A further 23 political prisoners were executed there in October 2001.

As of 2001 Abu Ghraib prison, west of Baghdad, may have held as many as 15,000 persons, many of who were subject to torture. Hundreds of Fayli (Shi'a) Kurds and other citizens of Iranian origin, who had disappeared in the early 1980's during the Iran-Iraq war, reportedly were being held incommunicado at the Abu Ghraib prison. Such persons have been detained without charge for close to 2 decades in extremely harsh conditions. Many of the detainees were used as subjects in the country's outlawed experimental chemical and biological weapons programs.

There have been several press reports of mass graves within the perimeter or near the prison, but this is not apparent from imagery alone. Further analysis using ground truth imagery and human sources may help confirm the existence and location of any mass graves."[47]

Where is the comprehensive coverage on prisoner abuse in the United States and around the world? Why are members of Congress and Senators not demanding answers and asking governors to resign over these horrible cases of abuse in their states? Why aren't Senators themselves held accountable for the abuse in their states and Congressmen held accountable for crimes in their districts? Where is the moral outrage over real abuse that injures people and destroys lives rather than guards putting women's panties on a prisoners head or making them create a pyramid while naked? Certainly one does not justify the other but we have to wonder why the media is so selective in their outrage over crimes against humanity. If the suffering of the Muslims held in Iraq was directly related to their humiliation, then the comprehensive coverage provided by the media and the constant flow of pictures of those men naked and ashamed only increased their suffering by displaying their shame before the world over and over again. In trying to humiliate the military and discredit the work of our nation, the press actually did more harm to the Muslim in Iraq than the half dozen soldiers ever could. Exploiting the prisoners for ratings or political commentary represents an abuse by the media that may be on par with the abuse they condemn. The hypocrisy of the media's coverage, ignoring the widespread and consistent abuse of prisoners around the world while fixating on the limited abuse of Iraqi criminals, betrays a bias and perhaps an agenda that should give us cause for concern and press the media to conduct institutional reform. The bias and agenda manifests itself in their willingness to accept worse cases of abuse in American prisons as ordinary and un-newsworthy while viewing the humiliation of prisoners in Abu Ghraib as extraordinary. Clearly there is an antimilitary bias or at least a desire for isolationism that exists either institutionally or subconsciously in the reporters. Since the broadcasts were saturated with the story for months, it appears that the media has an institutional bias that caused them to see an opportunity to discredit the military and the mission in Iraq. Otherwise, there would be equitable treatment or at least, comparisons drawn between trained civilian prison guards and their military counterparts. Fairness requires application of an equal standard to all.

The media has become a small looking glass that can present a distorted view of the world. Americans must regain the ability to discern truth and use the media as a tool for seeing rather than a window for understanding the world. America must regain an understanding of her destiny and the stewardship of Liberty that has been her responsibility to keep for the generations. If not, we will become like Alice in Wonderland, we will believe the unreal is the real, lose the ability to discern the difference, and lose a vision for our national purpose.

AN ANATOMY OF AMERICAN LIBERTY

"Freedom is that faculty that enlarges the usefulness
of all other faculties."
Immanuel Kant

"Our commitment to human rights must be absolute… ; the powerful must not persecute the weak,
and human dignity must be enhanced."
Jimmy Carter, Inaugural January 20, 1977

Eternal vigilance is the price of liberty.
John Philpot Curran, Speech, Dublin

"We must be the great arsenal of democracy."
Franklin D. Roosevelt, December 29, 1940

I am an American, fighting in the forces that guard
my country and our way of life. I am prepared to
give my life in their defense.
*Article 1 From the Code of Conduct of the
U.S. Armed Forces*

One day as Alice was sitting with her sister having nothing to do, she spied a rabbit that happened to check his watch and she heard him declare that he was running late. Alice had a great curiosity about the rabbit and followed him without hesitation down into his hole. The hole continued straight for some time and then suddenly turned down. It was so sudden that Alice couldn't stop herself from tumbling down into what seemed like a very deep well. Once at the bottom, she began a journey that took her far from the sane and peaceful world she had always known and deep into a new normal that was as mysterious as it was dangerous.

Chasing rabbit trails is a common cliché referring to a distraction that takes your attention away from more important tasks. What rabbit trails have Americans taken in our search for a national purpose and vision? Did a rabbit trail lead us to Iraq?

LIVING BY THE RABBIT'S HOLE

Many have wondered if we should be in Iraq. After all, why should Americans care about the politics of Iraqis? For that matter, why should Americans care what politics dominate the Middle East? Shouldn't we leave it to the Iraqis to take care of Saddam Hussein and the terrorists?

Historically Americans have taken an active interest in human suffering around the world. The progress of liberty anywhere was an American concern. John F. Kennedy said, *"Let every nation know, whether it wishes us well or ill, that we shall pay any price, bear any burden, meet any hardship, support any friend, oppose any foe to assure the survival and success of liberty!"* That is a vision for America rarely heard in today's debates.

There is still no unified vision for the war in Iraq. Some of those that once supported the war have become disenchanted. A minority even suggests that the Iraqis were better off under the administration of Saddam Hussein.

The debate centers on our justification for war. The US president suggested that America needed to remove Hussein because he represented a clear and present danger to the United States. He had demonstrated a willingness to use weapons of mass destruction and he couldn't prove he wouldn't use them today. After removing Hussein the weapons of mass destruction were not found. Were they moved to Iran, Syria, or buried in the vast Iraqi desert? The US administration is struggling to explain the war. Some have suggested that the decision to depose Saddam Hussein was more a family feud from 1991 than a strategy to protect America in 2003. There is no lack of speculation. Agreement is much harder to find.

The confusion stems from America's lack of retention and vision. When President George W. Bush took the case for war before the nation, he received widespread support from the nation as well as the Congress. Since then, voices of dissent have emerged and the case for war has become confused. Without weapons of mass destruction Americans wonder if the war was a mistake.

When President Bush addressed the nation on September 20, 2001 he described our vision in these words, *"The advance of human freedom – the great achievement of our time and the great hope of every time– now depends on us. Our nation – this generation – will lift a dark threat of violence from our people and our future. We will not tire, we will not falter, and we will not fail."*

Many Americans have forgotten the President's stirring words of comfort and direction. Many have forgotten the insecurity we all felt in the days after the trade towers fell. Many have forgotten how inspired we were when the President threw the first pitch at Yankee stadium. Many have forgotten the crews that worked night and day to clear the rubble from the trade towers. Life has moved on and left our fears and concerns behind. Now we must recapture a vision for our future. Do we continue the battle we have begun or is it time to thank our soldiers and bring them home?

In the early days of the war, several artist wrote patriotic songs. These songs brought us together and reminded us of the blessings of freedom and liberty. They gave America a unified voice and helped us mourn the early casualties of the war. Darryl Worley wrote a song titled, Have You Forgotten. His words touched the hearts of all Americans. He captured our desire to remember the dead and justify our war efforts.

"I hear people saying we don't need this war
I say there's some things worth fighting for
What about our freedom and this piece of ground
We didn't get to keep 'em by backing down
Now they say we don't realize the mess we're getting in
Before you start your preaching let me ask you
this my friend

Have you forgotten how it felt that day?
To see your homeland under fire
And her people blown away
Have you forgotten when those towers fell?
We had neighbors still inside going thru a living hell
And you say we shouldn't worry 'bout bin Laden
Have you forgotten?"

Americans have moved on with life since September 11, 2001. Have we forgotten more than the individuals that died on that tragic day in September? Have we forgotten the Liberty that our fathers fought and died for? Have we confused liberty with license? Have we cheapened the struggle and commitment of our forefathers by our quest for self-fulfillment? Have we forgotten what liberty means? Our generation is standing at the edge of a rabbit hole. If we fall in, we may never again know the rich blessings of the liberties we now enjoy.

LIBERTY MOVES TO AMERICA

Our pledge contains the phrase, "With liberty and justice for all." Liberty and Justice are separated as two distinct ideas. America is familiar with justice. We seem to be experts at litigation and incarceration. The generations following what news anchor Tom Brokaw dubbed, "The Greatest Generation", of the 1940's and 1950's have lost the concept of liberty. We have majored on justice and personal freedom but somewhere along the way, liberty became a quaint idea from the past. America must regain a love and commitment to liberty. Without liberty, there will be no tomorrow in America.

Liberty is not a law but it does secure the freedoms guaranteed by laws and regulations. Liberty is a paradigm for living. Liberty involves a mutual respect for one another and a commitment to integrity and virtue. Liberty flows from the desires of the heart rather than a judge's bench.

On "I Am An American Day" in 1944, Justice Learned Hand said, *"What do we mean when we say that first of all we seek liberty? I often wonder whether we do not rest our hopes too much upon constitutions, upon laws, and upon courts. These are false hopes; believe me... Liberty lies in the hearts of men and women; when it dies there, no constitution, no law, no court can save it... While it lies there, it needs no constitution, no law, no court to save it."*

Off the coast of New York City, within view of the site of the World Trade Center's destruction, stands the Statue of Liberty. In 1865, French intellectuals opposed to the oppressive regime of Napoleon III were at a small dinner party and happened to discuss their admiration for America's successful establishment of a democratic government and the abolition of slavery at the end of the Civil War. In the course of conversation it was decided that France should create a statue to give to America as a symbol of the two nations shared commitment to Liberty. Frédéric-Auguste Bartholdi would sculpt the beautiful lady and on October 24, 1881, the American ambassador to France, Levi P. Morton, drove the first rivet into the statue. On October 28, 1886, Lady Liberty was unveiled on what would later be called, Liberty Island. The road from the idea germinated first in 1865 to the finished Statue in 1886 was paved with thousands of patriots who sacrificed their own money and labor to deliver the enduring symbol of Liberty to the shores of America. A symbol that European immigrants would gaze at as ship after ship delivered generations of new Americans to the shores of North America.

In all of the years since, families have journeyed to the statue to teach their children the principles of liberty and tour the great statue. Those days truly represent an era that has passed. From September 11, 2001 to August 2004, Lady Liberty was off limits. After August, 2004, only the island itself and her pedestal were open to guests. A generation of elementary age children may not be able to visit Liberty Island in the near future. They might gaze at her only from distant shores. If the island remains open, people will be able to approach her pedestal but standing far beneath her shadow, Americans will not even be able to touch her toes. Liberty will be just beyond their reach. The experience of Lady Liberty is now relegated to television documentaries, museums, and postcards. Eventually, not only will an institutional memory of actual visits to the Lady be lost, but the idea of liberty may be a notion we can only see from the distance and admire as a quaint and mysterious idea of the past. An airplane trip into New York may give you the best view available of Lady Liberty because terrorist threaten to keep Americans away from our national treasures. The decision to limit visits to Liberty Island is practical and strategic; but, does it present us with a real metaphor to understand the dangers that Liberty faces now?

The threat against Liberty is more than a threat against individual lives; it is a threat against living. Our national survival depends on the removal of the threat. Just as we wouldn't feel safe when a forest fire rages only miles from our mountain home, neither can we believe we are safe simply because the threats to Liberty rage in the Middle East and Europe. William Allen White, famed journalist from Kansas said, *"Whenever a free man is in chains we are threatened also. Whoever is fighting for liberty is defending America."* The fight for Liberty has come to our generation. If we turn away from our responsibilites and defer to the United Nations or some other entity, we will condemn our children to forever lose the experience of Liberty.

The modern definition of liberty is usually confused with that of personal rights and priviledge. Abolitionist leader Reverend William Channing understood the difference between personal rights and liberty. He said, *"The spirit of liberty is not as multitudes imagine, jealousy of our own particular rights, but a respect for the rights of others and an unwillingness that any one, should be wronged or trampled underfoot."* In 1944, Justice Learned Hand conveyed the same understanding of liberty. He said, *"And what is this liberty which must lie in the hearts of men and women? It is not the ruthless, the unbridled will; it is not freedom to do as one likes. That is the denial of liberty, and leads straight to its overthrow. A society in which men recognize no check upon their freedom soon becomes a society where freedom is the possession of only a savage few-as we have learned to our sorrow."*

Liberty is freedom from fear and oppresion. Liberty is freedom to think and realize your potential. Liberty is freedom to be righteous in your conduct and benevolence. Liberty secures the individual freedoms we cherish and promotes the peace we so long for. Liberty is our responsibility! Without

Liberty, even personal freedom is meaningless. Inscribed on an old broken piece of metal, known as the Liberty Bell, is a quote from Leviticus 25:10. *"Proclaim Liberty throughout all the land unto all the inhabitants thereof."* Has the liberty bell that once sounded in the hearts of all Americans grown as silent as the relic on display in Philadelphia?

Our nation has always believed that Liberty could break the chains of fear, tyranny, and oppression. Our founding father's vision for liberty has directed our national affairs from our national birth. It compelled us to enter the European wars to liberate nations that had been trampled upon. It even caused brother to fight against brother and father against son to liberate American slaves from the yoke of bondage and deliver to them the same promise of liberty that was secured in the generation before.

THE NERO SYNDROM

Since the release of the first movie in *The Lord of the Rings* trilogy, audiences have enjoyed the mystical lands of Middle Earth. Young people have rediscovered J.R.R. Tolkien's literature and have explored the imagery presented in the series. The Lord of the Rings is full of analogy and metaphor that speaks to our time. J.R.R. Tolkien takes the reader back in time to an age of mythological creatures and men. In those ancient times Rings of Power were made by the Elven-smiths (like blacksmiths), and Sauron (a spiritual conscience that is the essence of evil), the Dark Lord, forged the One Ring. He filled it with his own power so that he could rule all others. Author, Mark Eddy Smith speaks to the spiritual themes in the original book series by Tolkien. One of the more vital themes is that of stewardship. In book three, Gandalf speaks to a character called Denethor and says, *"But all worthy things that are in peril as the world now stands, those are my care. And for my part, I shall not wholly fail of my task, though Gondor (the city of man) should perish, if anything passes through this night that can still grow fair or bear fruit or flower again in days to come. For I also am a steward. Did you not know"?*[48] In the last movie of the trilogy, the city of man is under siege by the demons of the underworld. The king of the City of Men was slow to prepare as he had no appetite for war and thought simply to avoid it by ignoring it. Sloth and distraction do not discourage evil, they only serve to give it opportunity to strike. In Christian scriptures, Satan is the personification of evil. Christians are warned, "Be sober-minded; be watchful, your adversary the devil prowls around like a roaring lion, seeking someone to devour".[49] The king saw the threat when he gazed out at the massive army of demonic Orcs gathered against him. He had not prepared his defenses or called for reinforcements. It was too late. His enemies were already in the field and prepared for battle.

Truth, liberty, and justice always offend evil. Evil can only be content when death, darkness, and fear enslave men. The King's sloth and inaction threatened not only his life but also the freedom of his people and the lives of future generations. Will Americans "fiddle while Rome burns" as Nero is reported to have done and the King of the City of Men did?

AN AMERICAN STEWARDSHIP

The idea of stewardship has been an essential element in America's self-identification throughout her short history. Senator Albert J. Beveridge in a speech before the U.S. Senate in 1900 said, *"He (God) has marked the American people as His chosen Nation to finally lead in the regeneration of the world. This is the divine mission of America, and it holds for us all the profit, all the glory, all the happiness possible to man. We are trustees of the world's progress, guardians of its righteous peace."* These words spoken on another occasion seem to fit the crisis of our time. *"Those who complain [about war] do so in ignorance of the real situation. We attempted a great task with insufficient means; we became impatient that it was not finished before it could fairly be commenced; and I pray we may not add that other element of disaster. We must stay engaged in the work until it is thoroughly and forever done. That is the gravest mistake we could possibly make, and that is the only danger before us."* He finished his speech with these words, *"Pray God that spirit never fails. Pray God the time may never come when Mammon and the love of ease shall so debase our blood that we will fear to shed it for the flag and its imperial destiny."*

Those who attacked us on September 11th didn't attack simply because they want Americans to leave the Middle East. They attacked because they are on a quest to see a different way of life everywhere in the world. A terrorist's only hope for eternal life comes through martyrdom and the murder of infidels. Anyone that disagrees with their interpretation of the tenants of Islam are infidels. Jihadists are threatened by modernization and globalization because those tend to liberate people from oppression. When people are kept isolated and ignorant they can be ruled by tyrants with ease but when common people glimpse freedom, even if it is through the medium of television or internet, the reign of tyranny begins to die. On December 5, 1810 James Madison said, *"It is universally admitted that a well-instructed people alone can be permanently a free people."* With missionary zeal, radical Islamic terrorists spread a form of Islam wherever there is a lack of resistance and seek to destroy anything that would instruct the masses on the concept of liberty and stifle their oppressive rule.

Some Americans struggle with the idea that we are at war because they can not identify a particular country or a singular entity that has declared war on America. They imagine our enemy is more like a street gang or city thugs that use drive-by shootings to disrupt shoppers at the local mall. Unfortunately, like a parasitic plague, our enemy has spread all over the world. Some have gathered in terrorists cells but there are potentially millions more that have yet to decide which side they will take in this global war against the freedom of Man. If Terrorists are able to convince moderate Muslims around the world that the West is a threat to them, by our way of life, and by our understanding of liberty, those moderate Muslims will become terrorists. If those moderate Muslims transition to terrorism, violence will erupt in every nation and in every community no matter how far from the Middle East they live. What is the vision of these terrorists? Their goal is to bring a radical form of Islam to every nation in the world. Nothing short of that will satisfy the most extreme of them. The way of life this form of Islam will provide has not been hidden. Time Magazine reported on the Islamic society installed by the Taliban in Afghanistan. The oppressive nature of Islamic society was exposed after American forces liberated the people of Afghanistan from the Taliban. In Afghanistan, the society terrorists want was displayed for the world to see. "In the streets of Kabul, you can see something these days that has not been glimpsed there for almost five years—women's faces. Now that the Taliban has fled the city, a few brave women have shed the burka—the head-to-toe garment, to Western eyes a kind of body bag for the living, made mandatory by the defeated Taliban leadership. Men sometimes look in astonishment at these faces, as if they were comets or solar eclipses. So do other women. [From their ascendancy to power in 1996 the Taliban sought to transform women from people to property.] They were required to be submissive and invisible. For five years, it almost succeeded."

The vision of these Islamic terrorists is not any different than other tyrants throughout history. They desire to oppress people and exalt themselves. Unable to change governments through free elections that are based on the will of the people, they use fear and violence to disrupt society and intimidate the weak. Violence has become a religious duty in their quest for domination. In Sura 61:4 the Qu'ran teaches the jihadists that, "Truly Allah loves those who fight in His cause in battle array, as if they were a solid cemented structure." This is a tyranny of an insane minority that seek to change America.

LIBERTY MEANS RESPONSIBILITY

The Declaration of Independence is stored in the National Archives. It was drafted by Thomas Jefferson between June 11 and June 28, 1776 and signed by 56 delegates from each of the colonies. It encapsulated the essence of America's character. It remains our most cherished symbol of liberty. The second paragraph reads, *"We hold these truths to be self-evident, that all men are created equal, that they are endowed by their Creator with certain unalienable rights, that among these are Life, Liberty and the pursuit of Happiness."* No distinction is made between men. All men were given the right to Liberty and America has served as the vanguard for truth and liberty since her inception. Thomas Jefferson knew what this commitment to liberty would cost. He said, *"The tree of liberty must be refreshed from time to time, with the blood of patriots and tyrants."* There are times and seasons when men are called upon to defend the liberty that preserves our freedom and way of life. If we do not defend her [Liberty] then we shall certainly loose her. Benjamin Franklin said, *"They that can give up essential liberty to obtain a little temporary safety deserve neither liberty nor safety."* Will America shrink back from our stewardship of Liberty? Will we stand for Liberty when she is threatened anywhere in the world? Are we undetermined to defend the very principle that made our nation great? Liberty is both the theological and political axiom that brought light into an oppressed world and caused the darkness to flee. Now, if the light of liberty is held in low esteem like a candle that has been covered, darkness will take the opportunity to occupy all the space in this world that it once called home.

Walter Lippmann said, *"The war for liberty never ends. One day liberty has to be defended against the power of wealth, on another day against the intrigues of politicians, on another against the dead hand of bureaucrats, on another against the patrioter and the militarist, on another against the profiteer, and then against the hysteria and the passions of the mobs, against obscurantism and stupidity, against the criminal and against the overrighteous. In this campaign every civilized man is enlisted till he dies, and he only has known the full joy of living who somewhere and at some time has struck a decisive blow for the freedom of the human spirit."* Lord Action said, *"The most certain test by which we judge whether a country is really free is the amount of security enjoyed by minorities."*

Where can we refuse to protect liberty? Can we ignore the plight of foreign nations when the people are under oppression and despotic abuse? Can we pretend to love liberty when we will not defend it wherever it is threatened? Perhaps the answer to our questions are found in George Bernard Shaw's observation that *"Liberty means responsibility. That is why most men dread it."*

America was attacked on September 11, 2001 but we have been attacked before. The rest of the terrorist's attacks against America failed to produce the public outrage and fear of future attacks that resulted from the Trade Center's destruction. We were then compelled to go to war. We cannot take revenge against the terrorists or obtain justice for those who were killed. Their lives are gone and only memories remain. We can refuse to be afraid and we can refuse to surrender our liberty to terrorism. We must not step away from our calling in history. We have a steward-ship of liberty and the world depends on our fidelity to our cause.

Patrick Henry addressed the Second Virginia Convention in March 1775. Britain had passed several laws that further restricted the liberty of Bostonians. The colonial leadership had lodged their protest but diplomacy had failed. Henry rose to speak to the crisis. He delivered these immortal words which are as contemporary to our time as his. *"If we wish to be free; if we mean to preserve inviolate those inestimable privileges for which we have been so long contending; if we mean not basely to abandon the noble struggle in which we have been so long engaged, and which we have pledged ourselves never to abandon until the glorious object of our contest be obtained, we must fight! They tell us, sir that we are weak, unable to cope with so formidable an adversary. This is no time for ceremony. The question before the house is nothing less than a question of freedom or slavery. When shall we be stronger? Will it be the next week, or the next year? Will it be when we are totally disarmed, and when a British guard shall be stationed in every house? Shall we gather strength by irres-olution and inaction? Shall we acquire the means of effec-tual resistance by lying supinely on our backs, and hugging the delusive phantom of Hope, until our enemies shall have bound us hand and foot? It is in vain, sir, to extenuate the matter. Gentlemen may cry peace, peace, but there is no peace. The war is actually begun. The next gale that sweeps from the north will bring to our ears the clash of resounding arms. Our brethren are already in the field. What is it that gentlemen wish? What would they have? Is life so dear, or peace so sweet, as to be purchased at the price of chains and slavery? Forbid it, Almighty God! I know not what course others may take, but as for me, give me liberty, or give me death!"*[50]

These stirring words President Woodrow Wilson spoke in 1917 are a fitting conclusion to an anatomy of stewardship.

> *"There are, it may be, many months of fiery trial and sacrifice ahead of us... To such a task we can dedicate our lives and our fortunes, everything that we are and everything that we have, with the pride of those who know that the day will come when America is privileged to spend her blood and her might for the principles that gave her birth and happiness and the peace which she has treasured. God helping her, she can do no other."*

This is only a diagnosis of a national problem. We have neglected the formation of our national character for too long. We have lost a vision for defending our liberty. Instead, we have pursued our personal interests and celebrated our personal achievements. We have sought the accumulation of wealth and the acclaim of our peers. This book ought to be the beginning of a national political and scholastic conversation. If a generation of Americans will reject moral relativism and embrace again the fundamental notions of virtue, character, courage, and liberty we may once again be a light unto the nations. Our laws, schools, technology, and benevolent giving will not secure our nation against the thieves that come in the night. Only vigilance and determination united with a national vision for liberty that is secured for all people will keep our nation safe for generations to come.

Considering our stewardship of liberty, the mission in Iraq is unavoidable and irreversible. Iraq is not a rabbit trail. Our addictions to entertainment and vice are rabbit trails that will lead us to a bottomless pit. We have taken advantage of our liberties to indulge ourselves beyond reason. We have pursued every rabbit trail that suits our fancy and become so lost that we wonder if we can ever get back. If there is a rabbit hole we have fallen into, it is not the pursuit of liberty for people everywhere. It is the self-indulgent lifestyles that have become so common in America. We must find a way off of the rabbit trail and back to a pursuit of liberty before it is lost forever.

> *"Posterity-you will never know how much it has cost my generation to preserve your freedom. I hope you will make good use of it."*
>
> John Quincy Adams

REFLECTIONS IN
THE GLASS

AN ANATOMY OF A
NATION'S CHARACTER

"Men do not differ much about what things they will call evils; they differ enormously about what evils they will call excusable."

G.K. Chesterton

"What a man believes upon grossly insufficient evidence is an index into his desires — desires of which he himself is often unconscious. If a man is offered a fact which goes against his instincts, he will scrutinize it closely, and unless the evidence is overwhelming, he will refuse to believe it. If, on the other hand, he is offered something which affords a reason for acting in accordance to his instincts, he will accept it even on the slightest evidence. The origin of myths is explained in this way."

Bertrand Russell

> "To every generation there comes that defining
> moment and if it is squandered, the chain of events
> is long and painful."
>
> *Ravi Zacharias*

Soon after the news and pictures of prisoner abuse flooded the media, unclassified portions of a detailed report by Major General Antonio M. Taguba was released. The Washington Post reported that when asked by a Senate committee on May 11, 2004 how the abuse of prisoners could have happened, General Taguba surmised that it was a lack of discipline, training, and supervision. He clarified the Army's official position on prisoner treatment when he noted that he could not find orders that would direct soldiers to conduct abusive interrogations with the prisoners. He blamed a *"failure of leadership"* for the problem but said he found no evidence that the soldiers who committed the mistreatment of the prisoners had acted on orders from commanders or supervisors. "I believe that they did it on their own volition and I believe that they collaborated with several (military intelligence) interrogators at the lower level."

Army Field Manual 34-52 lists some 17 interrogation techniques approved for use by Army interrogation specialists. In December 2002 the Secretary of Defense responded affirmatively to an October 2002 request to use 16 additional interrogation methods at Guantanamo. That approval was largely rescinded in January 2003. Any aggressive techniques used from that point required his direct and personal approval. A study group was erected to recommend a revised list of interrogation methods. That list was released in April 2003. Already, word was coming from Afghanistan that other techniques were being explored and as a result, there was some confusion in the intelligence community about what techniques were proper and which were forbidden. Iraq inherited the process being refined in both

Guantanamo and Afghanistan when Major General Geoffrey Miller presented the Secretary of Defense policy to the commanders in Iraq. In September 2003, Lieutenant Ricardo Sanchez signed a memorandum authorizing additional interrogation techniques for use in Iraqi prisons. All of these changes and revisions in search of a perfect policy resulted in a broad interpretation of the several policies issued from different sources. Additionally, attempts to classify prisoners as either criminals, Enemy Prisoners of War, or Unlawful Combatants further confused who should be treated by what standard of interrogation techniques. The 800th MP Brigade had assumed responsibility for the prisons in June and July of 2003. Obviously, they were operating in a changing intelligence environment with new directives and guidance being issued while operations were ongoing. Even then, the 800th was responsible for detention operations and the 205th Military Intelligence Brigade was responsible for interrogations, yet it is soldiers of the 800th MP Brigade posed with the Iraqis in the photos. Even after admitting that command guidance and official policy were confusing, none of the conduct displayed in the pictures is on an approved list in any theater of military operations. Was this abuse the result of institutional confusion, misleading orders, or unchecked depravity that has been stripped of moral guidance and the natural sense of right and wrong. If this is not a case of official misconduct, then what paths did these soldiers take to develop a character willing to abuse other human beings without permission or cause? Who or what do we blame for Abu Ghraib?

YOU WON'T LIKE THE ANSWER TO THE QUESTION

Following General Taguba's report to the Senate Committee, Sen. Carl M. Levin (D-Mich.), ranking Democrat on the committee said, *"The despicable actions described in General Taguba's report not only reek of abuse, they reek of an organized effort and methodical preparation for interrogation."* He said the collars used on prisoners, the military dogs that intimidated and bit them and the cameras that photographed them in sexually compromising positions *"did not suddenly appear out of thin air"* and that the abuses *"were not the spontaneous actions of lower-ranking enlisted personnel who lacked the proper supervision." Rather, Levin said, "These attempts to extract information from prisoners by abusive and degradation were planned and suggested by others."*[51] The senator's allegations remain unsubstantiated and aim to assign blame to individual leaders in the military or perhaps to indict the military system. Where do we assign blame if the military leadership never directed that prisoners should be abused? Will prosecuting the leadership fix the problem? Was this abuse designed and ordered by leaders in the military or was it the spontaneous actions of isolated and inexperienced young soldiers? There is a broader question of culpability that must be addressed. When the individual soldiers who abused the prisoners have been punished for their actions and the leadership has been reprimanded and removed, can we dismiss this issue and consider the case closed? Was the cause of the prisoner abuse unique to the command and environment of Abu Ghraib or do the conditions exist in America for it to happen again?

Growing up, I was taught that my actions were a reflection on my parents. That means that our parents are the architects of our character. One of the Ten Commandments requires us to honor our parents. That is usually taken to mean that we should be respectful towards them but it is much more. We are to respect their persons and also their teaching. It is dishonorable to condemn our parents teaching by rejecting it and adopting some ethical system foreign to our family. Of course, this command was given in the context of families guided by the unchanging law of God.

Today, we have forfeited the opportunity to form our

children's character. Given the opportunity to raise our children to respect life, we have taught them that life is only valuable when it is productive. Character formation has given way to tolerance. Virtue has been replaced by personal values and those values are not regulated by anything but personal convictions and the restraints of law. Abu Ghraib is the fruit of our fields of labor. Entertainment and self-gratification have become the highest attainments in life. Why are we surprised to see our values lived out in a new generation? Why did we abandon our calling to sculpt the characters of our children and teach them that values are guided by virtues which are informed by a law established not by man but by God? We have substituted godliness with indulgence and selflessness with selfishness thus proving the teaching from Proverbs 28, *"If you desert God's law you're free to embrace depravity."*[52] Our children are the casualties of our cultural war against the law of God. These are the two Americas at war to define the essence of morality. One defends a morality based on the extrinsic law presented by God to man. The other desires a morality that is guided by the consensus of opinion. This war has a battlefield and Abu Ghraib is evidence of the fight.

ENTERTAINMENT IS UGLY IN REAL LIFE

Childhood is a precious time. Children are a gift from God and their innocence should be protected and nurtured. Dr. David Elkind warned America that we were pressing our children to grow up to quick. In his landmark book, *THE HURRIED CHILD* Elkind said, *"The pressure to grow up fast, to achieve early is very great in middle-class America. There is no room today for the 'late bloomer' ... Children have to achieve success early or they are regarded as losers."* Elkind's concerns now dominate education philosophies in America. Children are encouraged to enjoy their childhood and leave adult issues for the later years. Children learn to love their youth and appreciate the freedom and license it affords them. Carnal behaviors that adults condemn are considered unavoidable actions every youth should be expected to enjoy. Hence, abstinence instruction is considered folly while contraception is considered a wise choice. Our children are ushered into a *Brave New World* while their custodians watch syndicated reruns of favorite programs. Instead of listening to the promise of Proverbs 22 that says, *"Point your kids in the right direction, when they're old they won't be lost."*[53] We have left them to find their own way. In matters of faith, parents often say they prefer to let their children choose for themselves what they should believe. In matters of vocation, rewards and ease are the strongest criteria to consider. Children are virtually taught irresponsibility. Food is placed on the table by adults, transportation is provided by adults, shelter is provided by adults, and technology provides entertainment and companionship. Everything is provided and sacrifices are made by adults. No wonder the toy store, Toys-R-Us, has used a commercial jingle with the words, *"I don't want to grow up, I'm a Toys-R-Us Kid..."* Who wants to grow up and lose all the fun of life? Proverbs 21 warns, *"You're addicted to thrills? What an empty life! The pursuit of pleasure is never satisfied."*[54] There is no positive vision for adulthood taught in America anymore. Becoming a man is chauvinistic and motherhood is a distraction from a successful career. Most kids believe growing up is a bane and a curse rather than a blessing. True, the driver's license and the freedom are tempting but not the responsibilities of adulthood. Movies reflect the desire we have to be free from the burdens of adulthood. In 1988 Penny Marshall directed Tom Hanks in a movie called BIG. Hanks played a young boy that made a wish to be an adult and overnight he grew into an adult but retained his childish mind. In April 2004 the movie,

"13 Going on 30" was released. It was directed by Gary Winick and starred Jennifer Garner and Mark Ruffalo. This romantic comedy presented a young girl near to her 13th birthday. All she wanted for her birthday was to be pretty and popular. Her wish came true, but with one catch... it's 17 years later and she's a 13-year-old trapped inside a 30-year-old's body. She skipped the hardening influence of her teen years and treats people with the innocent and unspoiled optimism of a 13-year-old girl. The movie shows how life can make people bitter and leaves us all feeling that we should soften up and care for one another a little bit more as we did in our childhood years. There is another side to the story that is not so funny. Skipping the teen years may avoid the trauma of puberty and teasing by peers but it also bypasses the life experiences that make us mature. Adolescence is presented as the most virtuous time of life. Maturing is presented as the physical process of aging. In fact, those in the movie who lived through the years she skipped are unhappy and unfulfilled. The movie is funny on screen, but what happens when it is an accepted paradigm for living? Is immaturity a virtue and is it as much fun in real life as it is portrayed on screen?

Personal maturity and character formation must be factors considered at Abu Ghraib. Americans have institutionalized immaturity on college campuses and in television sitcoms. The *Waltons* and *Little House on the Prairie* are out and *Sex in the City* and *Desperate Housewives* are in.

The Taguba report notes the inexplicable lack of moral restraint and presents a pessimistic picture of psychological and particularly moral maturity at Abu Ghraib:

"Between October and December 2003, at the Abu Ghraib Confinement Facility (BCCF), numerous incidents of sadistic, blatant, and wanton criminal abuses

were inflicted on several detainees. This systemic and illegal abuse of detainees was intentionally perpetrated by several members of the military police guard force. Detailed witness statements and the discovery of extremely graphic photographic evidence substantiated the allegations of abuse. Specifically, on 24 November 2003, Specialist Army Specialist Luciana Spencer, 205th Military Intelligence Brigade, sought to degrade a detainee by having him strip and returned to cell naked.

General Taguba listed numerous offences and acts of humiliation committed by American soldiers:

"Punching, slapping, and kicking detainees; jumping on their naked feet; videotaping and photographing naked male and female detainees; forcing detainees to remove their clothing and keeping them naked for several days at a time; forcing naked male detainees to wear women's underwear; forcing groups of male detainees to masturbate themselves while being photographed and videotaped; arranging naked male detainees in a pile and then jumping on them; positioning a naked detainee on a MRE Box, with a sandbag on his head, and attaching wires to his fingers, toes, and penis to simulate electric torture; Writing 'I am a Rapest' (sic) on the leg of a detainee alleged to have forcibly raped a 15-year old fellow detainee, and then photographing him naked; placing a dog chain or strap around a naked detainee's neck and having a female Soldier pose for a picture; a male guard allegedly had sex with a female detainee; military working dogs (without muzzles) were used to intimidate and frighten detainees, and in at least one case the dog bit and severely injured a detainee."[55]

On January 27, 2004 Investigators interviewed Army Specialist Jeremy Sivits. He served in the 372nd MP Company and was a prison guard at Abu Ghraib. In the investigative interview he provided a first-hand account of his actions as well as Staff Sergeant Ivan Frederick, Sergeant Javal Davis, Corporal Charles Grainer, Specialist Sabrina Harman and Private Lynndie England. Sivits claimed that Staff Sergeant Frederick invited him to go to the "hard site". The hard site was a detainee holding area with limited visibility from other areas in the prison. He mentioned that some new detainees had arrived and he wanted to go down and mess with them. When Sergeant Javal S. Davis was asked why the rules at the hard site were different than the rest of the prison, Sergeant Davis replied: "The rest of the wings hold regular prisoners and 1A/B [the hard site] are Military Intelligence (MI) holds."[56]

When they arrived at the hard site, the detainees were stacked into a pile on the floor. Sergeant Davis then ran across the room and jumped into the middle of the piled detainees. Then Corporal Granier invited Specialist Wisdom to join them in their harassment of the prisoners. Davis continued to escalate the abuse by stomping on the fingers and toes of the detainees. Sergeant First Class Snyder told Davis to stop. Davis left after the reprimand by Sergeant Snyder. Snyder's scolding discouraged the rest of the guards as well. The type of abuse shifted from physical to psychological. Grainer and Frederick proceeded to have the detainees strip off their jump suits. The detainees had sandbags over their heads the entire time. This added to the prisoner's psychological stress and in a strange twist, kept the guards from violating the Geneva Convention's prohibitions on taking photos of prisoner's faces. Grainer then escalated the abuse further by inexplicably striking a detainee's head with his fist. He struck him hard enough to knock the prisoner unconscious. Grainer checked him to make sure he was not seriously injured and then complained about hurting his hand on the detainee's head. After a couple of minutes Grainer moved over to the pile of detainees that were still clothed and climbed on them to have his picture taken by Sivits. Staff Sergeant Frederick then struck one of the detainees in the chest with a closed fist. The detainee began to struggle for breath. In his October 2004 testimony, Frederick was asked whether he believed the actions and pictures were "indecent." Frederick agreed that they were but tried to justify it by redefining the actions as humiliation rather than indecent. He blamed the U.S. military commanders for the abuse, suggesting he had been given no training and no support for the mission at Abu Ghraib. His lack of accountability, at least in his own mind, creates the impression that he is either not capable of moral thoughts and actions or is committed to immoral thoughts and actions unless constrained by the law. At the very least, that he and the other prison guards lacked a basic respect for the prisoners as human beings and they lacked an instinct for preserving their lives. Their thinking can only be described as confused. One minute the guards were abusing prisoners and then the next, Frederick called a medic to check the detainee for injuries. This duplicitous care and contempt creates a confusing psychological profile.

After calling for medical attention, Frederick ordered the rest of the detainees to strip down and put sandbags on their heads. Grainer stacked them into the pyramid structure that was broadcast so prominently on the news. Their antics began to gravitate towards sexual deviance and exploitation. They tried to get the detainees to stimulate themselves. At first the prisoners didn't understand but after some instruction from the guards, they began to feign masturbation. After about five minutes Frederick told them to stop and then moved them against the wall. Grainer then positioned one of the detainees on his knees in front of another detainee to simulate oral sex. The two females involved, Specialists Harmon and Private England took advantage of this time to have their pictures taken with their thumbs stuck up in the air as if gesturing to the detainee's gentiles. The abusive treatment of the prisoners falls into three categories; physical violence, sexual exploitation, and psychological terror. Each of these categories of abuse feeds the abuser's ego.

THE DANGERS IN TAKING CARE OF NUMBER ONE, OR SELF LOVE

Soldiers deployed in a war often develop a sense of helplessness and isolation. According to the results of a study posted on a forensic psychology website, feelings of insignificance or neglect may lead to aggressive and argumentative speech, passive manipulation of a situation, or actual physical attack. These are psychologically immature efforts to reestablish control and a chosen self-image. This is the route taken by the narcissist. It is as if they are afraid of non-existence. Only by being important or recognized, even if they have to imagine it to be true, are they sure they are alive. The official definition of a Narcissist is a person: *"who shows a pattern of traits and behaviors pointing to an infatuation and obsession with one's self to the exclusion of all others and the egotistic and ruthless pursuit of one's gratification, dominance and ambition."* In other words, the Narcissist is concerned primarily with their ego. Despite whatever the world around them may say, they will create a belief about themselves that is beyond criticism and when the narcissism becomes extreme, beyond any governing authority. They can potentially become a law unto themselves. That is what the world saw manifest at Abu Ghraib. Immature adults, used manipulation, humiliation, sexual exploitation and sexual gratification to reassure themselves of their own worth. Their concern for image, reputation, or self worth took a priority even above concerns for health and pleasure. While they are often pitied because of their depressed personalities, research shows that a narcissist is someone with a high self esteem rather than a low self esteem.

"Previous debates on what personality constructs lead to aggressive responses towards personal criticism have long focused on levels of Self-Esteem. The original belief was that low self-esteem underlies violence. With this theory violent offenders such as bullies and rapists were shown as low esteem individuals who acted aggressively to raise there self esteem. However, the scientific world has for quite a while believed that high self-esteem is actually the cause of aggression. In this case, violent individuals have inflated senses of self. When this unstable self-esteem was challenged the high esteemed individual would act violently to re-establish their previously high esteem. For example, a man who feels he has lost power and control in the home (i.e. from losing his job) may turn to violence against his wife or children to regain his lost power. This suggests that previous esteem research that indicated high self esteem as being the primary link behind aggression may not have been actually looking at self esteem levels. Rather, this study shows that narcissism is the key trait. Unlike high self esteem theories, the Narcissist approach does not believe that violent individuals themselves believe they have high self-esteem. However, such individuals feel superior to others and feel that they should have higher esteem then others.[57]

What we saw at Abu Ghraib was self-indulgence without regard to law or human dignity. Lost in the moment, the soldiers refused to consider the legal or moral consequences of their actions. The pictures that show American soldiers at ease with the abuse and taking pleasure in their dominance over their captives demonstrate a lack of respect not only for the law, but for humanity. They had lost their moral bearings because of a lack of intrinsic moral development and commitment to anything outside of themselves, including the law.

COMMON AGREEMENT ON RIGHT AND WRONG

Moral theorists have often defined humanity's common agreement on right and wrong as "Natural Law." There are two senses of Natural Law. The first is the law that governs nature. By that we mean gravity, the sun rise, the tides, and the seasons. These are set and we depend on them for balance in nature. We can't live without them. The second sense of natural law promotes the idea that the moral standards governing human behavior are, in some sense, objectively derived from the nature of human beings. That explains why murder, stealing, and lying are against the law in nearly every culture and in almost every time. The laws that govern nature bind the entire animal kingdom. Fish must live in water and mammals must breath the air. While man is bound by the same laws of nature, he has a more sophisticated morality than other animals. Man has used his moral nature to construct societies that reflect a respect for the dignity of life and the civility of relationships. Theologians have taught that the law common to all men regardless of their religious beliefs is evidence of a divine hand in creation. Evolutionists have struggled to explain the common moral development of man apart from a divine influence.

In William G. T Shedd's *Dogmatic Theology,* he writes,

"Revelation in its general and wide signification is any species of knowledge of which God is the ultimate

source and cause. In this sense, all that man knows intuitively is revealed to him; for even his axiomatic knowledge does not originate from himself independently and apart from his Creator. All that he knows in this manner, he knows through his intellect, and this intellect is the workmanship of God. Man cognizes in accordance with the laws of human intelligence, and these laws are established by his maker."[58]

Now, man has divorced himself from his maker and has begun to see himself above the natural law, or as it is normally called, the *moral law*. Since this has happened, men have become a law unto themselves. Any common notion of right and wrong that is consistent between generations and cultures is rejected and a system of self indulgence takes it's place. How was the moral progress of man arrested and where did a strange new vision of morality and ethics develop?

MORALITY IN AN ELECTRONIC AGE

Children growing up in the late 1980's and 1990's have been raised on audio visual programming, internet, and video games. Homes and classrooms alike use video for instruction and distraction. TVs and video games may work as a baby-sitter but they actually work counter to educational goals. Most reputable psychological testing demonstrates that the constant stimulation from external media stunts the development of thinking skills and keeps a persons thinking immature. It also robs young adults of a personal value system. Instead of living by a personal ethic, they emulate the programs they watch and speak the words they hear on TV and in music. When you consider networks like MTV and shows like Sex in the City, we shouldn't have to wonder where the behaviors of Abu Ghraib were learned.

The soldiers at Abu Ghraib struggled with a lack of external stimulation. When they searched themselves for substance, they found a strange and uncomfortable silence. Deprived of their electronic distractions, they acted out what was usually saw played out on the screens of TVs and the internet.

When I traveled to the field for military exercises with the 101st Airborne, I anticipated being alone and unoccupied for the first few days. The soldiers all felt good and were oblivious to any issues they needed to talk about with the chaplain. After three or four days, soldiers began to walk over and sit down close to me. They began to ask questions about the meaning of life, the role of a husband or wife in a relationship, their struggle to find meaning in life and their search for God. Only after they were deprived of noise and entertainment for a few days did they begin to search for a deeper meaning in life. The soldiers of Abu Ghraib were no different.

Silence was the topic of an address given at a student banquet for Westminster Theological Seminary students in 1967. The speaker noted that in the biblical account of the end of time, seals are opened on a great book and when the seventh seal was broken open, there was a silence in all of heaven for about thirty minutes. The speaker draws a sharp distinction between sounds of nature and noise.

"There is a qualitative difference between the screech of auto brakes, the roar and throb of electric motors, the din of heavy roadway construction, and a difference there from the insistent hum of locusts in the night..." "Silence gives a person room to move around in oneself, presents a reserve for regrouping one's forces; instead of needing to keep on responding outwardly, a person can in silence, consciously or subconsciously, concentrate on ordering one's

past thoughts, intentions, desires, one's present makeup..." "The truth is, people do try naturally to escape facing the ultimate questions (silence brings) and prefer to live, day in night out, as if who they are and why is sufficiently taken care of not to need reflect on the matter. Long ago the mystical saint Augustine chided others, somewhere in his Confessions, for traveling abroad while leaving themselves undiscovered." "It would not be hard to make a case that the maximum of machine-made noise people have in their hands today is used – teenagers hugging blaring transistor radios to their breasts, adults fastened fascinatedly to the smoky blue screen is used wittingly or not to avoid the silence which is an ordinance of creation inviting one to self-knowledge. Because the modern person seems bent on ruining the opportunities of silence to know one's self and thus runs from God-knowledge too, it is no wonder a Western civilized trend seems to be toward a youth of frenetic movement, middle age of luxurious boredom and an old age of operations and medical complaint, rather than a Christian joy, leadership, and elderly wisdom."[59]

Deprived of a lifetime of character development, a present source for answers and the ceaseless noise and distraction of entertainment, the soldiers of the 327th MP Company turned to the prisoners for distraction and relief.

The investigator asked Sivits to describe the soldier's attitudes during this incident. Each of the soldiers seemed to have lost their individual discretions and became lost in what Aldous Huxley describes as a *"Herd Mentality"*. "Herd mentality" is a term that describes an irrational sentiment that directs individual behavior based on the behavior of others. 'Herd mentality' is often used describe an irrational sentiment that hits the financial market. People will tend to behave as they perceive others do and sell their stocks and portfolios when there is no logical reason. Herds provide a sense of anonymity and safety. Going along with a group consensus seems to release an individual from an obligation to follow personal convictions. Before the young MP's went to Iraq, their behavior reflected the values and social norms of the small communities they lived in. Once in Iraq, they were removed from frequent contact with the chain of command and moral prohibitions. Their behavior changed and the ethical boundaries evaporated. They seem to have possessed no internal barometer to discern right from wrong. Moral relativism came into full bloom just as they have been taught it in a morally relativistic society. A society that claims truth depends on the individual. A society that has adopted the motto: *"What's true for you isn't true for me"*.

Sivits described Grainer as joking and laughing while Frederick quietly watched. Private Lynndie England laughed at each of the different incidents while Specialist Harmon reacted with a mixture of nervous laughter and disgust. She participated by unceremoniously writing the word "rapist" with a dry erase marker on one of the detainee's legs. The detainee had an official record of committing rape. Sivits confessed that he was laughing during the incident as well despite his personal feelings of disgust. As he reflected on his reaction later, he related that he did not find any of it funny now. That is consistent with a "Herd Mentality". When individual reservations are set aside and the individual runs with the herd, he participates in actions he otherwise wouldn't condone. This also explains why their family finds the actions of the soldiers so inconsistent with their upbringing.

When the interviewer asked him directly if he felt the incident was wrong he said that all of the incidents were wrong. When he was asked why they were wrong he confessed he knew mistreating prisoners was against the Geneva Convention. Sivits did not report the incident to his chain of command because he was told not to by Grainer and the others who participated.

Several facts have emerged. The chain of command was not informed of the abuse. Therefore, while punishing the chain of command is always required because leaders are always held responsible for the actions of their subordinates; to scapegoat the leadership and believe that we have solved the institutional and societal problem is a mistake. The American soldiers laughing at the humiliation and abuse of the Iraqis demonstrate a disturbing lack of individual moral development and cooperate ethical clarity. In fact, their animalistic behavior may betray a retarded ethical system or a complete lack of moral conscience. Their behavior prior to their deployment to Abu Ghraib compared to their treatment of the prisoners in Iraq demonstrates a frightening development of moral relativism. Good behavior occurs in situations where a majority upholds moral law but when the attending population relaxes their commitment to moral law, the absence of personal virtue becomes apparent. Sorrow is evidenced only during the legal proceedings. Sorrow is connected with the accused soldier's personal misfortune rather than the suffering and misfortune of others.

WHO ARE THE SOLDIERS OF ABU GHRAIB?

The facts in the prisoner abuse at Abu Ghraib are clear and the pictures that were taken seem to support the story given by Sivits. After reading what these soldiers did, we must wonder what sort of monsters they must have been all of their lives. Surprisingly, none of the soldiers involved have records that would indicate this could happen. Specials Charles Granier was 35 years old when he was sent to Abu Ghraib. He joined the Marines in 1988 after completing high school and still sports a tattoo featuring the Marines' eagle emblem and the letters USMC on his right arm. After leaving the Marines he worked as a prison guard at a high maximum-security state prison in Greene County, Pennsylvania when he was not in military uniform. Friends and neighbors know him as a hard working man that always took time to care for his children ages 13 and 11. He was divorced in 1997 and joined the Army Reserves to try and better himself. In 2001, his wife filed an affidavit claiming that he had come to her house and dragged her by the hair down the hall of her home. When neighbors heard about the accusations against him for prisoner abuse, they found it hard to believe. They suggested he must have been following orders from those in authority.

Private Lynndie England lived in the small town of Fort Ashby, West Virginia, population 1,354. She is the daughter of a CSX railroad worker from Fort Ashby, a remote and quiet West Virginia town. The median age in Fort Ashby is 38.7 years and the median household income in 2000 was $32,375. A home in Fort Ashby costs around $86,900 in 2000. The community is 98.4% white. The unemployment rate and the college graduate rate are both well below the state average. Private England was 21 years old when the abuses at Abu Ghraib occurred. She joined the Army Reserves while she was still a high school student and married when she was 19 years old. The marriage lasted only a year. She worked the night shift at a chicken processing plant a full hour from her home. She wanted to go to college and work as a meteorologist. While she was serving in Iraq, she became romantically involved with Granier and she became pregnant. Both England and Granier feature prominently in pictures taken of naked Iraqi men positioned in humiliating poses. Her family and friends claim she was only visiting Granier in the inmate section when the abuses occurred and she was not a prison guard at all. They claim she was just in the wrong place at the wrong time. Puzzled to explain England's lewd behavior, former Staff Sergeant and fellow Reservist, Tanya Vargas described Lynndie England as quiet and reserved. Her friend Destiny Goin told The Washington Post, "It just makes me laugh because that is not Lynn. She wouldn't pull a dog by its neck, let alone drag a human being." Her mother, Terrie England insisted in a CBS interview that her daughter is innocent because, "She has more values than that! She is a good girl." Her sister Jessica told ABC news on May 13, 2004 that she is convinced England was taken advantage of by her superiors. The family is at a loss to explain the pictures of England showing her smiling with a cigarette hanging from her mouth as she points at a naked mans genitals and another showing her holding a leash attached to a naked man lying on the floor. Kenneth England, her father suggests that the Army is just looking for scapegoats.

On May 5, 2004, attempting to quell the outrage in the Muslim communities over the abuse, President Bush spoke on Arab TV assuring those listening that "people will be held to account" for the "horrible" and "abhorrent abuses." Bush was passionate to make sure the Arab world knew that these few soldiers did not represent America. "What took place in that prison does not represent the America that I know." Where did these people come from then? Why is there so much inconsistency between a person's background and their conduct? Why is everyone closest to those who commit such vile acts against humanity so surprised to learn about the misdeeds of a family member or a neighbor?

It is rare to find a young American that has not been required to read the "Lord of the Flies" at some point prior to graduating from High School. William Golding authored the book in 1954 when American values were still solidly conservative and overtly Christian. The book describes the exploits of a number of children who undergo a societal transformation from ethical to barbaric. Lord of the Flies teaches that without an inner commitment to unchanging principles, we will become savages with little value placed on life.

In a commentary on the Lord of the Flies Scott Gerenser suggests "William Golding presented numerous themes and basic ideas that give the reader something to think about. One of the most basic and obvious themes is that society holds everyone together, and without these conditions, our ideals, values, and the basics of right and wrong are lost. Without society's rigid rules, anarchy and savagery will emerge.

Golding is also showing that morals come directly from our surroundings, and if there is no civilization around us, we will lose these values.

Gerenser's explaination is framed in a humanistic inter-pretation of human motivations and moral development. He presupposes that society is defined differently from place to place and time to time. In every society, societal architects strive to mold civilization to in their own image. Terrorists use violence to influence culture. The American Civil Liberties Union (ACLU) uses litigation to change societal norms. Christians use rhetoric to present theological precepts as an appeal to a natural law given by a divine authority to influence society's world and life views. Other groups from veterans to Planned Parenthood seek to pass legislation to force society to accept their views of right and wrong. Sociologists observe and report trends in civilization but have no means to direct it. Unless theology directs a civilization, there will always be chaos. Any foundation established in time rather than in eternity will shift from generation to generation. Enduring values and a permanent vision for right and wrong can only come from theology. Theology teaches that we should treat others as we would want to be treated. It teaches us to love God with all our heart and mind and to love others as we do ourselves. It teaches us to turn the other cheek rather than seek litigation and extortion for every misdeed we discover. It teaches us to

pray for our enemies rather than destroy ourselves by culti-
vating hatred. Compare these enduring principles to those
presented in a humanistic society like William Golding's
"The Lord of the Flies".

According to Gerenser, other themes in "The Lord of the
Flies" include:

- People will abuse power when it is not earned.
- When given a chance, people often single out
  another to degrade to improve their own security.
- You can only cover up inner savagery so long before
  it breaks out, given the right situation.
- It's better to examine the consequences of a decision
  before you make it than to discover them afterward.
- The fear of the unknown can be a powerful force,
  which can turn you to either insight or hysteria."[60]

Golding's humanistic presentation of man is pessimistic
at best. He seemed to have little faith that anything but law
and the threat of punishment would restrain man from
becoming a savage. Without an internal theological barometer for judging right from wrong, people will sacrifice
anything and anyone for their own advancement.
Unfortunately, Golding's fictitious prophecy is today's reality. In February 2004, Nicole Townes, a 12 year old girl,
attended a friend's birthday party. While she was there a
little boy accepted a dare to kiss her on the check. The kisser
was the boyfriend of the birthday girl and her mother, 36
years old, urged her daughter to handle her business.
"Nicole was scratched, pummeled, kicked, and stomped by
as many as six women and girls, police said. She was in a
coma for nearly three weeks and her family said that she
may have permanent brain damage."[61]

We must admit that there has been a serious decline in
America's moral and ethical climate. "In a 1994 issue of the

Heritage Foundation's Policy Review, former Secretary of Education, William J. Bennett, compared and contrasted the concerns of teachers in two different generations: '*In 1940 teachers identified [the top problems in America's schools] as talking out of turn, chewing gum, making noise, running in the hall, cutting in line, dress code infractions, and littering. When asked the same question in 1990, teachers identified drug abuse, alcohol abuse, pregnancy, suicide, rape, robbery, and assault.*" Bennett also made the observation that between 1960 and *1990 "there has been a 560 percent increase in violent crime; more than a 400 percent increase in illegitimate births, a quadrupling in divorces, a tripling of the percentage of children living in single-parent homes, more than a 200 percent increase in the teenage suicide rate, and a drop of 75 points in the average SAT scores of high-school students.*"

Few subjects have received more attention over the last twenty-five years than the declining moral literacy in our society. In our schools, no doubt out of good intentions, we shifted from teaching character formation to values clarification while at the same time refusing the idea that there are moral absolutes. Humanistic thinking prefers to see every individual as an autonomous and personally sovereign person. Each person unfettered by any external theological or moral authority except the law of the land. Yet law is itself based on some other moral authority. Without agreement on a theological or even a lasting philosophical foundation for our ethics and morality, the proverbial lights are on in the house of morality but no one is home. Now we have moved on to a plethora of new but confused agendas, and we are genuinely nonplused by all of the practical consequences. Our children are not only more lawless in school, as evidenced by the astounding increase in crime, but are too often without any apparent moral consciousness regarding their actions.[62] J.C. Ryle describes youth as *the planting time* of life. He contends that you can judge the type of person a young man or woman will be by the character they demonstrate while they are young just as you can tell what a fall harvest will produce by observing it in the spring. Habits of good or evil are daily strengthening in your hearts.[63]

William Bennett along with other social critics and political theorists have argued that this radical change in our culture and its institutions is not merely the result of misguided public policies, though they no doubt have made a contribution, but rather, they are the result of a change in how people think about morality and civic culture. Instead of thinking that ethical virtue and vice are based on unchanging moral laws that transcend cultures and individuals, many people today embrace moral relativism. This views morality as relative to cultures and/or individuals. According to this view, moral law is mutable, able to be changed by the collective political and social will."[64] Virtue has come unhinged from any external and authoritative truth. We have shifted from an open system of thought to a closed system. An open system allows for the mystery of God, the creative influence of man, miracles, and even for moral initiative and first causes *[First cause is used to argue for the assistance of God as the creator]*. An open system is not limited by simple cause and effect. Life was not viewed so mechanistically that we have to be limited by the factors that determine us such as genetics and environment. Those limitations produce a nation of victims that cannot dream or truly love. A closed philosophical system based on the idea of cause and effect has resulted in pragmatism. Pragmatism has displaced virtue and is embraced by most Americans and seems to dominate business and personal strategies. It produces a people of experience rather than thought. *"When people began to think in this way, there was no place for God or for man as man. When psychology and social science were made a part of a closed cause-and-effect system, along with physics, astronomy and chemistry, it was not only God who died. Man died. And within this framework love died. There is no place for love in a totally closed cause-and-effect system. There is no place for morals in a totally closed cause-and-effect system. There is no place for the freedom of people in a totally closed cause-and-effect system. Man becomes a zero. People and all they do become only a part of the machinery."*[65] *"This is the first time that a civilization has existed that, to a significant extent, does not believe in an objective right and wrong."*[66] Yet, we want to judge right and wrong when we are offended or embarrassed. 21st Century America may represent the most schizophrenic culture in history. We believe in justice with moral absolutes but refuse to be held to those absolutes as a way of life. We are double minded. We love the truth but prefer to live the lie. Clearly we cannot continue much farther in history with such conflicted life views. If we can't agree on the rules, eventually people will refuse to participate in our great society and the end of our Republic will come by our own hands.

BREAKDOWN OF SOCIETY

In a conversation between Alice and the Cheshire cat, Lewis Carroll wrote, "But I don't want to go among mad people,' Alice remarked. 'Oh, you can't help that,' said the Cat: 'we're all mad here. I'm mad. You're mad.' 'How do you know I'm mad?' said Alice. 'You must be,' said the Cat, 'or you wouldn't have come here.' Alice didn't think that proved it at all; however, she went on' And how do you know that you're mad?' 'To begin with,' said the Cat, 'a dog's not mad. You grant that?' 'I suppose so,' said Alice. 'Well, then,' the Cat went on, 'you see, a dog growls when it's angry, and wags its tail when it's pleased. Now I growl when I'm pleased, and wag my tail when I'm angry.

Therefore I'm mad."

Is this a metaphorical picture of modern America? Up seems to be down and down seems to be up. You can go to jail for leaving your pet in a hot car but sex with a minor sometimes earns probation. Smoking in a park is against the law but smoking marijuana should be a protected right. Spotted owls have more rights than full-term infants before they are born. Common sense has become a rare commodity in America. Our founding fathers seemed to have prophetic insight into our loss of reason and common sense.

> *"At the conclusion of the Constitutional Convention, a Mrs. Powel of Philadelphia asked Benjamin Franklin, 'Well doctor, what have we got? A republic or a monarchy?' 'A republic, Madame,' Franklin replied, 'if you can keep it."*

Keeping our republic has never been so difficult as it is now. No longer is it even referred to as a republic but rather, democracy is the preferred title. "Democracy" has an emphasis on the sovereign individual that "Republic" seems to lack. But is a true democracy what we want in America or will that spirit of the autonomous self bring down the great society of America? As we continue to implode upon ourselves and concern ourselves with only our own comfort and happiness, we will miss the gradual erosion of our society until the waters of chaos begin to beat against our shore. Already, signs of breakdown are all around us and under the banner of personal liberty, the breakdown is being accelerated at an alarming pace.

One of the most unsettling scenes from the pictures of Abu Ghraib pictures an Iraqi man lying in the floor with a female American soldier holding a dog leash attached to the man's neck. Our discomfort involves the unseating of several passionately held ideas. One is the maternal role of women. To see a young woman treating a human in such a cruel way disturbs American sensitivities. Additionally, to see a person captured in a moment of inhumanity scares us and we wonder if we are capable of doing the same. There seems to be a disconnect between our view of ourselves and the reality created by our actions. We live with a romantic view of the past while we are dismantling our future.

Americans have passively accepted anything the film and television industry has presented. When Howard Stern announced his agreement with CBS television in 1998 he said, "Television is ready for someone like me... standards have gone to an all-time low, and I'm here to represent the change." Charles Krauthammer observed, "Until now, no society had combined total liberty with mass culture, let alone with technology that hard wires the stuff into the brain. History is therefore no guide as to what happens next. The mayhem in the streets, however, tells the story." An enthusiastic acceptance and then reliance on technology and automation have turned Americans into virtual sociopaths. According to the Diagnostic and Statistical Manual of Mental Disorders, a Sociopath, (or anti-social), is a term given to people who "have a pattern or disregard for, and the violation of, the rights of others". When barbaric acts are committed on the silver screen, we are not concerned with the morality of it because it is only entertainment. Over time, we become conditioned to accept barbarism as normal as long as it doesn't visit upon us personally.

In the summer campaign for the 2004 presidential election, then Democratic candidate John F. Kerry demonstrated his ability to make a disconnect between morality and reality when he announced his belief that life begins at conception. Since scientific research and discovery continue to advance the idea that life does begin at conception, his announcement is less controversial than it would have been several years earlier. His conflicted positions on abortion and life create a striking illustration of America's disregard for life. While claiming life begins at conception, he also upholds a woman's right to have an abortion for non-medical reasons. This essentially makes conception a capital offense for the child that has been conceived. It would be far more consistent for him to declare that life begins only when an infant is viable outside the womb than to promote the idea that killing a living being is acceptable if it is done before you can experience life as a child.

Clearly there is dysfunction in most of our relationships. Men and women take vows when they marry wherein they pledge their support for one another no matter how good or bad the times become. Their commitment to their promise leaves much to be desired. The divorce rate in the United States has generally been going up throughout the 20th century until its peak in the late 1970s. In fact, the divorce rate has been climbing in every industrialized country in the world. This reflects a growing lack of commitment to civic life in America. "Americans who came of age during the Depression and World War II have been far more deeply engaged in the life of their communities than the generations that have followed them."[67] In the America of yesterday, communities were close knit and neighbors frequently socialized together. Each one depended on the other. Today we rely on the internet for communication, we insert our debit card into the gas pump to fill our tanks, and we pay our bills on-line with electronic banking. No longer do we sit at the laundry mat, walk with our neighbors, or even go to grandma's house after church. We have become a nation of isolated and disconnected people. Image has replaced character and relationships are so spontaneous and temporary that people rarely know the substance of themselves much less one another. Francis Beckwith captured this problem with a lack of substance and relativistic thinking in the title of his book, "Relativism: Feet Firmly Planted in Mid-Air"

ABANDONMENT

The isolation of Americans stems not only from a break-down in our commitment to theology or some unifying philosophy, but from the breakdown of the American family as well. Isolation is often associated with a childhood disorder called autism. Autism is characterized by a child's withdrawal into their own world presumably to protect their own sense of worth. Fear of abandonment or simply lacking the psychological coping skills and social communication skills, children retreat into a world of their own creation where they are safe from outside anxieties. It has been suggested that autism is growing at a rate of 10-17% per year. At that rate the incidence of autism could reach as high as 4 million Americans in the next decade. Autism is a brain disorder that affects an individual's ability to communicate, to reason, and to interact with others.

One out of every 250 babies born today will develop some form of autism affecting five boys to every girl. Autism is more common than multiple sclerosis, cystic fibrosis or childhood cancer.

Autistics have been described as being in their own world. An autistic child may appear deaf, unable to speak or if speaking, only with difficulty. An autistic child will engage in repetitious behavior, becoming upset for no apparent reason, they will be oversensitive to pain, and engage in self-stimulating behaviors to include rocking and hand flapping. According to the American Academy of Pediatrics and the Centers for Disease Control and Prevention the rate of children being diagnosed with autism is now as high as one in 166. Ten years ago it was one in 2,500. It is not just autism that has increased. There have been similar increases in attention deficit hyperactivity disorders as well as and cases of childhood depression.

Given the increase in three different clinical syndromes we can not simply lay the blame on genetics. Since there is so much mystery still surrounding autism in children, we can only suggest this is one of the possible contributing factors. Yet, as we look at society, the incidence of autism seems to have paralleled the breakdown of the family and the change in social priorities. In fact, autism may help us to characterize the behavior of our society at large. Withdrawn, overreacting to pain, and struggling to communicate are apt descriptions of our culture in the early 21st century. Our behaviors and actions are often disassociated with penalties. We act before we think and we judge our actions as wrong only if we get caught. What role has the devaluation of family had in the breakdown of our nations collective commitment to morality and social ethic.

Since the industrial revolution of the 1940's the family has been in steady decline. Father's used to spend the entire day working with and talking to their sons. Questions about life and love were asked spontaneously and the mysteries of life and a commitment to family and virtue were bred in each and every child.

When the industrial complex began to displace agriculture as a primary vocation in America, fathers took jobs with long hours or on swing shifts. Often they would take two jobs because manhood was more often than not identified with economic stability and improved living conditions for the family. Good fathers and husbands improved the quality of life for the family. As men began to disappear from the cultural and parental scene, roles usually occupied by men were turned over to women. Sunday school and secular education was handed over to be taught by women. Boys didn't have the exposure to manhood that they once had and instead, academics became the goal. During the last few hours of his life on September 4, 1965, Albert Schweitzer said, "Example is not the main thing in life, it is the only thing." Young men were now left without the example set by their fathers. As we moved into the 1960's the results became apparent. Young people born after the industrial revolution lacked direction and conviction. "What is called matriarchy is simply moral anarchy, in which the mother alone remains fixed because all the fathers are fugitive and irresponsible."[68] They wanted experiences and meaningful purposes in life. Drugs and sexual freedom erupted into the culture and brought with it devastating affects. The entire worldview of American's was changed in a single generation. Now instead of a commitment to the family and community, the focus of every individual was expected to be on themselves. While used little in the 1960's and 1970's, divorce became more common in the 1980's and 1990's and produced wrecked homes. Disassociated parents began carting children back and forth for visitation rights but never gave them a sense of security and permanence. More often than not, fathers were relieved of the responsibility of raising their families and mothers were granted the duties of child rearing by the courts.

Christian Philosopher Os Guinness notes, *"Fathers are vanishing legally as well as physically. About one-third of all childbirths in the nation now occur outside of marriage. In most of these cases, the place for the father's name on the birth certificate is simply left blank. In at least two of every three cases of unwed parenthood, the father is never legally identified. Not surprisingly, paternity suits are on the rise. Imagine something big, made out of glass, called fatherhood. First imagine it slowly shrinking. Then imagine it suddenly shattering into pieces. Now look around. Try to identify the shards. Over here is marriage. Over there is procreation. Over here, manhood. Over there, parenthood. Here, rights. There, responsibilities. In this direction, what's best for me. In that direction, what's best for my child..."*[69]

In 1970, children in the South and in most of America

would often leave their homes first thing in the morning, return briefly for lunch, and then come in only when they heard the voices of their parents calling them in for dinner or a bath. Neighbors were friends. Bicycles could be seen riding up and down the roads and the sound of children laughing was everywhere in the summer. People were trusted until they proved otherwise and the community looked out for one another, often to a young man's chagrin when he was up to no good. Parents did not teach their children much about strangers because strangers were not always strange. That was then. Today's children are growing up in an entirely different world.

Lacking the social and interpersonal intimacy we used to enjoy, people turn to the world of fake relationships. The mildest form of faking a relationship is the internet chat rooms and the more extreme actions result in addiction to pornography.

The crucial moral change that resulted from this development, cultural historian Jackson Lears has written, 'was the beginning of a shift from a Protestant ethos of salvation through self-denial toward a therapeutic ethos stressing self-realization in this world... the cultivation of satisfaction, pleasure, and emotion now takes precedence over the nurturing of moral and institutional character."[70]

"In the United States, people spend more on porn every year than they do on movie tickets and all the performing arts combined. Each year, in Los Angeles alone, more than 10,000 hard-core pornographic films are made, against an annual Hollywood average of just 400 movies."[71] With both chat rooms and pornography, no substantive contact is made between people and no real relationship is formed yet the mind is convinced that it is in a relationship but the heart knows it is alone.

America has been at an ethical crossroads at least 40 years. Perhaps never before have we seen such conviction to opposing views of life and faith, ethics and morality. Each presidential election galvanizes opposing viewpoints. Individual character once seperated law and personal freedom but now, character has given way to legal restraints and personal freedom is exercised without considering ageless principles such as honor, duty, selflessness, and courage. Religious convictions are relegated to personal preferences and the right to consider God's law or even Natural Law (Natural law is less authoritative than a revelation from God, and more authoritative than human pragmatism.) to be universal is publicly mocked. The odd thing about natural law is that it is not natural for man. Christianity teaches that the law of God is written within the heart of the individual Christian. That refers to the 10 Commandments of course and their New Testament summary that men must love God with all their heart, soul, and mind and also love their neighbor as themselves. If this type of ethical behavior represents civilized man, what trends can we detect in American society today? Francis Schaeffer is quoted saying, "I have come to the conclusion that none of us in our generation feels as guilty about sin as we should or as our forefathers did"[72]

Consider these high profile incidents that have occurred in the last ten to fifteen years.

The Army gives soldiers a pocket card and classroom instruction on values. While they are going through their basic training classes they are given thorough instruction on Loyalty, Duty, Respect, Selfless Service, Honor, Integrity, and Personal Courage as well as examples to demonstrate what these values actually look like in real life. Even in this controlled and overtly ethical climate, in 1996, Army Staff Sgt. Delmar Simpson, a drill instructor at Aberdeen Proving Ground, was accused and subsequently found guilty of raping ten female recruits. In some cases he was accused of raping them multiple times. He was also charged with forcible sodomy, indecent acts, extortion, robbery, larceny, indecent assault, and maltreatment of a subordinate. It is said that values are caught not taught. That is not entirely accurate. Values are taught but they fail to be internalized without the critical role of example. Today, "role model" is an overused and misapplied title given to rock stars and sports figures. To feature a public personality as a role model reinforces a belief that substance is in image rather than character. A role model is a person whose behavior is worthy of imitation and emulation. The application of the term today indicates more of a desire to emulate a lifestyle than a character.

We are pummeled every day with stories of misconduct in value-based organizations. Whether it is Jim Baker stealing money and having an affair at the religious based PTL or a police officer accused of beating a man during an arrest, there seems to be little connection between what an organization publicly stands for and what their membership actually live by. America seems to have reached what Russell W. Gough defines as ethical complacency. That is the point when individuals and in this case, an entire culture ceases trying to improve as people. Civilization begins to slide backwards even as technology marches forward. If Dwight Moody was correct when he said that character is what we are in the dark then we need to be afraid of the dark.

Like the Army's system of Core Values, the Boy Scouts have a code of conduct contained in the scout oath and law that they usually recite at each weekly scout meeting. By the time a scout reaches the rank of Eagle, they have memorized the code of conduct and demonstrated their understanding of it by multiple community service projects. In addition to being an Eagle Scout, "Gary Hirte, 18, of Weyauwega, was a member of the track, wrestling and football teams at Weyauwega-Fremont High School. He is quoted as telling his girlfriend in a secretly taped call that 'he wanted to see if he could get away with (murder)'.

He is charged with first-degree intentional homicide. The victim, Glenn Kopitske, 37, and a substitute teacher who was described as the "local eccentric with mental health issues", who his mother said was lonely, and living on Supplemental Security Income. He was not only shot in the back of the head with a 12-gauge shotgun, but then he was stabbed three times."[73] Where was Gary Hirte's ethical core? His ethical training in the scouts seems to have been compartmentalized and treated as theory rather than a code for living.

Consider Luke Woodham, a solid A and B student, was convicted of killing three people, including his mother in Pearl, Mississippi. On October 1, 1997, he entered Pearl High School at 7:55 a.m. carrying a 30-30 rifle in hand and opened fire for 11 minutes, killing two students and injuring seven more. He had already killed his mother, 50-year-old Mary Woodham, who was beaten and stabbed. His first victim at the school was his ex-girlfriend, Christian Menefee, 16. Six other students in a cult like club they dubbed the Kroth, had plotted with and encouraged Woodham to go on the killing spree. After being sentenced, Woodham spoke briefly to the court.

"I'm so sorry. I'm so sorry," he sobbed. *"It wasn't me. I didn't want to do it."* *"I am sorry for the people I killed and hurt. The reason you see no tears anymore is because I've been forgiven by God,"* Woodham said.

"If they could have given the death penalty in this case, I deserve it." The Prosecutor John Kitchens suggested that most of Woodham's problems — the breakup with his girlfriend, his lack of friends and his problems with his parents — were common to most teen-age boys. In his own testimony, Woodham confessed that he didn't have much of a home life after his parents separated and he was an *"outcast"* at school. A breakdown in his civic world, his family, had devastating results on his

social and spiritual development.

How can we explain such random and extreme decisions to commit the worst forms of violence. Americans love to know a criminals motivations. We always want to know why something happens but in the spiritually fragmented and psychologically fragile world we have created as a society, there is often not enough material available to create a conviction strong enough to dissuade a persons brutal nature. Immaturity seems to characterize America now more than anything else. Children can be heard arguing on the playground using words like, *"Gimme", "that's mine"*, and other self-centered demands. Now, that type of social interaction has become the norm for adults as well. While it is phrased more sophisticatedly, the intent is the same. A relentless pursuit of self-interest and self-gratification has driven us further and further apart and has trained us to respect one another less. We have lost our moral compass. That compass resided in our conscience and our firm sense of right and wrong as defined by external authority and the common good. Isolation from other people and transient communities have created an environment devoid of individuality. Add to the loss of identity, a conviction to embrace relativism and moral chaos is the result.

In *"Why Johnny Can't Tell Right from Wrong"*, William Kilpatrick suggests, "...one of the main thrusts of recent moral education has been to set reason up on its own: to create, in effect, a culture-free morality. Kohlberg, for example, thought that children should become autonomous ethical agents, independent of family, church, and state."[74] Morality cannot be taught independent of an external authoritative ethical system. Character education without some guiding light or foundational ethic, is subject to either abuse by manipulation or inconsequence because of it's relativism. During WWII, children were indoctrinated into the thinking of the Third Reich by placing them in an organization called,

Hitler's Youth. They were given a strong academic and "moral" education yet there was not a respect for all human life that was taught. Islamic Jihadists are bound to observe a strict religious code and in their own communities demonstrate a degree of ethical behavior, yet without a respect for the dignity of man and without ethical directions from a deity, they are left with a totalitarian and violent ethic for life. Our behavior is based on our context rather than an inner sense of identity. *"Who we understand ourselves to be is significantly affected by interpersonal relations, beginning in the family, but also extending beyond that. There is constant affirmation or denial of who we are in these settings. It is here that we are first taught whether or not we have value and, if so, on what basis."*[75]

One of the people who have written most cogently about this topic is Professor E. D. Hirsch of the University of Virginia. Hirsch's book *Cultural Literacy* created a stir and became a bestseller largely because he dared to make a list of 5,000 things that people in a literate society ought to know. Unfortunately, many of his critics tended to concentrate on the list and ignore the argument of the book. Hirsch's argument was basically this: *Communities and cultures depend for their existence on shared knowledge. Without such specific knowledge and a shared ethos, it becomes difficult for members of a community to communicate and cooperate. Those without this knowledge will always be condemned to the margins of society. If the knowledge deficit becomes widespread, the culture will collapse.*

A good deal of past and current history supports this hypothesis. Contrary to the claims of advocates of "cultural diversity," the actual history of culturally diverse societies is one of discord and bloodshed. Unless there exists a common language, common religion, or common traditions to bind them, people in such societies tend to be at each other's throats. By contrast, a country with many racial and ethnic groups can remain relatively peaceful for decades if these groups share the same language or values.

Such stability is endangered, says Hirsch, when educators neglect specific content in favor of critical thinking skills. And ironically, critical thinking itself will be one of the first casualties. A youngster won't learn to think critically if he doesn't have anything to think about. He won't learn to read or write very well either, nor will he have much grasp of history or current events."[76]

Children in the boomer and buster generation were taught American history in a way that connected them with the historical figures and events. Christopher Columbus was a courageous explorer that believed in his ideas enough to risk his life searching for them. Now he is demonized as a slave holding capitalist that didn't care if he exterminated an entire Indian civilization to line his own pockets with gold. When asked about teaching children religious values today, many will answer that they prefer to allow their children to make their own decision about religion and faith. That answer is perhaps one of the most uncaring and reckless answers any parent could give. In the first place, if a person holds a conviction that their belief system is true, then certainly they would want their children to come to the truth as well if they were to have any hope for salvation. Secondly, if a parent is not the one to provide guidance, then who will? Wisdom comes through knowledge and experience. When parents withhold knowledge then children are only left with experience that is not a good teacher on its own. Like a ship let loose from its moorings and set on a journey without a compass or a captain on board, our children are drifting at sea willing to land on any beach they can find since no one shore is better than another. The goal of life has degenerated into a quest for good experiences rather than noble and purposeful living. Without parents and communities to model themselves after, they have patterned their behavior after media personalities, MTV and internet perversions. "Once you deprive children of the content of serious culture, do they become their own persons or simply more enthrall to popular culture?"[77] Whatever attraction is loudest, most popular, and generates the highest energy gets their attention. It is no wonder we do not recognize the current generation as traditional Americans. Style and appearance have replaced character as the criteria of judgment. A world of sound bites and flashing images create affection for the appearance of someone without ever knowing their character. College graduates are encouraged to look people in the eye to win them over on the first handshake rather than building a reputation for ethical decision making and integrity.

President Clinton's term in office was hobbled by investigations into his misconduct and abuse of his office. Throughout his defense, image was maintained.

Where can we recover our moral center? Where is the school of ethics to be found?

"One group, represented by people like Diane Ravitch, Chester Finn, and William Bennett, has called for a renewed emphasis on the unifying themes of Western culture and history."[78] As we continue to struggle to understand the lack of character and poor decisions made by the coming generation, perhaps we should look at the culture we have handed them. The Boomers and Busters have not hesitated to indulge their senses. Whether it cost a man his integrity or his family, he has chased whatever desire he has wanted. Children were left standing in the door, crying for him at night all while he chased whatever indulgence or financial dream he had. Not to be outdone, mothers then began to leave homes as well. Deprived of any affirmation in their roles as wives and mothers they went back to school and then to work seeking their fulfillment through the recognition of others. Children were left with Barney the Dinosaur to teach them ethics and relationships. Unfortunately, indulgence comes full circle and now those children lack any sense of their own personal identity and worth and cannot see others in any high regard either.

What can we do? My daughter spent the summer working as a cashier in a grocery store. She brought me a homemade religious tract left at her register one night. "Is Repentance Old Fashioned?" was displayed prominently on the front. I began to think about the concept of repentance. Normally it is exclusively associated with religious practices. Can a society repent? Repentance does not mean being sorry, it is not turning over a new leaf. Repentance is a cognitive action. It means to completely change your mind and attitude. America has developed some bad habits that reflect our lack of conviction about the value of life, the necessity of character education, and our importance in the history of our nation. Most children know the Bible story of Jonah and the Whale. Jonah was a Jewish prophet in ancient Israel. He was commanded by God to go to Nineveh and urge them to repent of their licentious living and wicked idolatry lest God destroy them. Jonah did not want to go because the Ninevites were mortal enemies of the Israelites. Jonah decided to run the other way and forgo his mission from God. While he tried to make good his escape by the sea, a terrible storm overcomes the crew of the ship and they are convinced that the only way to save the ship is to throw Jonah overboard to assuage the anger of God. They toss the fleeing prophet overboard and Jonah is swallowed by a huge fish and delivered to the beaches of Nineveh courtesy of God. He reluctantly carries the message to the people of the city. Much to his chagrin, they listen to him and repent. They entire culture changed and the people abandoned their lifestyles of corruption and self-centered living. We can not continue to imagine that how we live is somehow disconnected from who we are. "Every day you are either getting nearer to God or further off. Every year that you continue unrepentant, the wall of division between you and heaven becomes higher and thicker, and the gulf to be crossed deeper and broader."[79] If America is to have any hope for the future, we must look at our children with compassion. We must see them as the future of our nation rather than siphons of our time and resources. We have to remember how much we needed the love and counsel of our parents and how alone we felt when they were gone.

> *"John Adams wrote, 'There never was a democracy yet that did not commit suicide.' And James Madison observed that democracies had always been 'spectacles of turbulence and contention' and 'as short in their lives as they have been violent in their deaths.' Freedom is never stable and lasting. As corporations and great commercial enterprises age, so do great societies and civilizations. However, because it is the product of human choices, the grand cycle of the birth, growth, and decline of nations is never deterministic. It is always potentially reversible, and in that sense quite different from the lifecycle of plants and other living things."*[80]

Lewis Carroll wrote in "Alice in Wonderland", *"'Who are YOU?' said the Caterpillar. This was not an encouraging opening for a conversation. Alice replied, rather shyly, 'I—I hardly know, sir, just at present— at least I know who I WAS when I got up this morning, but I think I must have been changed several times since then."*
Who are we going to become in the essence of our being? What sort of character will America have when the culture wars have ended? What sort of people will become American' in the next generation? The often-quoted poem by Robert Frost could very well be the best illustration of

where we stand now.

> Two roads diverged in a yellow wood,
> And sorry I could not travel both
> And be one traveler, long I stood
> And looked down one as far as I could
> To where it bent in the undergrowth;
>
> Then took the other, as just as fair,
> And having perhaps the better claim,
> Because it was grassy and wanted wear;
> Though as for that the passing there
> Had worn them rally about the same,
>
> And both that morning equally lay
> In leaves no step had trodden black.
> Oh, I kept the first for another day!
> I doubted if I should ever come back.
>
> I shall be telling this with a sigh
> Somewhere ages and ages hence:
> Two roads diverged in a wood, and I –
> I took the one less traveled by,
> And that has made all the difference.
> Robert Frost (1874–1963)

ENDNOTES

1 http://www.2020democrats.org/page2/node/view/254

2 Cloning of the American Mind, B. K. Eakman (Huntington House Publishers, Lafayette, Louisiana, 1998), p. 212

3 Ibid, p. 213

4 ibid, p. 214

5 A Conversation with Lt. Gen. H Steven Blum, National Guard Bureau Chief, National Guard Magazine, August 2004, p. 23

6 Steven Strasser, editor, The Abu Ghraib Investigations, (PublicAffairs, New York, NY 2004), p.11

7 David Wells, Losing our Virtue (Eerdmans Publishing Co., Grand Rapids, Michaigan 1998), p. 133

8 Ravi Zacharias, Deliever Us From Evil, (Word Publishing, 1996), p. 148

9 Adam Smith, The Theory of Moral Sentiments (Regnery Publishing, Inc., Washington, DC, 1997), p. 2

10 The Union Leader, http://www.utterspeculation.com/archives/000660.html

11 http://faculty.ncwc.edu/toconnor/429/429lect14.htm

12 http://www.jewishvirtuallibrary.org/jsource/Holocaust/Gestapo.html

[13] Federal News Service, Friday, April 9, 2004; Page A10

[14] Daniel Johah Goldhagen, Hitler's willing Executioners (Alfred A. Knoph, New York, 1996), p. 167

[15] ibid, 217-218

[16] ibid., 369

[17] M. Scott Peck, M.D., The People of the Lie (New York, Touchstone Press, 1988, pp 213-214)

[18] http://www.centurychina.com/wiihist/confess/demondoc.html

[19] Aleksandr I. Solzhenitsyn, *The Gulag Archipelago (1918-1956)*. New York: Harper & Row Publishers, 1974, p. x.

[20] Ibid., p. 168.

[21] Ibid.

[22] Mark 7:20-21, New International Version of the Bible.

[23] Charles Colson with Ellen Santilli Vaughn, *The God of Stones & Spiders*. Wheaton, Illinois: Crossway Books, 1990, p. *viii*.

[24] In ibid.

[25] In Charles Colson with Ellen Santilli Vaughn, *The Body*. Milton Keynes, England: Word Publishing, 1992, p. 191,

[26] Ravi Zacharias, *Can Man Live Without God*. Dallas: Word Publishing, 1994, p. 172. Zacharias is referring to Christopher Browning, *Ordinary Men*. New York: HarperCollins, 1991, jacket cover.

[27] Jeffery Goldberg, The Great Terror (New Yorker, 3/25/2002), http://www.newyorker.com/fact/content/?020325fa_FACT1

[28] Neil Postman, Amusing Ourselves To Death (Penguin Books, New York, New York 1985) p.159

[29] William J. Small, former CBS Washington Bureau manager, "Political Power and the Press" (W.W. Norton, 1972)

[30] L. Brent Bozell III, Weapons of Mass Distortion (Crown Forum, New York, New York, 2004), p.224

[31] http://www.cnn.com/2004/US/06/26/beheading.backlash.ap/

[32] Bernard Goldberg, Bias (Perennial, One Massachusetts Avenue, NW, Washington, D.C. 2002), p.35

[33] Bernard Goldberg, <u>Bias</u> (Perennial, One Massachusetts Avenue, NW, Washington, D.C. 2002), p. 31

[34] April 29: TREATMENT OF PRISONERS; G.I.'s Are Accused of Abusing Iraqi Captives N

May 1: CAPTIVES; Bush Voices 'Disgust' at Abuse of Iraqi Prisoners

May 2: DETAINEES; OFFICER SUGGESTS IRAQI JAIL ABUSE WAS ENCOURAGED

May 3: PRISONERS; COMMAND ERRORS AIDED IRAQ ABUSE, ARMY HAS FOUND

May 4: PUNISHMENT; ARMY PUNISHES 7 WITH REPRIMANDS FOR PRISON ABUSE

May 5: INMATE; Iraqi Recounts Hours of Abuse By U.S. Troops

May 6: THE PRISON GUARDS; Abuse Charges Bring Anguish In Unit's Home

May 7: THE SOLDIER; From Picture of Pride to Symbol of Abuse

May 8: COMBAT; G.I.'S KILL SCORES OF MILITIA FORCES IN 3 IRAQI CITIES

[NOTE: Abu Ghraib mentioned in first paragraph]

May 9: THE MILITARY; In Abuse, a Portrayal of Ill-Prepared, Overwhelmed G.I.'s

May 10: PROSECUTION; FIRST TRIAL SET TO BEGIN MAY 19 IN ABUSE IN IRAQ

May 11: THE REPORT; Head of Inquiry On Iraq Abuses Now in Spotlight

May 12: Afghan Gives Own Account Of U.S. Abuse

May 13: PRISON POLICIES; General Took Guantánamo Rules To Iraq for Handling of Prisoners

May 14: THE WHISTLE-BLOWER; Accused Soldier Paints Scene of Eager Mayhem

May 15: MISTREATMENT; Earlier Jail Seen as Incubator for Abuses in Iraq

May 16: THE COURTS-MARTIAL; ACCUSED G.I.'S TRY TO

SHIFT BLAME IN PRISON ABUSE

May 17: PRISONERS; SOME IRAQIS HELD OUTSIDE CONTROL OF TOP GENERAL

May 18: INTERROGATIONS; M.P.'s Received Orders to Strip Iraqi Detainees

May 19: ABU GHRAIB; Officer Says Army Tried to Curb Red Cross Visits to Prison in Iraq

May 20: THE COURT-MARTIAL; G.I. PLEADS GUILTY IN COURT-MARTIAL FOR IRAQIS' ABUSE

May 21: THE INTERROGATORS; Afghan Policies On Questioning Landed in Iraq

May 22: THE WITNESSES; Only a Few Spoke Up on Abuse As Many Soldiers Stayed Silent

May 23: SUSPECT; Translator Questioned By Army In Iraq Abuse [Page 12]

May 24: ABUSE; Afghan Deaths Linked to Unit At Iraq Prison

May 25: ARMY SHIFTS; No. 2 Army General to Move In As Top U.S. Commander in Iraq

May 26: INVESTIGATION; ABUSE OF CAPTIVES MORE WIDESPREAD, SAYS ARMY SURVEY

May 27: Three Accused Soldiers Had Records of Unruliness That Went Unpunished

May 28: U.S. Releases More Prisoners From Abu Ghraib

May 29: Cuba Base Sent Its Interrogators to Iraqi Prison

May 30:Scant Evidence Cited in Long Detention of Iraqis

May 31: Army Is Investigating Reports of Assaults and Thefts by G.I.'s Against Iraqi Civilians

[NYT Memorial Day Special]

June 1: Searing Uncertainty for Iraqis Missing Loved Ones

June 2: Afghan Prison Review [This was not on front page]

[35] John Blanchard, Sifted Silver (Evangelical Press, England), p. 220

[36] Seymour M. Hershs, Torture at Abu Ghraib (The New Yorker, May 10, 2004)

[37] Robert Spencer, Islam Unveiled (Encounter Books, san Francisco, California), p. 75

[38] ibid, p. 76

[39] ibid, p. 79

[40] ibid, p. 82

[41] CBS News, 60 Minutes, 60II Classic: A Brutal Prison, New York, 1999

[42] Human Rights Watch Children's Rights Project, November, 1999

[43] By Rob Johnson, 06/10/04, The Tennessean

[44] Florida Prison Legal Perspectives, Inc., http://www.geocities.com/connect_threads/inmate_abuse.htm

[45] Human Rights Watch, http://www.hrw.org/prisons/abuses.html

[46] Amy F. Bailey / Associated Press, June 2, 2004

[47] Global Security.org

[48] Mark Eddy Smith, Tolkien's Ordinary Virtues (InterVarsity Press, Downers Grove, Illinois, 2002) p.107

[49] 1 Peter 5:8, English Standard Bible

[50] Liberty Speech in S.G. Arnold, *The Life of Patrick Henry of Virginia* (New York: Hurst & Company Publisher, 1845), pp. 107-111

[51] Washingtonpost.com, http://www.washingtonpost.com/wp-dyn/articles/A17088-2004May11.html

[52] Proverbs 28:4 taken from The Message

[53] Proverbs 22:6, The Message

[54] Proverbs 21:17, The Message

[55] Article 15-6 investigation of the 800th Military Police Brigade, p. 16-17

[56] Article 15-6 investigation of the 800th Military Police Brigade, p. 18

[57] http://flash.lakeheadu.ca/~pals/forensics/index.html

[58] William G. T. Shedd, <u>dogmatic Theology</u> (P&R Publishing, Phillipsburg, N.J. 2003), p. 85

[59] Craig Bartholomew, <u>In the Fields of the Lord</u> (Piquant, Carlisle, UK 2000) p. 300

[60] http://www.rit.edu/%7esjg2490/lotf/index.html

[61] www.journalnow.com/servlet/Satellite?pagename=WSJ/MGArticle/WSJ_BasicArticle&c=MGArticle&cid=1031775107221&path=!

[62] David Wells, <u>Losing our Virtue</u> (Eerdmans Publishing Co., Grand Rapids, Michigan 1998), p. 13

[63] J.C. Ryle, <u>Thoughts for Young Men</u> (The Vision Forum, Inc, San Antonio, Texas, 2003), p. 20

[64] http://www.npri.org/books/relat.htm

[65] Francis A. Schaeffer, <u>How Should we Then Live?</u> (Crossway books, Wheaton, Illinois, 1976), p. 147-148

[66] David Wells, <u>Losing our Virtue</u> (Eerdmans Publishing Co., Grand Rapids, Michigan 1998), p. 17

[67] <u>Robert D. Putnam, The Strange Disappearance of Civic America,</u> (The American Prospect, vol. 7 issue 24)

[68] - *The Everlasting Man, CW II, p.186*

[69] Os Guinness, <u>The Great Experiment</u> (NavPress, Colorado Springs, CO, 2001) p.246-247

[70] David Wells, <u>Losing our Virtue</u> (Eerdmans Publishing Co., Grand Rapids, Michigan 1998), p. 98-99

[71] http://www.smh.com.au/articles/2003/11/21/1069027323201.html?from=storyrhs&oneclick=true

[72] http://en.thinkexist.com/quotes/francis_schaeffer/

[73] *Polly Drew, <u>OnWisconson</u>, Feb. 22, 2004*

[74] William Kilpatrick, <u>Why Johnny Can't Tell Right from Wrong</u>, (Simon & Schuster, NY, NY 1992), p.112

[75] David Wells, <u>Losing our Virtue</u> (Eerdmans Publishing Co., Grand Rapids, Michigan 1998), p. 142

[76] William Kilpatrick, <u>Why Johnny Can't Tell Right from Wrong</u>,

(Simon & Schuster, NY, NY 1992), p.117

[77] William Kilpatrick, <u>Why Johnny Can't Tell Right from Wrong</u>, (Simon & Schuster, NY, NY 1992), p.116

[78] William Kilpatrick, <u>Why Johnny Can't Tell Right from Wrong</u>, (Simon & Schuster, NY, NY 1992), p.122

[79] J.C. Ryle, <u>Thoughts for Young Men</u> (The Vision Forum, Inc, San Antonio, Texas, 2003), p 24

[80] Os Guinness, <u>The Great Experiment</u> (NavPress, Colorado Springs, CO, 2001) p.19